Coffee Connect Campaign

Are you in your 20's and feeling a bit meh? A little stuck? A bit lonely sometimes? You are not alone!

Loneliness is a global epidemic – and it is you Quarter-Lifers who are suffering most.

I know you know social media is a false friend – it only creates the illusion of connection.

Building genuine connections in real life is the only solution.

Which is why I'm on a mission to bring 20-somethings together at a community level, and it all starts with a cup of coffee.

So look out for the YELLOW HEART EMOJI, wear something yellow and pop along to your local coffee shop to say HI!

A warm cuppa, a warm smile and a warm welcome awaits you.

Look out for my Coffee Connect Meet-ups around the UK and further afield. #CoffeeConnect

KB x

Kate Berski asserts her moral right to be identified as the author of this book.

All rights reserved. No part of this publication may be reproduced, stored in a retrieval system or transmitted in any form or by any means, electronic, mechanical, photocopying, recording or otherwise without the prior permission of the copyright owner.

A CIP catalogue record for this book is available from the British Library.

Publisher: Café Publishing. Stratford Upon Avon. UK

Layout design and front cover: Tarik Halil

Editor: Sally Bee

ISBN: 978-1-0687860-0-6

Printed in the UK by Adlard Printing, Nottingham. UK.

About The Author

Kate Berski is an entrepreneur turned writer and content creator. She's also a married mum, avid tea drinker, horror film fanatic and recovered '30-Phobic'. Having successfully overcome her own quarter-life crisis, she now advocates for 20-somethings everywhere - by sharing the real facts and expert mindset hacks to help them get unstuck and start building their best life.

Kate is living proof that life really does start at 30. At 29, she was broke, burned out, unmarried and living in a damp flat in London. She felt like she was failing at life. By 39 she was a married mother of one and self-made millionaire, living her lifelong dream of writing a book from sunny Spain.

Kate credits her transformation to a simple shift in mindset and a radical rejection of societal expectations. She will be sharing her secrets, and her story, inside this book.

Follow Kate on Instagram!

"The world needs this book!"

"I feel like we are the same person a decade apart, you made me feel so seen!"

"Kate, you have inspired me to have hope and not succumb to societal pressure to live to a specific timeline"

"I felt the world had come to an end, and your words lifted my spirit again"

"This book changed my life!!"

Dedication

For Kate 'Pembo', who always knew the value of friendship, and never put happiness on hold. And for Quarter-Lifers everywhere and the women who lift them up.

Contents

Introduction	1
30 Phobia Is Real	4
So You Don't Have A Partner	20
So You Don't Have A Ring	43
So You Don't Have Friends	61
So You Don't Have Bank	81
So You Don't Have A Place	111
So You Don't Have Immortality	131
So You Don't Have Kids	151
So You Don't Have Calm	172
So You Don't Have A Dream Job	197
Life Starts At 30	225
Epilogue	238
Notes	242
Acknowledgements	252
References	254

Introduction

"I'm almost 30, I'm happy here. If you're not going to propose, I'm not coming back!"

Meet twenty-nine-year-old me, ugly crying over Zoom from Sydney Australia to my boyfriend of three years, finally kissing my 'cool girl' persona goodbye.

Spoiler alert, the above marriage ultimatum was politely declined. I turned 30 with no ring on my finger, not to mention zero savings in the bank, no car, no confidence and no real sense of direction.

Always an ambitious over-achiever, my situation simply didn't compute. How could I be falling behind now? Why was I nowhere close to having my own sh*t together, yet drowning in invites to other peoples' house warmings, engagement parties and weddings? I was still young, so why couldn't I shake the rising panic, the growing sense of dread that I was running out of time?

Maybe the constant questions had something to do with it. As a 20-something woman, it can feel like all your life choices, or lack thereof, are constantly up for interrogation. Why aren't you married yet? When are you having babies? What about getting your own place? Where are your savings? What are you actually doing with your life...? All under the guise of light conversation. At a time of life when often the only certain thing is uncertainty, these well-meaning enquiries can lead to only one thing – major anxiety.

It was only when my own life failed to conform to the 'conventional' timeline that I started to push back on all the pressure. I began to question where all the life goals, expectations and milestones that were giving me such anxiety came from anyway. I started looking IN instead of OUT for validation.

It was at this time that I finally felt free to build a life on my terms. And you can do the same.

This book will give you the ammunition you need to question the established questions, and all the best hacks to help you take back your 20s – one life goal at a time. But first, we need to figure out what we're working with. Which means asking one BIG question...

Where Do You See Yourself At 30?

This might sound like bullet point 101 from The Big Book of Job Interview Clichès, but it's important, so bear with me.

Since you're reading a book called 30-Phobia, and fears and anxieties tend to be future-orientated in nature, I'm going to assume that you haven't yet turned 30. I'll also hypothesise that you're a goal-orientated person. That you have a picture in your mind of where you want, or hope, to be in life by the time you turn 30. I want you to bring that image to mind now.

What do you see?

Try to summarise your biggest life goals into 3 to 5 things you want to achieve by the time you're 30. These might have to do with career, relationships, friendships, family, finances, travel or anything else that's important to you. Scribble them down below, or note them on your phone, post-it, journal, close-by cave wall or wherever you usually capture your thoughts.

Write them in priority order, number each one and be as clear and specific as possible. Don't feel that this is something you MUST do – but it's something that you might find helpful to do.

These are your Turning 30 Goals.

My Turning 30 Goals

By the time I turn 30, I will...

1.

2.

3.

4.

5.

Before we move on, read over your list a couple of times and pay attention to how you're feeling about these goals.

What emotions come up for you?

How achievable do they feel?

How will you feel if you don't achieve them by 30? Or ever?

Keep these notes somewhere safe (or in your head) – we will be revisiting them often.

30-Phobia Is Real

29 was quite possibly the worst year of my life. The year in which all the 'lifegoals' pressure that had been simmering since my mid-20s started bubbling up – finally boiling over on my 29th birthday when it dawned on me;

"I'm not going to reach a *single* one of my milestones by the time I turn 30"

I've always been the kind of woman who knows what she wants and makes it happen. Even from a young age, my life goals were based on my future career. At 15, I announced to my high school class that I was going to work in advertising. By 22, I'd made it happen. I'd never felt outside pressure to achieve – my motivation came from within.

A podcast host recently asked me where my self-motivation came from. And my best guess, apart from 'I was born with it,' is my dad. A Doctor of Psychology with a strong internal drive himself, he drummed into me from an early age the importance of doing things to your own satisfaction, instead of trying to please everybody else. Today, I love the sense of accomplishment and mastery that comes from creating something that *I* think is good before showing anybody else. But my natural self-assuredness took a turn for the worse in my mid-20s.

As I closed the established playbook of the Education system and started making my way in the 'real world,' I started looking outside for inspiration, and guidance. Other people's expectations and choices started to carry more influence. By 26, the invites for house warmings, engagement parties, weddings and baby showers were rolling in thick and fast. I was constantly scrolling social media, comparing my *actual* life to other people's perfect-looking lives. I started avoiding social events because all the well-meaning *'When are you getting mar-*

ried?' and *'What about babies?'* questions made *me* question what I was doing with *my* life. I started to add things to an invisible 'To Do' list – get promoted to Director, get engaged, save £50k, buy a house... And I assumed I'd do it all by 30.

I did what I'd always done and continued working diligently towards my goals. But as the decade wore on, and my approach wasn't working, my patience grew thinner. I had a happy relationship but no long-term commitment. A good career but no money. A lovely home, that I had to share. Wonderful friends who were increasingly unavailable thanks to the aforementioned marriages, mortgages and the like.

By 29 I'd developed full-blown 30-Phobia. I was terrified to turn 30 because I felt like I was running out of time to get my sh*t together. I lived in a constant state of anxiety, verging on panic. I felt like I was failing at the game of life.

So, I decided to take myself out of the game. I upped and moved to Sydney, Australia. I wanted to take a break from the turning 30 pressure. Having lived abroad before, I wanted to surround myself with Expats, the 'Peter Pans' of adult life for whom timelines and traditional expectations are often sidelined in favour of new opportunities and great lifestyles. And if I'm going to be really candid here, I was secretly hoping that absence would indeed make the heart grow fonder, and my man would finally seal the deal. (This idea got into my head after a co-worker told me that her boyfriend had flown out to propose to her during a stint abroad.)

For the most part, it worked. I switched the *grizzle* of London for the blue skies of Bondi, steamy pub pints for breezy beach walks, a settled friend group for a gaggle of wild adventurers, a gruelling commute, and 9 to 9 work schedule for a short stroll to my 9 to 5. I was taking good care of myself and embracing the carefree Aussie lifestyle. I slept better than I had in years. I felt relieved, like I'd hacked my way out of a crisis. But the feeling wouldn't last.

It seems I hadn't quite dropped my nasty 'compare and despair' habit. A month or so after moving, I caught wind that both my best friend and my boyfriends' (much younger) sister were engaged. And the news hit me like a tonne of bricks. I spiralled – telling myself that the reason I wasn't wifed up was because I was inferior to these other girls, not pretty enough, slim enough or funny enough to be marriage material. Naturally I took it out on my boyfriend. I did what I swore I would NEVER do. I issued my long-distance boyfriend with an ultimatum: propose before I'm 30, or I'm not coming back! My 30-Phobia had taken hold again.

Spoiler alert - I did not get the Instagram-worthy long-haul proposal fantasy, or tick off any of the other items on my life list by 30. And that 'hard stop' forced me to have a long hard chat with myself. I knew it was time to stop looking outside for answers and start looking in, instead.

So, I started to question every assumption I'd ever made. I faced up to the existential questions that were troubling me most. Why was marriage so important to me? Why now? Why did I feel the need to own a property? Was getting promoted going to make me any happier? Why were my expectations of life so out of whack with my reality? Where did the dreaded timeline in my head come from? When did I sign up for the 30 deadline? What was actually going to happen to me if I didn't tick all the boxes by 30?

Or ever?

And that's when it clicked.

The timelines, deadlines, the visions of success that I'd internalised to the point of panic, were not real. That time bomb was a big fat fake. And most of the pre-30 goals (marriage, kids, babies...) that had been filling me with fear since 26 were not mine at all. They were other people's expectations.

The identikit, socially accepted model of success that I'd never thought to question. My goals were things I felt I *should* do, not things I actually needed to be happy and fulfilled.

So, I stopped *'should-ing'* all over myself. I unfollowed social media accounts that left me feeling less than. I pursued internal validation over external. I focused less on how my life *looked* and more on how it *felt*. I finally asked myself – what does success look like to *me*?

Then I wrote a new life list – with NO deadline attached: Travel the world, find a life partner, become my own boss and finally start enjoying my life...

At 30 I started writing the blueprint for the life I wanted, not the life that was expected of me.

And I stopped looking at 30 as the deadline – instead, it was going to be my start line.

It sounds awesome, doesn't it?

But in reality, making different choices to the people around me wasn't always the easy option. Alternative milestones like starting a business or quitting a toxic job are rarely celebrated as traditional trophies like engagement rings, bonnie babies and shiny new job titles are. And being different can be lonely at times. I certainly drifted from a few old friends when our life paths took us in different directions. And I often had to defend my unconventional choices – like going part-time *without* being a parent or giving up a six-figure job to start a beauty business with a starting salary of zero. I had to dig really deep to stick to my guns at times, especially in moments when my 'brave choice' wasn't exactly paying dividends.

My path to life satisfaction has been squiggly for sure. But like many of the incredible women who have contributed to this book, while my 20s were a bit of a sh*t show, things really started to come together in my thirties.

The irony is, that once I took the pressure off myself, I achieved even more than I ever expected. I got promoted at 30, married at 32, went freelance at 33, co-founded a beauty business at 34, bought a house and had a baby at 35, sold my business at 38 and achieved the financial freedom that enabled me to follow my lifelong passion for penmanship at 39. Now at 40, I'm starting a whole new life overseas.

Of course, all of this inner work is easier said than done. Action requires far more effort than inertia. Letting go of lifelong habits, ingrained thought patterns and internalised societal expectations is an ongoing process. Subverting societal norms demands more thought than blindly following them.

Letting go of external expectations is a work in progress. But for me personally, the toughest has been silencing my inner critic. As a self-directed person with glass-half-empty inclinations and a penchant for the dramatic, it's all too easy for me to give in to my inner Negative Nancy. Especially when I'm feeling tired, overwhelmed or under the weather – all of which happen often now I have a toddler in tow. Mindfulness, gratitude and positive thinking do not come naturally to me. Self-compassion still requires continuous, conscious effort, even ten years on, even after I wrote the book on it.

So, I'm still a work in progress. But I'm fine. Because like you, I have a lifetime to figure it all out. Real women continue to prove that there IS no deadline on dreams and no stopwatch for success.

And yet, 'Milestone Anxiety' persists. And I wanted to work out why. Why do so many of us feel pressure to reach certain milestones *before* our 30th birthday? Where does 'Birthday Anxiety' come from anyway? And why is society so hell-bent on promoting the 30 Deadline, with all their '30 Under 30' and '30 Things to Do Before 30 Bucket lists?' I wanted to answer all of these questions and some. The biggest question of all is – *"If our 20s are supposed to be the best days of our lives, why does this all feel so damn hard?"*

In researching this book, I've bent the ear of every past, present and future 20-something woman I know; I've poured over every scientific journal and news article available; I've interviewed over forty experts - from Psychologists and Medics to Coaches and Comedians. And I've surveyed 2,500 20-something women across every part of the UK and the USA.

My mission is to tell the truth about 20-something life and challenge outdated 'milestone myths' that make you feel like you're failing, when you're not. I'm going to show you how false deadlines, invisible timelines and unrealistic expectations are standing in the way of your success, and happiness. I'm going to **help you** reframe your goals and get unstuck, so you can start building a better future, while celebrating every inch stone along the way.

This is the book I wish someone had given me on my 26th birthday. It is the antidote to 30-under-30; the solution to 'birthday blues', and the definitive cure for 30-Phobia.

Why Do Milestone Birthdays Give Us Anxiety?

The terms 'birthday blues,' 'birthday anxiety' and 'birthday depression' are trending on TikTok and rising up the Google search ranks. So, if you're feeling less than thrilled about your upcoming birthday, you are most definitely not alone.

The anxiety can get even more real in the run-up to big birthdays like 20, 30, and 40. The term 'Milestone Anxiety' encapsulates the feelings of stress, pressure, overwhelm, panic and even fear experienced by those fast approaching the end of a decade.

'30-Phobia' (this book's title) might sound a tad dramatic, but so are our 20s. I wanted to create a new term to communicate the unique and specific combination of fears and anxieties reported by many women on the cusp of turning 30.

Psychologists and Founders of The Core Therapy Centre in Canada explain how this shows up in their patients:

"Milestone anxiety comes from comparing yourself to others at various stages in life and feeling pressure to achieve certain milestones by a particular age (For example: I should be getting married, I should have kids, I should know what I want to do for my career, I should have the money to buy a house). Not achieving these milestones can leave you feeling behind or like a failure."
    (Tonya Kelly, MSW, RSW and Dr. Erica Martin, Ph.D. C. Psych.)

30-Phobia, like all anxieties, is innately future-focused. Contrary to what popular culture would have us believe, the 20-something experience appears not to be characterised by carefree *living in the moment* – but by projection. Worrying about what *will* happen in the future, what hasn't happened *yet*, or what may never happen *at all*.

As a former Market Researcher, I'm obsessed with understanding my audience and reflecting reality. So, I didn't want to rely on my own subjective experience in writing this book. I commissioned a survey of 2,500 20-29 year old women across the UK and USA, to understand what life is *really like* for today's 20-somethings. I asked them about their biggest priorities, hopes, dreams and fears for the future.

I found that 61% of young women have negative feelings about turning 30, with 'anxiety' topping the emotional charts at 40%. Singles, women identifying as LGBTQI+, low earners and non-homeowners were more likely to experience negative feelings, including worry, sadness and fear. 64% of all 20-something women agreed they felt 'under pressure to reach certain goals by 30,' and 57% felt they were 'running out of time' to achieve their goals, the closer they got to 30.

The evidence for 30-Phobia is real, but nothing brings women's turning 30 anxieties to life better than their own words:

"I'm scared that I won't have achieved any of my goals by 30, and that I won't like what my life will look like"
(21yrs, UK)

"I feel as if I'm running out of time to accomplish my goals before I turn 30. The things I want to accomplish take a lot of time and energy from me and I don't always have the resources to do so"
(24yrs, USA)

"I have so many things I want accomplished before I turn 30 and I only have 4 years, I don't have enough time or money to accomplish my goals"
(26yrs, USA)

"30 feels like a turning point where you should have your act together and know exactly who you are, have a career etc, which I don't feel like I have"
(27yrs, UK)

"It's a big milestone and I'm not where I thought I would be or who I thought I would be at this age"
(29yrs, USA)

Professionals supporting 20-somethings recognise 30-Phobia too. Anxiety around this milestone birthday came up time and again in my interviews with experts, almost regardless of the topic. From friendships and financial security to finding love and family planning, the experts often explained their clients' fears in relation to the invisible 'checklist' of goals they expected to achieve before turning 30.

IFS Therapist Caitlan Siegenthaler explains:

"In my clients, I see all this pressure, 30 under 30, I need to be married by 30, I need to have my life together by 30... When they're in a different space than what they imagined, there's this huge sense of overwhelm, anxiety, this panic about running out of time"

With so much internalised pressure to achieve before milestone ages, it's no surprise that the consequences of perceived 'failure' to reach our goals, can be extreme. It seems the countdown to a milestone birthday really *does* hit different.

Scientists have found strong correlations between being a 'nine-ender' (having a '9' at the end of your current age) and significant, even deadly changes in behaviour. A 2014 study by Alter and Hershfield in the USA reported that people aged 29, 39, or 49 are more likely to run a marathon, cheat on their partner or tragically end their own life. The study highlights the darker side of placing arbitrary meaning on the 'end of eras.'

Understanding the dark consequences of milestone anxiety helped keep me motivated to continue researching transitional life stages, even when TikTok followers criticised my 'whining' and 'middle-class privilege' in response to posts about the challenges of Quarter Life.

The under-29s are not exempt by any stretch. In fact, one of the things that surprised me most in researching 30-Phobia is that it's not limited to those in their late 20s. I've had DMs from people as young as 20 suffering from severe anxiety and fear of turning 30.

My data shows that 30-Phobia can actually be most extreme in the early 20s, with women aged 20 or 21 significantly more likely to say they feel 'afraid' of turning 30 than those aged 25-30. In fact, contrary to my personal experience, negative feelings about the big 3-0 seem to taper off somewhat the closer we get to the big day. 30-Phobia in the early 20s appears to come along with fear of the unknown and/or feeling greater pressure to achieve, given that there's 'still time' to tick off major life goals. Women in their late 20s on the other hand may be more accepting of their current life circumstances, or familiar with the life changes that come with it.

My survey suggests there could be a generational effect at play too. 65% of our 20-somethings agreed that 'life is more difficult for people my age than previous generations'. Arguably, the generation now coming of age has been exposed to more global instability and uncertainty than my cohort of Geriatric Millennials, thanks to global pandemics, climate change, and constant political and economic shifts, all amplified by 24/7 media coverage. Negative perceptions of the state of the world appear to be feeding young peoples' anxieties about growing up and adding 'make the world a better place' to the growing list of already overwhelming adult responsibilities. The result? Women are becoming *more* afraid of ageing, not less. Their 'scary ages' are moving forward, and not back.

Digging into the comments sections of my survey, it struck me that younger women often use the most fearful language to describe their feelings about getting older:

"The thought of getting older frightens me"
    (20yrs, UK)

"I am scared I won't be where I want to be by 30"
    (20yrs, UK)

"I'm absolutely terrified of getting older"
    (23yrs USA)

"I don't know what the future will bring so it's scary"
    (24yrs, USA)

For many young adults, the run-up to 30 appears to trigger an internal 'life audit' – in which we weigh up our expectations of how our life would pan out versus where we actually are. If we identify any disparities, it can make us very unhappy indeed. I call this phenomenon **The Expectation Gap** – and it helps explain many of the negative emotions we experience in the run-up to 30. In my Turning 30 survey, only 5% of women strongly agreed *'life has turned out exactly as I expected.'* Meaning for everyone else, life hasn't quite matched up to expectations.

One 26-year-old explained:

"I am not content with many important areas of my life currently and do not see myself being able to change that by the time I turn 30. I had a 30-year plan growing up, and I am nowhere close to being in line with that plan which is making me depressed and regretful"
    (26yrs, USA)

The Expectation Gap relates to *if* life events happen – if you always expected to buy your own place, then the financial reality hit home. It refers to *when* events happen – when you assumed you'd be 'wifed' up by 30 but you're still swiping right at 32. It applies to the *order* in which milestones are reached – like the feeling that you *should* have been married before getting pregnant. It applies to *how* an anticipated event unfolds – like the time I expected a proposal from my boyfriend and the bomb got accidentally dropped by my dad.

And finally, the Expectation Gap is felt acutely when we reach a milestone and it doesn't *feel how* we expected it would – like not experiencing that rush of love everyone talks about when meeting your baby for the first time. Or finally making the pay grade, only to find money didn't buy happiness after all.

Comparison culture further compounds the Expectation Gap. When we can see others around us getting everything we always wanted, with apparent ease, it can make us feel inadequate, like we're falling behind or failing somehow. And our mid to late 20s can be a time of particular disparity when it comes to our peer group. While one friend might be married with two kids at 29, another might be interning and living at home with her parents. Another still might be going through a divorce and contemplating starting over. At some point in our 20s, salaries start to stretch apart, creating huge financial gaps within friendship groups which can in turn lead to tensions.

Obsessive Comparison Disorder, as it's now being termed, can be really toxic in our 20s. Survey respondents habitually measured their own achievements relative to their peers, often leaving them feeling worse about themselves:

"I'm already years behind people my age due to my autism and don't know if I will catch up"
  (20yrs, UK)

"I feel like I'm further behind in life than others around my age"
  (28yrs, USA)

"I'm way behind where I want to be, and it depresses me when I see other people my age who have accomplished more in their lives than me. I feel defeated sometimes like I'm not going to get it together before I turn 30"
  (29yrs, USA)

It's almost impossible to talk about the comparison culture without Social Media rearing its beautifully filtered head. External pressure to tick through your timeline has always existed, but social platforms exacerbate the gap between unreal expectations and experienced reality. As digital natives, all of us are immersed 24/7 in the perfectly curated and heavily photoshopped lives of others. Privilege is over-represented and 'normalised' online. We see the edited highlights, but rarely behind the scenes – which can make it feel like everyone else is smashing through life while we're barely able to drag our sorry selves through the day.

61% of our 20-somethings feel that *'social media makes me feel worse about my life'*. And 64% agree *'Others seem to find life easier than me'*. A data point which I hope will bring comfort. If the people who feel like they've got their sh*t together by their late 20s are in the minority (just 9% to be exact) then admitting you still have a way to go makes you entirely normal.

Why Is 30 Such A Big Deal Anyway?

Age 30 isn't just emotionally significant, it appears to have great cultural, scientific and spiritual meaning, which may help explain why this milestone age has become emblazoned on our collective consciousness.

In the Bible, male 'heroes' typically find their true calling at age 30. At 30: Jesus started his ministry (Luke 3:23); Joseph became 2nd in Command to the Pharoah (Gen 41:46); David became King (2 Sam 5:4); Ezekiel was called to be a prophet (Eze 1:1).

In the Torah, 30 is considered a key 'moment of transition', when men graduate from the training phase, acknowledging the realities of life and start to reach their 'full strength' or leadership potential.

During the Roman Empire, men were not considered legal 'adults' until the age of 30 - sounds about right!

In Numerology, 30 symbolises limitless opportunities, creativity and spiritual awakening. There appears to be a cyclical nature to 30 years too. Economists recognise roughly 30-year cycles of economic growth and decline. The United States stock market has been described as moving in 30-year cycles since the 1890s.

In Astrology, the 'Saturn Return' is an astrological cycle that comes about roughly every 29 years, whereby the planet Saturn comes back to the same location as the day you were born. It is said that Saturn drives us to solidify our foundations – which could help explain why we freak out about not having all our ducks in a row.

Other thrilling 30 facts include:

30 is the minimum age for United States Senators and the age at which Jewish priests traditionally start their service.

Neuroscientists have found that human brains are not fully developed until age 30. A fact which you may consider whipping out at a party if challenged on your life choices, or lack thereof. *"I'm not falling behind Brenda, I'm waiting to reach peak cognitive potential before making that critical life choice"*

In Chinese culture, women's 30th birthdays traditionally go un-celebrated. 30 is considered a 'Forbidden Age,' a year of such uncertainty and danger, that women will choose to remain 29 for another year rather than face the bad luck.

So far, so interesting, but perhaps the most helpful insight for the Birthday Anxious and 30-phobic comes from modern Developmental Psychology.

Developmental Psychologists have long considered the ages of 18 - 45 'Early Adulthood' – a fact which makes this almost 40-year-old feel very happy indeed. Science says I'm still young! More recently, Psychologist JJ Arnett suggested an additional pre-adulthood phase, 'Emerging Adulthood' (from 18 to 25 or even 29) a time in which we lay the foundations of adult life. This life stage is characterised by identity exploration, self-development, infinite possibility and – get this – feelings of instability, inadequacy and stress.

It seems to me that regardless of your take on turning 30 - historical, cultural, philosophical or scientific – everyone agrees on a few things:

1. Your 20s are a time of huge transition and turmoil.

2. Turning 30 is absolutely a big deal.

3. Nobody has it all figured out by 30.

If you take one thing from my fun facts section (aside from some cracking trivia to impress your friends with) make it this – if you're losing your mind about turning 30, give yourself a big fat break. Or if all else fails, book a one-way ticket to China and live up your 20s for another 12 months.

What Are We So Afraid Of?

Mindful not to project my own former fears about turning 30 onto the current generation of 20-somethings, I surveyed Quarter-Lifers about what, if anything, scared them most about getting older. Their answers enabled me to identify the Core 4 Turning 30 Fears:

1. **Health Fears – 69%** fear declining mental and physical health, and visible ageing.

2. **Financial Fears – 55%** worry about financial insecurity or not affording a home.

3. **Relationship Fears – 47%** have anxiety about finding love and friendship.

4. **Career Fears – 36%** are concerned about finding their purpose or path in life .

So, I'm 30-Phobic, Now What?

Each chapter of this book breaks down a specific turning 30 anxiety. I'm going to show you why the fear you're feeling is very real, and normal, and I'm going to explain why it's absolutely not your fault. I'm going to show you where your biggest turning 30 anxieties are coming from and crucially, how you can move past them – with the help of my expert panel of fantastic females.

Now, the first step in any recovery journey is admitting you have a problem. So, if throughout this chapter, you've identified as 30-Phobic, congratulations you just completed Step 1!

The next great bit of news is that you already have the only tool you need to overcome any turning 30 fear – your own mind. At the end of each chapter, I'll be sharing expert mindset hacks and practical first steps to help you get unstuck and get set for success.

When it comes to overcoming fears, I've done my homework, so you don't have to.

And when I asked the experts, their advice was incredibly consistent, almost regardless of the topic. This enabled me to identify 4 steps to overcoming any turning 30 anxiety.

Get Unstuck In 4 Steps

1. **STOP Looking OUT**
   Stop allowing external pressures and external validation to dictate the way you live your life. Let go of false deadlines and outdated and unrealistic societal expectations. Stop people pleasing and 'comparing and despairing.'

2. **START Looking IN**
   Start living for YOU – seek internal validation and personal fulfilment. Sit with your feelings and take time to get clear on your personal priorities.

3. **REFRAME Your Goals**
   Set new life goals that feel achievable, positive, motivating and authentic to you. Make the shift from a milestone mentality to process positive.

4. **CELEBRATE The Small Wins**
   Practice celebrating the baby steps, the micro successes and the little moments of joy in life. Embrace the possibilities of the future and be open to new experiences to set yourself up for success.

At the end of each chapter, I'll be sharing the best expert advice for overcoming your specific turning 30 fears, following this simple framework.

How To Read This Book

30-Phobia tackles the hottest turning 30 topics. From finding a partner to financial insecurity and fertility fears – we'll be breaking down your biggest birthday anxieties one by one and building you back up in the process.

Much like the number 30, the order of chapters in this book is somewhat arbitrary. In real life, everyone has their own unique journey, and life isn't linear. So, I invite you to dip in and out, choosing the topics that most speak to your life experiences, your biggest anxieties, or your mood on the day.

And finally... This isn't just a book, it's a small part of an ongoing live conversation. As I put pen to paper, I also put myself out there, sharing my writing journey, emerging insights, mindset hacks and relatable memes with a growing community of 20-somethings on Instagram **@kate.berski** and TikTok **@30_phobia**.

Feedback from my community helped shape the writing of this book in real-time. I've paid close attention to what you relate to, what makes you laugh, and what freaks you out. I've noted your questions, concerns, and constructive challenges – and zoomed in on the topics that affect you most in this book. If you've been following along, thank you. I hope you'll see a little bit of your story reflected in these pages. You might even find your comments in print!

So You Don't Have A Partner

"I'm single because nobody believes that I am single"
(Anon)

I'll start by saying, it is perfectly possible, and valid, to be happily single at any age. However, it seems that being a single pringle in the run-up to 30 can be a source of significant anxiety, especially for those in their early 20s. While nearly half (47%) of all women aged 20-29 worry about finding a partner, single anxiety affects 60% of women under 23.

Single Anxiety Is Real

When I was turning 30 a decade ago, relationship status was the biggest culprit behind big birthday freak-outs. So naturally, as I started researching this chapter, I collared some of my closest friends to relive our almost-30 relationship angst:

"I was extremely anxious in my late 20s. I thought I needed to be sorted at 30. I wanted to be engaged or at least know it was going that way. I was afraid of being single at 29. I thought it meant being an old maid. That was definitely the main concern for me"
(Tess, 40yrs)

"I was obsessed with getting things in my timescale – that meant marriage at 29 and baby at 30. In hindsight, I wish I'd taken my time and enjoyed myself rather than rushing along trying to get it all ticked off asap"
(Charlie, 40yrs)

I wanted to understand whether today's 20-somethings feel the same way as my friend group did. And my research indicates that they do.

The majority of women, across cultures, who are unattached in their late 20s are not especially thrilled about it. What's more, relationship status appears to have a disproportionate and overriding impact on young women's general mindset and feelings about the future.

67% of single women in my survey, say they feel 'behind where they want to be' in their relationship goals, indicating a significant Expectation Gap between women's romantic ideals and their relationship realities. It doesn't end there. Unpartnered women are less likely to say they feel 'happy with where they are at in their life right now', less likely to truly 'believe in themselves,' and more likely to feel like they're 'running out of time to achieve their goals' compared to those in relationships.

It is no surprise then that single status is highly correlated with more negative emotions around turning 30. Nearly half of single women say they feel 'anxious' about turning 30, compared to just over a third of those in relationships. Singletons are also more likely to say they feel 'depressed' or 'sad' about their upcoming birthday:

"I'm anxious because I thought I would be in a steady relationship at this point"
    (23yrs, USA)

"I don't feel like I've achieved a lot. I don't have a partner at the moment, and I would love to have kids and be married someday, but I am nearly 30 and I'm worried that my window is closing, which makes me really sad"
    (28yrs, UK)

"I recently had someone I considered to be my soulmate break up with me, which has put me back on my family goals, put me back financially, and put me back on my house goal, too. I've had to take on another job so I don't get evicted. All my friends are now married with kids and I'm nowhere near where I thought I'd be"
    (29yrs, UK)

Reading through these comments I don't feel surprised, but I do feel sad. Mostly because I can relate. In my 20s, my self-esteem was tied up in the opinions of others, and nothing felt more validating than attention from cute boys. This also meant that romantic disappointments, of which there were many, felt especially painful. Looking back, it seems unbelievable that I would entrust my sense of self-worth to some silly drunken nitwit at a bar. Or feel like my entire future was resting on the success or failure of a first date at Pizza Express. But I did. Because the more my friends got whisked off the market, the more I felt like the market was closing, leaving me to root around in the bargain bin for a slightly wonky, cut-price consolation date. Yes, Quarter-Life relationship panic is very real.

But when logic (and the celebrity gossip columns) tells us that we could find love at any age, why does turning 30 feel like such a pivotal moment for locking love down? The experts spoke of a late 20s perspective shift that drives women to lay the foundations for the future:

"In our early 20s life just feels so abundant, you don't feel that sense of time shortening yet. And then when the 30 gets close, life starts to come into perspective a little bit. Your identity starts to change, your values are shifting, you start to want to settle down a bit, set down roots I think some natural shifts happen around that age"
(Dani Weiss, Dating Coach)

"The Saturn Return is an astrological event that happens every 27 to 29.5 years. It's when the planet of Saturn returns to the exact sign, place and location that was in when you were born. And this is significant because astrologically, Saturn rules structure. It wants to make sure that we have a really solid foundation in all areas of our lives - like this astrological push into adulthood. So as women start to turn 30 they start to solidify their partnerships – they get married, think about having babies..."
(Caitlan Siegenthaler, IFS Coach & Podcaster)

Interestingly, it's not just unpartnered women who suffer single anxiety. Women who are currently in failing relationships can feel further behind than those on the starting blocks. Which can lead to significant stress and anxiety around milestone birthdays: Dating coach Dani shared her late 20s breakup story – an experience so profound that it led to her re-training as a dating coach.

Love After 30: Dani Weiss, Dating Coach

"At 28/29 I was in a long-term relationship. And then when I was approaching 30, I had this come-to-Jesus moment where I was like this isn't it. It looks good on the outside, it checks all the boxes. It's what I thought I wanted. But, in my heart of hearts, this isn't the relationship that I want for my life partner. And so, I went through a breakup when I was 29, two months away from turning 30. And then I was single on my 30th birthday...

It was such a painful time, and all those months of dating and being single and 30 were just so scary for me. I would wake up with anxiety in the middle of the night, thinking oh my god, what if this never happens for me? What if it's too late? What's wrong with me? I felt like I was missing something that other people knew about...whenever you want something so badly that you don't have there's a lot of pain there... that's when I read all the books and listened to all the podcasts. I learned about attachment styles and I trained as a coach.

What I couldn't have known then was that nine months later I was going to meet my person who is now my husband and is the most amazing life partner, and most amazing human being I could ever have dreamed of"

Single at 30: Am I Normal?

If you are single and struggling right now, it might help to know you are not alone. The data doesn't lie friends!

The Myth: LOVED-UP AT 30. Being single at 30 is ABNORMAL. Everyone else is paired off well before 30, and if you're not, you've 'missed the boat.'

The Reality: SINGLE OR NOT AT 30. Being single in your 20s is entirely NORMAL. My survey shows that 37% of women aged 20-29 across the UK and US are currently single, and nearly half under 25's are unattached. Those in their early 20s or who identify as gay, bisexual or other are most likely to be single.

Single Anxiety: It's NOT You

Clearly there are strong evolutionary factors at play when it comes to our innate desire to find a mate fast. But there's immense social pressure too. And after diving into the research, data and opinion on this, my hot take is that society has really got it in for single women. It seems to me that a variety of forces outside our control are negatively influencing the way we feel about flying solo, and by extension, the way we feel about ourselves. This is especially worrying in light of recent predictions that by 2030, 45% of women aged 25-44 will be single. The pressure to partner up could be taking a dent out of the self-esteem of half the female population.

Some of the most pervasive external influences I've identified include:

1. Peer Comparison

2. Women's Worth

3. Single Tax

4. Dirty Words

5. Appy Days

6. RomCom Effect

Peer Comparison

At a certain point in your mid-20s, your entire social calendar will be taken over by Other People's Relationships. The Engagement parties, The Hen Dos and Bachelorette Bashes, The Destination Weddings... If you haven't reached that stage yet, my first piece of advice is to book a holiday right this minute to somewhere you REALLY want to go. Because as soon as those dominoes start to fall, your travel plans will be 100% dictated by a succession of bridezillas with big ideas.

This stage of life can be particularly tough for single women, because at no time in our entire lives are the romances of others quite so in our faces. As a single woman in receipt of yet another ivory embossed envelope, you can't help but compare your non-existent love life to the romantic bliss of the latest happy couple - and feel like you're falling short. Where you may have felt just 'one step behind' when your friend had a boyfriend, now she has a fiancé and you're 2 steps back by default!

The thing about being in your late 20s is that a formerly level playing field starts to feel decidedly uneven, and nothing divides a group quite like relationship status. Groups of same-age friends can range from majorly married to steadfastly single. This can be an alienating experience whichever side you're sitting on – but I believe it's the unhappy singles who are hardest hit, watching their girlfriends fall into serious relationships with apparent ease, while they're left standing at the start line. Of course, you're always happy for your friends, but it's hard to avoid feeling like a romantic flop when you're always the best friend, never the main character. In their words:

"Most of my friends are in relationships and I'm hopeful that I will find a partner to eventually have kids with, as I feel like time is running out. But I still worry it won't happen"
   (28yrs, UK)

"I feel like I am nowhere near where I would like to be in life. I see friends and others around me advancing past me. I am still single and not very happy"
   (29yrs, USA)

I can relate. For most of my 20s I felt like I was the only single girl in the world. Never the one cosying up with my beau in the corner of a bar, or smugly picking out kitchen implements at Ikea. And no stranger to third-wheeling when pitying coupled-up friends invited me along for dinner (I actually don't think they expected me to say yes, but a girls gotta eat right?!)

Singledom is especially trying in early adulthood, thanks to all the celebrating that goes on around traditional relationship milestones. Society really bigs up anniversaries, engagements and weddings, but last time I checked nobody ever got a cute poker chip to celebrate another year of romance-freedom. Side note – there probably should be, since being functionally single seems a step ahead of being stuck in a dysfunctional relationship.

Women's Worth

In my 20s, I distinctly remember the guy sitting opposite me on our first date asking, Why are you still single?! What's wrong with you? The irony of the question was completely lost on him.

Sadly, such leading questions, often asked in mock jest, are all too familiar to those of us who've done time on the single bench. And aside from being incredibly annoying and potentially embarrassing, I believe the casual acceptability of these enquiries is indicative of a culture of single blaming. First off, they assume that there is something fundamentally wrong with the currently unpartnered – leaving little room for personal choice, or circumstance. And pointing this out matters, because when someone's relationship status is repeatedly questioned, especially by people they love and trust, it can make them start to question themselves, which can gradually erode their self-worth.

Dating Coach Dani Weiss explains how her 20-something clients can start to create false, and often damaging narratives to fill the explanation void:

"There's a lot of shame and anxiety around being single for women. They start to think there must be something wrong with them, something about them that's undesirable. I've heard all kinds of explanations, like men only want women with brown straight hair and I have curly red hair... often they want a relationship to prove their worth, to prove that they're likeable, or lovable"

Dani believes there's a wider patriarchal narrative at play here, in which a woman's relationship status is perceived as directly proportional to her value. Society tells us that there is something fundamentally 'wrong' with unattached women, that they are of lower value, particularly past a certain age:

"In a patriarchal society, women's value comes from being desired by

a man. We are only deemed valuable and worthy if we are desirable, particularly by men. Even as Feminists, it is the soup we swim in, the air we breathe... and society puts end dates on finding a man while we are still young, like at 30, because it values youth. Younger women are deemed more valuable."

I'm literally sighing as I read this back. Which is why I'm making it my mission to change the narrative around single women. As are my beautiful community. Just the other day, I received this DM, in which Jasmin shared a refreshingly real perspective on being single in her 30s:

"In my 20s, I was nervous about turning 30 and being unmarried, especially since I'd never had a long-term romantic relationship. Now at 31, and still single, I savour all this time to myself and don't feel pressured to get married anytime soon, or maybe ever. Funny how things change..."
    (Jasmin, 31yrs)

Single Tax

Personal finance emerged as a hot topic for all Almost 30s – which is why I've devoted an entire chapter to it later on. But since it's single women who appear to be hardest hit by Quarter-Life financial insecurity, it feels pertinent to include it here.

My survey found that single women are more likely to fear future financial insecurity than those currently in relationships. They're also more likely to say they're 'behind where they thought they'd be' on their financial goals, and more worried about not being able to afford their own property. The implication is that being single doesn't just affect our romantic prospects, but our broader life prospects too.

It turns out, being single comes at a heavy cost. A 2022 study by Ocean Finance found that the monthly cost of living is £630 higher in the UK for singles compared to those in relationships. Each month, unpartnered people pay an average of £363 extra on bills, £241 more on rent, £90 more on groceries and £33 more on streaming services.

The subtle financial penalties of singledom are endless. There's the small stuff, like not being able to split a cab, or a kebab, on the way home. Or going to a wedding and paying for the hotel room, the gift, the petrol, all by yourself. Then there's the big stuff, like stumping up for the full rent on your own or saving for a house deposit solo, which potentially puts dreams of independent living, or property ownership out of reach.

My survey showed that single 20-somethings are more than twice as likely to be living at home with their parents - 47% compared to just 21% of those in couples. This figure really brings home the lifestyle compromises singles are potentially forced to make for financial reasons. Financial Educator Ellie Austin-Williams frequently comes across this amongst her clients:

"The single tax comes up a lot. The system just doesn't work for single people. Like if you live on your own you get a 25% council tax discount. Why wouldn't it be 50%? And it doesn't feel fair that if you're single you have to spend double the money as someone in a couple for your own flat, or live in a house share when you're past the age when you want to do that"
(Ellie Austin-Williams, founder of This Girl Talks Money)

To add insult to expensive injury, todays singles mostly have to pay for the privilege of finding a partner too. A 2019 study by UK dating site Plenty of Fish reported that dating costs an average of £1,349 a year, with dating subscriptions at around £30 a month and the typical date setting people back over £100, including pre-meet preparations.

To finish on a particularly cheery note, the singleton tax doesn't even end when we die! While married partners can access spousal benefits over inheritance tax, the estates of singles are subject to the full 40% tax. Talk about kicking a gal when she's down.

Dirty Words

Why is 'single' such a dirty word anyway? I blame the English language. Seriously. The theory of linguistic relativity states that the language we are exposed to directly impacts the way we think about the world.

Experts have argued that language can be inherently sexist, with female versions of words often carrying far more negative connotations than their male equivalents. The word 'bachelor' for example has come to mean a handsome, eligible young gentleman, whereas 'spinster' is giving more 'crusty old witch.' There's good reason why the female-led version of the TV dating franchise went with 'The Bachelorette.'

The wild part is, that in the true sense of the word, spinsters really aren't that old anyway. The word 'spinster' was traditionally applied to unmarried women UNDER the age of 30. Any unmarried woman OVER 30 automatically graduated into a 'thornback'. Personally, I think it's about time we bring this back. 'Thornback' sounds far more badass than Spinster or Singleton, don't you think?

Now here's a classic - enter the 'Old Maid.' Popularised in the 17th Century to refer to the paradoxically 'old' (read 26) yet unmarried, virgins. Equivalents of the term are also used in Spain, Poland and other European countries. To be fair to the 17th Century bigots, at that point in time, average life expectancies were around 35, so not being married at 26 probably did seem like more of a 'missed the boat' type situation than it does today. But given that today's women can expect to live past 80, it really does seem like time's well and truly up for these old-school single slurs.

The single bashing doesn't stop with European languages. In China, women who remain unmarried in their late 20s and beyond are referred to as 'Sheng Nu,' or 'leftover ladies.' In Japan, the term 'Parasaito Shinguru' or 'parasite single' was recently coined to describe any single person in their 20s or 30s still living with their parents. It appears to be disproportionately applied to women.

When women grow up with such unequivocally negative and judgemental terminology around being single, is it any wonder that we end up internalising some of it?!

On a rosier note, there are efforts afoot to remove the stigma of singledom and reframe relationship status by introducing more neutral or positive language. Actor Emma Watson (of Harry Potter fame) for example, has emerged as a role model for single women. She famously described herself as 'self-partnered' as she turned 30, to demonstrate that she feels perfectly happy and fulfilled as a solo individual.

Romcom Effect

Would you describe yourself as a 'hopeless romantic?' Do you believe in love at first sight? Do you dream of being swept off your feet? Do you believe that the right partner will 'complete' you? That friends with benefits could potentially lead to love? Do you believe your secret crush is just one monologue away from becoming your lover? Or that 'happily ever after' comes right after you meet 'the one?'

If you've answered yes to any of the above, you may be subject to subconscious media conditioning, or as I call it, the 'Romcom Effect.' And you wouldn't be alone. Recent studies have found that the TV and movies we are exposed to significantly shape what we expect romantic relationships to be – leading to inflated, unrealistic or downright damaging expectations of love.

I, for example, grew up in the '90s, a decade in which movies brought us all manner of misguided lessons in love. Here are just a few of the messages my teenage self eagerly absorbed:

- *A glow-up is the fastest way to find love* (She's All That)

- *The fuckboy will fall for you in the end* (Cruel Intentions)

- *You need a man to complete you* (Jerry McGuire)

- *Kidnap is a great basis for romance* (Beauty and the Beast)

- *It's cool to be second best, just hang on in there* (Four Weddings and a Funeral)

- *Lies are a solid foundation for love* (The Proposal, While You Were Sleeping, How To Lose a Guy in 10 Days, Never Been Kissed... need I go on?)

I very nearly called this section 'The Disney Effect,' because of the huge influence animation has had over our world views, and from a precariously young age. A study by Hefner and Wilson found that repeated viewing of Disney princess movies, in which romantic ideals such as 'love at first sight' and males as the dominant pursuers are commonplace, was correlated with greater idealisation of one's partner (which has been linked to unrealistic expectations, lower relationship satisfaction and other inequalities). Interestingly, these kinds of romantic messages were most prevalent in movies from 1989 to 1998 – meaning that those currently in their 30s may be most likely to harbour unrealistic, or even toxic, expectations about romantic relationships.

Just think about the love story presented in the original Little Mermaid (1989) for a second, a film I watched daily, and on repeat, throughout my childhood. In it, an impossibly beautiful woman with no voice is pursued by a handsome prince. To win his love, she is required to completely change her physical appearance and disconnect from her entire family in order to marry post haste. Suffice to say, if this happened to one of our friends IRL, we would be seriously concerned.

Relationship status is a clear contender for the biggest Expectation Gap of 20-something life. When we are constantly immersed in over-the-top, big-budget, unreal romantic ideals, it's hardly surprising that we can feel confused, disappointed and let down by real-life love, or lack thereof. And the myth of 'happily ever after' lives in the real world too. Well-meaning people are constantly reassuring struggling singles that 'it will happen' and 'he's out there' – empty platitudes which can be more than a little frustrating for single women for whom there are no real guarantees.

A good friend of mine explained:

"I wish people would stop telling single women that it will all be OK and it will all work out in the end. What if it doesn't? We need to start getting real and accepting that staying single is an option, then we can plan for that"

If I can offer any platitude-free words of reassurance here; If your love life feels more like a dark comedy than a romcom right now, remember it's not you, it's Netflix.

Appy Days

Technology is arguably the external factor that's had the single biggest impact on this generation's approach to finding love. Statista projects that by the end of 2023, there will be 441 million online daters worldwide, with nearly 22% of Americans and 20% of Brits being active users. The most recent data suggests that around a third of couples now meet online, and this is soon set to rise above 50%.

It's not difficult to see why. On the surface, dating apps are the perfect tool for finding a partner. They give us access to a much larger pool of potential dates than we'd otherwise encounter. They allow us to meet, and 'screen' suitors in the safety of our own homes and are better suited to introverts than traditional dating. What's more, their huge popularity and complex algorithms have us believing that scores of high quality, available partners are only a few clicks, and a credit card number, away.

On the surface, the odds of finding love online seem great – especially if you're a woman seeking a man. According to Statista, 85% of current dating app users are men, and on Tinder, the most popular app, there are 9 male users for every 1 woman. Moreover, if you're in your 20s, the chances of meeting an age-appropriate partner look good, with 60% of Tinder users being under 35.

The question is – can you actually access these age-appropriate matches? Online dating, unlike real-world meets, emphasises age upfront – making claimed age, and perceived visual age, the first filter for both searching and matching. This isn't always helpful, especially for hetero females past 25, since research has shown that straight men of all ages are most attracted to women in their early 20s – an irritating phenomenon I like to refer to as 'DiCaprio's Law.'

Meanwhile, women's age of attraction tends to increase proportionately with their own age. Commentators have speculated that people habitually lie about their age on dating profiles in part to 'beat the algorithm' – and that those approaching milestone birthdays are more likely to age down to fit the filters.

Age-based deception is the tip of the iceberg when it comes to the myriad ways online dating can unnaturally elevate, and skew, our expectations, leaving us sorely disappointed IRL. Speak to almost any girl who's done time on Tinder, and you'll be hit with a handful of horror stories and a whole new vocabulary. From benching and breadcrumbing to cookie jarring and catfishing. Grifting to ghosting. Hesi-dating to haunting. Roaching, stashing, submarining, orbiting, zombie-ing... In the era of apps, there appears to be no end of new ways to be let down by love.

Journalist Alyssa, 28, painted a bleak picture of how apps have impacted the New York dating scene:

"I have very mixed feelings about dating apps. I know they work because my friends have met people that way. But I really think they're reaching burnout, it's so much worse than even a few years ago. People are just always thinking about the next person, just constantly swiping on to the next one, like we are not even human beings. People will use them to find quick validation, not to find someone – they'll focus on how many likes or matches or dates they've got. But that's not really the point"
   (Alyssa Montagna, Hearst Magazines)

Recently, a close friend explained in plain English why finding a serious relationship on dating apps is far trickier than it may first appear:

"I feel like most quality men who want commitment are already committed. So, dating apps are flooded with people looking just for fun. The fuckboys, the jaded, avoidant divorcees, the closet commitment-phobes, the married men... It seems like there are a lot of guys on there – but finding a decent one is complicated. It's a lot of work, a lot of disappointment and compromise. It gets exhausting"
   (Ang, 40yrs)

Whilst some girls do get lucky on the apps, others, like my friend, are left with chronic dating fatigue - each false start weighing heavier on her heart than the last. The irony here is that whilst it may seem like taking proactive steps towards our relationship goals, and 'playing a numbers game' must pay off eventually, constantly dating the wrong people can make us feel further away from our relationship goals than ever before.

As one Quarter-Lifer explains:

"I never took the time to just stop and think about everything. I'm going to be 30 next year and I'm still single. It really freaks me out. I've entertained the wrong guys for too long and I've wasted too much time"
(29yrs, USA)

The mental health professionals and dating coaches I spoke to were wary of dating apps, suggesting they may not be the healthiest, or even the most efficient way to find romantic partners. Rather than helping you find your match fast, the constant rotation of apparent options and 'gamefied' nature of the interface actually reinforces unproductive dating behaviours such as dismissiveness, indecision and commitment phobia:

"Dating apps present too many apparent options – it creates a decision paralysis, the feeling that there is always something better out there. It encourages you to keep swiping forever... it's actually way harder to settle with someone than it would be if there were fewer choices"
(Dani Weiss, Dating Coach)

"Prior to the emergence of technology, finding a partner was limited to who was in your community and small social circle. Currently, however, online dating has created the 'swipe culture'. We keep swiping with the thought that maybe there will be someone better "next." This can lead us to not appreciate what's already in front of us because we wonder if there is something or someone 'better' right around the corner"
(Tonya Kelly, MSW, RSW and Dr. Erica Martin, Ph.D. C. Psych)

If you're curious about my own history with dating apps, I'm going to show my age here by sharing my somewhat limited experience. Believe it or not, I am old enough to remember My Single Friend, one of the OG dating sites (we didn't even have smartphone apps back then!) happily endorsed by TV's Sara Beeney, in which a mate 'presented' each single to prospective partners. The logic being that it's far easier to fan girl your friend than for her to blow her own trumpet. I remember my flatmate filling in a profile for me when I was about 25. A slightly cringey, yet edifying process in itself. And if I'm honest, that was the most fun I ever had on MSF. Even my best friend would tell you that my unique brand of beauty cannot be captured in two-dimensions, so the floodgates didn't exactly open for me and my lacklustre profile pic. A smattering of interest trickled in from a selection of wildly unsuitable-looking men, mostly residing far outside my age bracket, and my postcode.

When I eventually agreed to a date with a guy who looked relatively normal, and London-based, it transpired that he had 'been creative' with his height measurement (why do they do that? We are going to notice when we meet them...) As superficial as it sounds, at 5 ft 4 myself I wasn't looking for a male counterpart I could see eye to eye with, so to speak. And whilst he was a perfect gentleman, I knew in the first five seconds he wasn't for me, so I'm ashamed to say I pulled the emergency rip-cord after only thirty minutes. When I got home, I deleted my account and never looked back – vowing to stay single and celibate rather than waste another moment on fruitless dating admin. As it turned out, I would meet my match in real life less than six months later, and it would only take moving abroad, and breaking several of my cardinal relationship rules, to do it.

Having sworn off dating sites and eliminated all friends-of-friends as sources of potential partners, I was left with only two options: The bars, and the office. One of the best things about being twenty-something is that you may actually have some single colleagues. And in my early days at the ad agency, I had plenty. Friday night drinks with nothing but a late lunch to line our stomachs, often took a romantic turn. And once in a while those flirtations turned into something more. But I found out the hard way that office romances are pretty great, as long as you end up married. If things go sour, things get a tad awkward to say the least. After my own attempt at an office fling ended in tears, I swore I'd never look at another co-worker in that way again. Which only left the bars. In which I met a string of reasonable-looking, yet decidedly dull and commitment-phobic gentlemen, few of whom made it past the first drink, let alone the first date. The only one that stuck around was a romantically inclined Italian chap. He was beautiful, and refreshingly keen, but he spoke very little English. And it turned out after a couple of dates, even I wasn't superficial enough to date someone with whom I could not converse at all, so I told him I didn't want to see him anymore. He said 'no,' a response I wrongly assumed was not allowed in a break-up scenario. And he didn't stop protesting until I moved to Amsterdam and changed my phone number. Andre, if you're out there, I really am sorry for that. After experiencing the language barrier, I decided that fluid conversation was a must, so only a British bloke would do.

The good thing about being commitment-free at 26 was that I was also free to take up any opportunities life threw my way. So, when I was unexpectedly offered a job in The Netherlands, I jumped at the chance. I'll just go there for a year, I reasoned. So, no point bothering with boys at all. Yes, a year of being single and fabulous would be just the ticket. You know that old cliché about meeting the one when you least expect it? Well, it's me. I'm the cliché. One week into my Amsterdam adventure the love of my life slid into the desk next to mine. He was a co-worker, he was a foreigner, and I was smitten.

In my mind, the following few months were the stuff of movie montages – a soft-focus blur of riding bicycles alongside glittering canals, cradling lattes in cosy cafes and pitting my Welsh wine-drinking skills against his Polish penchant for vodka shots. Everything seemed easy, inevitable, exactly how it was supposed to feel. Cut to now - fourteen years, six countries, seven house moves, one failed marriage ultimatum, one actual wedding and one baby later. Me and my former desk mate are married (five years after the aforementioned ultimatum I might add), as well as co-parents, business partners, and most days, best friends. But that's leaving out the squiggly bits. If finding true love takes graft, then boy, maintaining it is a whole other level of work. But that friend, is for another book.

Single And Anxious? Get Unstuck In 4 Steps

OK, so we have established that the idea of being single at 30 can give us serious anxiety, and we also know it's really not our fault for feeling that way. Now what?

When you're approaching 30 and looking for love, it's tempting to rush towards your happily ever after. But think about it for a second. If you're lucky, you'll be on this planet for another 60 years or more. And if you're even luckier, you'll be with your partner for the rest of your life. That means, 60 more years with the person you're potentially panic coupling with right now. Big gulp.

As they say in therapy, slow is fast. And you might find that being single opens the door to experiences you wouldn't otherwise have. I speak from experience. Despite being anxious about my single status for most of my 20s, looking back I'm glad I settled down a little later than expected. Being un-attached for most of my 20s gave me the freedom to invest in myself, travel the world, live abroad and build incredible friendships - without having to consider a plus one in the process.

I consulted some of the world's wisest Therapists, Relationship Experts and Recovered 30-Phobics, for specific advice on overcoming single anxiety and putting yourself in the best position to find your person, whenever that may be. Get ready for some red-hot expert tips.

How To Stop Looking Out

- **Drop False Deadlines**

"Clients will say, if I don't find someone by 30, then I'm never gonna find someone. But is that true? Probably not. If you can let go of that story, that's when that breakthrough happens. Realise that the timeline is actually not that significant. You might find someone at 33, or 42. Finding the person, that's the real point"
　(Caitlan Siegenthaler, IFS Therapist & Podcaster)

- **Stop 'Should-ing'**

"Don't waste energy on what society says you should be doing or what other people expect of you... the thing that matters long term is what you want to do"
　(Karina Valencia, COO Wheely)

- **Prep A Comeback**

"If other people are questioning your relationship status, prepare a response that makes sense to you. You could say 'I don't have a partner yet because that doesn't feel aligned to me,' or 'that's my business,' 'there's a lot more to me than my relationship status', or 'my career's going great"
  (Caitlan Siegenthaler, IFS Therapist & Podcaster)

- **Flip The Script**

"When you go on a date, don't worry about whether the other person likes you, think about if you like them first"
  (Dani Weiss, Dating Coach)

How To Start Looking In

- **Banish Self-Trash-Talk**

"Start recognising your negative thinking – when you start thinking maybe it's me, maybe they won't like me, maybe I'm not good enough. Take note of it. Start reversing that negative self-talk"
  (Vassia Sarantopoulou, Psychologist)

- **Understand Your Needs**

"Think about why you want a relationship – relationships are not for the faint-hearted, and you certainly don't go into them if you want an easy life. Staying single is perfectly valid and there could be other ways to meet your needs. So, you obviously want something. You want companionship, or togetherness or someone to share your interests, cook your dinner... it's important to start with what you do want"
  (Mary Hutchings, Relate Counsellor)

- **Love Yourself Too**

"I don't advise women that if they love themselves first, then they will find love. Self-love is a parallel journey. Know that you are inherently loveable already. You do not need to arrive already 'healed' or become

'perfect' to be worthy of a relationship. Just keep going down the path you're already on, and keep dating at the same time"
(Dani Weiss, Dating Coach)

- **Invest In Yourself**

"You are the best investment you will ever make. So, enjoy being self-centred for now. Take every opportunity to work, learn things, travel the world and make connections. It will never be easier than it is right now"
(Kate Berski, Author)

How To Reframe Your Goals

- **Meet Your Person, Not Your Deadline:**

"Place less emphasis on the right time, and more emphasis on the right person, because there's no point rushing into a relationship or a marriage. You could end up even further behind in your timeline if you commit to or get involved with the wrong person and it doesn't work out. It's much better to take your time to make such important decisions"
(Caitlan Siegenthaler, IFS Therapist & Podcaster)

- **Seek Connections, Not Tick Boxes**

"Most daters are picky about the superficial factors. They have a checklist saying he has to be six foot tall, earn X amount of money, wear X type of shoes or have these hobbies... but they are not picky enough about the human connection. So let go of the surface checklist but be picky about how that person makes you feel, the deeper emotional needs they meet, the kind of life partner they will be... Do they make you feel safe? Loved? Understood?"
(Dani Weiss, Dating Coach)

- **Think Long Term**

"Fast connections often burn really hot, and then burn out. Instant good chemistry can be a sign that you'll have good sex, but not nec-

essarily a good relationship. And that 'spark' can mean the person is poking at an old wound... they're a little bit unavailable, a little bit narcissistic, a little self-centred. And because of your history, that really lights you up"

(Dani Weiss, Dating Coach)

- **Live For Now**

"You have time to meet your person... for now, be present, enjoy the moment, be silly, make mistakes, drink too much, think too little. Visit people and places, try weird things, talk, listen, try, fail... live for now, not the future"

(Rosanna Ruff, Life Coach & Co-Founder of Tapestry)

- **Do The 4-Date Rule**

"Slow is fast when it comes to love. If you want a lasting relationship, getting to know the person slowly is the only way. I encourage women to go on four dates. If you don't hate this person on the first date, if there are no big red flags, if they're a good person who treats you with respect on the first date, give it three or four more chances. Online dating inhibits that process, we are very quick to write people off and move to the next, instead of letting relationships develop and seeing where they go"

(Dani Weiss, Dating Coach)

- **Bid For Connections**

"Practice putting out conversational 'bids' every day – when you're in line at the coffee shop, in a store or at an event. Comment on the weather or ask someone for their opinion. Don't have any motive other than forming the habit – any real connections will be a bonus"

(Tricia Rosas, Travel Influencer & Opera Singer)

How To Celebrate The Small Wins

- **Celebrate The Learnings**

"The bad dates, the heartbreak... they're almost a prerequisite for

coming into greater alignment and finding the right relationship. So, every time you date the wrong person, think of it as a stepping stone, you're getting a little closer to what you want. Take a growth mindset - what did I learn? What did I figure out that I do or don't like?"
(Dani Weiss, Dating Coach)

- **Enjoy Your 'Single Moon'**

"Enjoy this single season as if it's going to end soon, like when couples go on a 'baby moon.' Because if you're on this path, it is going to end. So, celebrate the freedom of travelling solo, the peace of living alone and enjoying your own company while it lasts"
(Dani Weiss, Dating Coach)

- **Identify Your Virtues**

"Don't make relationship status your identity. You have so much more going on, other more important things that define you than who you're with... Make a list of your great qualities and achievements. Remind yourself that being single is not your identity"
(Caitlan Siegenthaler, IFS Therapist & Podcaster)

MINDHACKER QUESTIONS

- Is it more important that I meet my timeline, or my person (at any time)?

- What compromises or changes would I need to make to my life(style) or life plan if I met my person right now? Am I ready and willing to make these changes at this time?

TURNING 30 GOALS - REGROUP

Take a look back at your original list of Turning 30 Goals – did you write a relationship goal on there? How high up your list is it sitting? What words did you use to express it?

Now you've learned more about the external influences that might have shaped your romantic expectations, does finding a partner still feel like a top priority for you?

If yes, that's great. Now you know for sure that this is a genuine life goal. But does it feel any more or less important on your life list? Would you now articulate the end goal any differently? For example, if your original goal was 'Find a partner by the time I turn 30,' your new goal might be 'Find my person when the time is right.' How can you reframe your relationship goals to be less about mountainous milestones and more about small steps to help you get there? Instead of 'Find someone to marry' could it be 'Find one new person to have coffee with every month?'

Before moving on, take a minute to re-write your relationship goals, in your own words, on the 'NEW GOALS' list at the back of this book, or wherever you're taking your notes. And if you feel ready to move forward, add a 'BABY GOALS' list too. Jot down two or three simple things you can commit to doing that will put you on the path to finding your person when the time is right. I don't believe in putting deadlines on end goals but timings can be helpful when it comes to process goals – so while the goal to 'meet someone by 30,' might be unrealistic and pressurising, a plan to 'invite one new person to coffee every month' could be motivating. Remember to keep your commitments small, achievable, and within your control. There really is no step too small here.

So You Don't Have A Ring

"It's better to be single wishing you were married than married wishing you were single"
(Unknown)

Engagement Anxiety Is Real

Engagement anxiety was a BIG pressure point for me and my friends in our late 20s. And honestly it took me by surprise. Having always been wildly ambitious, fiercely independent and disinterested in settling, I resolved to stay unmarried at an early age. I'd developed commitment phobia in my early 20s, not symptomatic of my parents' divorce, but rather their staying together. With them role-modelling marital success (at the time of writing they've just celebrated their 50th wedding anniversary), anything less than a guaranteed lifetime commitment and a best friend for life seemed barely worth the bother.

Yet here I was, aged 29, three years into my first serious relationship, the last of my close friends to seal the deal, and panicking. I never wanted to be the ultimatum girl, but when push came to pre-30 shove, I saw no other option than issuing the infamously uncool 'commit or quit' ultimatum. In my 20s, relationships felt like a race – with a big fat ring at the finish line.

Therapist Caitlan Siegenthaler observes a similar mindset in her clients today, particularly those whose 30th birthdays are looming:

"Women in their late 20s are looking at this milestone birthday, the dawn of a new decade, and it really creates a reflection point. They become anxious that they've not done enough at this point, that they're behind. What they are most anxious about is being in the right rela-

tionship or getting married. Many feel this pressure to get married by 30"
 (Caitlan Siegenthaler, IFS Therapist)

I wanted to understand if this engagement pressure was something all 20-somethings felt – so I consulted my data. The reality surprised me, in a good way. While finding a romantic relationship remains a priority for women now in their 20s, it is equally important to other life goals, such as finding a great job. Moreover, today's 20-somethings appear to be prioritising mental health and financial security above relationship status, which I believe indicates a positive shift towards self-development before settling down.

Hearst Journalist Bethan explained:

"I like the idea of marriage, and many friends are doing it. But I would much rather be on my own, doing my own stuff than be married to someone who isn't 100% right. I don't even necessarily have to get married. If I'm in a long partnership with someone, that's also fine"
 (Bethan Rose Jenkins, 29, Hearst Magazines)

Despite these findings – engagement anxiety still exists, with some groups of women, as we'll explore later, feeling greater pressure than others to tie the knot. In my survey 67% of single women said they feel behind where they expected to be on their marriage goal. Their comments indicate a significant gap between their expectations about when they'd get married and their experienced reality:

"I planned much more for myself by this age, let alone 30. At 25 I thought I would be married with children and own a house, I do not have any of these things which puts more pressure to achieve it by 30"
 (25yrs, UK)

"I aways thought I'd be married by 30, and now I'm anxious because I'm unsure if I will ever be married. I hope my life will turn around by 30"
 (24yrs, USA)

Whilst engagement pressure can feel very real in our 20s, what's interesting is that in hindsight, few women who marry after 30 feel they tied the knot too late. Many of my expert interviewees met their partners in their 30s and 40s, and all took the view that it's more important to meet the right person than to meet an age-related deadline.

Marriage After 30: Laurie Jennings, GM Good Housekeeping Institute.

"I met my husband at 35, we were married at 40... I always believed in marriage, that lifelong partnership, but before I met my husband there really wasn't anyone I could see myself spending my life with..."

Engagement Anxiety: It's NOT You

When we can theoretically get married at any legal age, I wanted to understand where the expectation of being married by 30 comes from, why women still feel under pressure to lock it down by the end of the decade, and why they may feel like a failure if they don't.

It is apparent that external influences can really ramp up the pressure when it comes to if, and when we tie the knot. Some of the biggest pressure points I've identified include:

1. Generation Gaps

2. Cultural Pressure

3. FOMO

4. Content Vs Contentment

5. Fast-Tracking

Generation Gaps

Despite the aforementioned marriage ultimatum (which failed spectacularly) me and my boyfriend did wind up getting married. In 2016, when we were both 32. Three years after my self-imposed deadline.

My mother, by way of contrast married in 1974 aged 21. And according to the UK Office of National Statistics, this generation gap in marital age is bang on trend. Back in the mid-70s when my Mum tied the knot, a whopping 91% of women were married by 30. Today, it's less than 33%. According to the US Census Bureau, Americans are still more likely to be married by 30, at 50%, though this figure has also dropped by almost half, from 90% in 1962.

This could help explain why Millennials like me (broadly people born between the early 1980s and the late 1990s) with Boomer parents feel this pressure particularly keenly. A 2017 study by UK dating site Match.com found that Millennials are 177% more likely to feel an overwhelming pressure to get married, than other generations. Which I feel can only be a positive shift for the current generation.

Whether consciously or not, parental marriage age can create an implicit expectation, prompting negative comparison down the line ('my mum was married with two kids at my age, and I don't even have a boyfriend!'). That was almost certainly true in my case. Knowing that my mum had been married at 21 seemed to set off an unconscious timer that I felt I was racing against from that point onwards. I was behind before I'd even begun seriously dating!

While my own time pressure was mostly self-imposed, for many women it's more overt. Often manifesting as constant questioning around relationship status, light-hearted 'banter' towards partners, or well-meaning meddling. It all sends the message to women that they really should be settling down by now. This is bad enough when we want to get married (cue conflict behind closed doors), let alone when we don't. Nobody can ever know what goes on inside another couple's relationship – so piling on the pressure is usually unhelpful, and potentially even dangerous, in the instance of abusive relationships for example.

While my parents acknowledge that getting wed straight out of university seems ridiculously young and 'times are different now,' I'd convinced myself they secretly despaired as I trundled along ring-free into my late 20s. And if I'm honest with myself, wanting to please them did have something to do with my desire to get engaged by the time I turned 30. Having grown up with 'problematic' siblings who were unlikely to live conventional lives, I felt compelled to be the 'good girl' by default. I wanted to do all the right things, live a straightforward life, and make my family proud. Full disclosure, I probably read a little too much Jane Austen in my teens too, fancying my dad would be highly relieved at marrying off his only daughter for a modest dowry.

Of course, looking back these marriage motivations seem fairly ridiculous. My family would much rather I lived happily single than miserably married. And since I would be the one actually doing the marriage, surely pleasing myself should have carried more weight than pleasing my parents? But in my 20s, I didn't always know my own mind. I was easily swayed by the (real and perceived) opinions of others and overly eager to follow the crowd.

My current anti-pressure stance makes my own 'engagement' story seem all the more ironic. In fact, my current relationship status presents something of a riddle – I'm married, and yet I was never proposed to. And I have the meddlings of my mother and father to thank!

Two years post-ultimatum. My boyfriend is chatting to my dad over a G&T one evening. He casually floats the subject of marriage in a vague, future-oriented type of way. Dad is so thrilled at the prospect of finally getting shot of me, that he jumps the gun and announces it the very next evening over dinner. Much to the surprise of both myself and my groom-to-be. I wasn't mad about it mind you. I secretly believe that I'd still be waiting for that elusive proposal without a bit of well-meaning parental pressure at that critical juncture. Dad, if you're reading, thank you!

Cultural Pressure

If you've never indulged in the Netflix series Indian Matchmaking, you are in for a real treat. As well as being wildly entertaining viewing, it represents an intentional approach to coupling that flies in the face of other 'suck it and see' dating formats like Married at First Sight and Love Is Blind. I'm a huge fan of Reality Dating, can you tell?!

In the Indian Matchmaker, 'Aunty' Sima, puts great effort into making marriageable matches between couples whose situations, values, goals, and family cultures are deeply aligned. What strikes me most though is just how invested the singles' families are in the process – they hire the matchmaker, attend the initial 'briefing,' sometimes even the dates themselves, and are very vocal about the suitability of the match.

Whilst parent-dating isn't something all Indian women buy into, my survey suggests that South Asian women do feel greater pressure to settle down by 30. A fact which several members of my Instagram community agreed with:

"Since childhood, we are told that one should get married by 30. I feel we are slowly / gradually programmed into believing that by 30 we should get married"
(24yrs, from India, via Instagram)

"I deal with this pressure from my family, relatives and even colleagues – they say you're 26 years old, why don't you get married?!! It comes from the cultural belief that a girl should be married at 20 to 25. But I want to pursue my studies at this time"
(26yrs, from Pakistan, via Instagram)

Instagram followers from India informed me that the 'right marriageable age' for women tends to be between 22 to 28 for women, and 24 to 30 for men. Fascinatingly, the legal marriageable age in India also differs between genders, 18 for women and 21 for men.

Several other cultures came up in my conversations around marriage pressure. Italian American Journalist Alyssa explained how the well-meaning questions of her close-knit Italian family can unwittingly pile on the pressure:

"I come from a big Italian family, and our culture is really all about family – marriage and kids and big family gatherings... so everyone is always asking me when are you going to meet someone, when are you getting married, what about kids...? They are only asking because they care, but it does add to that pressure"
(Alyssa Montagna, Hearst Magazines)

Chinese women have also reported extreme pressure to marry at a young age. Chinese parents will visit 相亲角 (xiāngqīn jiǎo) or Matchmaking Corners" to post 征婚 (zhēnghūn) "marriage-seeking" ads for their children. Such is the marriage culture in China, that a specific word exists to describe it - 催婚 'cuīhūn' meaning pressing or urging someone to get married.

My data indicates that marital pressure doesn't just make women feel pressured, it encourages them to act on it. For example, Asian women are more likely to actually be married by 30 than white women (38% are married at 29 Vs 28% of white women).

But I believe things are starting to change. Young women from cultures with a tradition of early marriage are beginning to challenge the accepted norms. Tired of being torn between the expectations of their families and their own personal goals, they're pushing back on pressure and taking the time to figure out a future that fits, choosing to marry, or not, for themselves, and not only to please other people. Which I feel is inching us closer to a more equal world. My hope is that every woman is afforded the luxury of getting married if or when it feels right, and not because the outside world is telling her it's about time.

FOMO

Please excuse the achingly Millennial acronym, I promise it's relevant. I don't know about you, but I have to confess to having mixed feelings in my 20s each time another close friend glowingly announced her recent engagement. Yes, I was so happy for my friend, and yes, I was also sad that it wasn't me.

When you want to get married (and I fully appreciate not everyone does), watching friend after friend walk down the aisle ahead of you can create a lot of 'outsider' feelings - missing out, being the odd one out, running out of time... The changing marital status of others can trigger our unconscious desires to fit in, to avoid falling behind the pack – all perfectly functional survival instincts that don't serve us quite so well in this context. As this 21-year-old put it:

"30 seems like a hard place in life. What if I'm the only one not mar-

ried or with kids or a good job? What if I'm unhappy?"
   (21yrs, USA)

Celebrity Wedding Planner Georgie Davies observes that external pressure is a powerful driver for couples getting engaged:

"People are surrounded by others who are starting to settle down. Couples see everyone else getting engaged or married or having children and feel they need the next 'thing'- typically the wedding comes first"
   (Georgie Davies, Wedding Planner)

Now, I was queen of FOMO in my 20s. Forget 'always the bridesmaid, never the bride,' I was never a bridesmaid, and often relegated to second-tier guest status too. Sidebar – what is with the British tradition of 'evening guest' lists? Yes, the after party is the best bit, but there's something strange about turning up, stone-cold sober, to celebrate someone's nuptials when you've missed the main event, not to mention the fancy sit-down meal. But I digress. By the end of my 20's I was so over other people's weddings. The sitting awkwardly next to my non-fiancé as our closest friends made the commitment I coveted, the cringing as yet another auntie probed into our plans to tie the knot, the wondering why I wasn't marriage material after all... I tried my best not to make it about me, but I'd be lying if I said that other people's weddings never made me feel worse about myself.

Maybe that's why when it was, eventually, my turn, I did away with almost all of the traditions. We never 'announced' an engagement. We just got married, quietly, in a small church near my parents' place in Wales and walked back to their garden to celebrate. There were 12 of us in total. No 'wedding party', no top tables, no wedding breakfast, no tiered wedding cake, no first dance, no cheesy disco, no diamond rings... and no bank loans required. This approach would not be to everyone's taste it's true. Georgie the wedding planner described this set-up as 'her worst nightmare.' But it was right for us. And the best part was that NONE of our friends got FOMO. They all respected our decision to keep things on the down low. And I'll bet, they felt more than a bit relieved too.

Content Vs Contentment

91% of 20-somethings completing my Turning 30 study, admit to using social media every day – with scrolling socials emerging as the most popular leisure activity by far. It's no surprise then to see that social media has a powerful impact on women's perceptions, expectations and decisions around milestone moments like weddings.

Instagram and TikTok are flooded with viral videos of picture-perfect proposals, exotic engagement trips and wildly glamorous weddings - typically featuring abnormally attractive and unfeasibly wealthy young couples. And while I'm all for a bit of good-natured 'inspo,' my hunch is that most of these videos leave the average gal, betrothed or not, feeling less than adequate in the romance department.

The culture of content creation is clearly putting pressure on regular people to up their game. In 2019, the UK National Wedding Survey found that 42% of couples feel 'under pressure' to have a Pinterest or Instagram-worthy wedding. In 2022, the NWS reported that 60% of couples shared their engagement on social media before telling anyone face to face.

I don't mean to rain on anyone's wedding parade – but I can't help but worry that we are focusing on the wrong things here. Emphasising the event of the wedding over the lifelong commitment of marriage. Seeking external validation above internal certainty. And for those whose ultimate goal is to get, and stay, married – could our insta-inflated expectations actually be standing in the way of us getting the one thing we want?

In a recent study by Bookatable.co.uk, 33% of women said they'd be disappointed if their partner failed to plan an elaborate proposal. And 20% were looking for a proposal to brag about on their socials. If you find yourself agreeing, imagine being in your partner's shoes for a second. Maybe they're socially anxious and dread being the centre of attention? Maybe they're feeling the pinch and the thought of shelling out tens of thousands on one day is giving them major anxiety. Maybe they're time-poor and don't have the capacity to take on a side job in event planning. Maybe taking the pressure off would be the fastest way to get a ring on that finger. I can't speak for your partner, but I can tell you that the moment I let it be known that my goal was to have a marriage, and not a wedding, suddenly marriage was on the cards.

My husband, a natural introvert, and at the time a cash-strapped entrepreneur, breathed a visible sigh of relief when I suggested a guest list of close family and a budget of £2k for our 2016 wedding. I say this not to do anyone out of their dream day. There is nobody more You Do You than me. I merely mean to offer up alternatives, just in case the thing that's standing in the way of the marriage you want, is the thought of the wedding your partner doesn't want. So, if you're working with a reluctant fiancé, or you're the one dragging your feet, I highly recommend asking these questions – what do I want more, the wedding or the marriage? Or to put it another way – what is holding me back, the thought of the wedding, or the thought of being committed for life?

In our case, letting go of traditions and external expectations allowed me and my partner to have the wedding we really wanted. And it appears that many couples are tempted to do the same. According to a 2022 survey, 62% of engaged couples are considering a scaled-back wedding or an elopement, in light of the rising cost of living and the appeal of a more relaxed, intimate set-up. My hunch – most of them will end up doing things the traditional way to keep everyone happy, and I know there are a lot of opinions and expectations around weddings. But if deep down you know that a big white wedding is not for you, this is me giving you permission to pull the plug on tradition.

I've been married for eight years now, most of them very happy. And I've never once regretted our low-key wedding. I like being married too. I still get a childlike thrill from saying 'my husband,' like somehow, I'm playing at being a grown-up. It feels legit rolling up to a hotel as a Mr and Mrs. And I find comfort in being legally bound together – the unspoken promise that we try a little bit harder to make things work. I *have* adopted one tradition I didn't expect to. Whilst I didn't plan on changing my surname (I wanted to retain my personal and professional identity after marriage), I changed my mind a few years later when we became parents. There's something cute, and convenient, about having a common team name – and whilst it didn't feel important to take my husbands' last name, it suddenly felt crucial that

I share my daughters. That's the beauty of tradition – it can be wonderfully comforting when it works for you. And I feel lucky that I've been able to pick and mix the best bits.

Fast-Tracking

The process of researching and writing this book has shown me just how insidious societal conditioning can be when it comes to our life goals, and the 'proper order' of things that gets drilled into us almost from birth. I distinctly remember, aged about six, chanting the lyrics to a popular playground rhyme - 'first comes love, then comes marriage, then comes baby in a baby carriage...' Harmless perhaps, but nonetheless indicative of the type of external influences that cement the dreaded 'internal timeline' in our heads, compelling us to march through the milestones in the expected order, and making us feel like failures when we dare to deviate from the beaten track.

This brings us to babies... We will explore fertility pressure in great detail in Chapter 8, however, it definitely deserves an honourable mention here on account of how often it appears to be grouped in with getting married. We might be long past the era of shotgun weddings, but the good old Ticking Clock remains a key marital trigger for today's 20-somethings:

"I'm anxious because I don't have a spouse, and my biggest dream is to get married and have kids"
   (24yrs, USA)

"I feel like I'm in a sinking relationship and in order to have kids and get married I would have to have a better relationship before I'm 30"
   (25yrs, USA)

So far nothing new. Except, marriages are happening later than ever before. According to the ONS in 2019, the average age of men marrying women in the UK is now 34 and women marrying men is 32 (the ages are slightly younger in the USA). Same-sex couples tend to marry later, men at 38 and women at age 34.

Now, I'm a great believer in taking your time to make most big life decisions, including marriage - marry in haste, repent at leisure and all that. However, when it comes to female fertility, time is not always on our side. This puts some women under incredible pressure to procreate at warp speed, particularly those following a traditional 'marriage first' timeline. No sooner have they said 'I Do' to becoming two, than the race is on to make three.

I'd count myself among the more leisurely of family planners. Before we got married, we both felt strongly that children were not for us and decided on a child-free path (I think we even shook on it). But I changed my mind a few years later, and luckily my husband was on the same page (PSA: It's OK to change your mind!). It felt like we took our time to come to the right decision for us, and yet, we were married for just three years before taking the plunge. My young-married parents on the other hand enjoyed 9 years of marital bliss before baby #1 came along. Later marriage it seems, isn't necessarily changing the timeline, it's simply compressing it.

Unmarried At 30: Am I Normal?

If your ring finger is feeling decidedly light right now, it may help to know you're not alone.

The Myth: MARRIED AT 30. Everyone is married, or at least engaged, by 30. If there's no ring on it at 29 you've missed the marriage boat.

The Reality: UNMARRIED AT 30. According to our study, the majority (72% to be exact) of women are NOT married, or engaged by the time they turn 30. At 29, 28% are married and 13% are engaged.

Unmarried And Anxious? Get Unstuck In 4 Steps

OK, so we have established that marriage pressure is real, and being unmarried, when we want to be engaged, can give us anxiety. So short of hypnotising an unwilling partner into popping the question, how do you get unstuck?

First things first, do a sense check. Take a deep breath and think about what your end goal really is. Be brutally honest with yourself. There are no wrong answers.

People want to get married for myriad reasons, some more valid than others. Arguably, over-focusing on short-term goals like the engagement announcement, the wedding, the honeymoon or even the generic outcome (being a Mrs by 30!), could lead you to overlook the ultimate end goal – finding and committing to the right person, and making it work for the rest of your lives. It is widely said that your choice of life partner is the single most important decision you will ever make – dictating everything that happens from here on in, from your financial situation to your career prospects, family set-up and friendship groups.

So, while milestone birthdays can pressure us into rushing down the aisle, try to keep the big picture in mind. If you're lucky, you'll be on this planet for another 60 years or more. And if you're even luckier, you'll be with your partner for the rest of your life. That means, 60 more years with the person you're potentially panic coupling with right now. Big gulp.

The reality is, thanks to the emancipation of women, few of us actually NEED to get married any more. Marriage is a WANT. A positive decision made between two consenting adults when the time is right for them. Nobody else need apply.

How To Stop Looking Out

- **Drop The Deadline**

"Deadlines create stress when it's not there. They're constructs of our mind that aren't real. Let yourself off"
    (Laurie Jennings, GM Good Housekeeping Institute USA)

- **Lose The Pressure**

"Put less pressure on yourself to be married by a certain point – realise that it's actually better to get wherever you want to go in your own

time. Once you're on the other side of the deadline you will realise that it didn't actually matter in the end"
(Caitlan Siegenthaler, IFS Therapist & Podcaster)

- **Don't Live To Others' Timelines**

"Ask yourself to what extent other people's timelines are influencing your own internal marriage deadline. How old were your parents when they married (if they did?) Which of your closest friends are already married? Aim to live to your own timeline instead"
(Kate Berski, Author)

- **Let Go Of External Validation**

"Making people happy and meeting others' expectations are the wrong reasons to get wed. The approval of others is fleeting, but marriage is a lifelong commitment. Remember that you and your partner are the decision-makers here"
(Kate Berski, Author)

- **Push Back**

"If people are asking questions around when you're getting married, it's totally acceptable to say you're not happy discussing that. Recognise that it's more about them than you"
(Georgie Davis, Wedding Planner)

- **Don't Compete**

"Remember that early marriage is no guarantee of a successful marriage, so don't use that as a barometer of other people's relationship success"
(Kate Berski, Author)

How To Start Looking In

- **Write A Pros List**

"Ask yourself why you want to become a wife. List all of the positive reasons that are attracting you to marriage right now. Then cross out anything that sounds like a 'should.' For example, 'because that's just what you do,' or 'because all my friends are married.' These are external expectations and not genuine internal needs"
(Kate Berski, Author)

- **Do An Impact Audit**

"Think about if and how your life will change when you get married. Look at every angle – the emotional, social, professional, financial, practical and any other implications. They might be positive, negative or neutral. Talk about it with your partner. Will you do anything differently after you're married? How ready are you for these changes? Does this change anything about your marriage plans?"
(Kate Berski, Author)

- **Know Your Needs**

"Conversations between two people are so often about an individual. In any relationship, you need to understand yourself and your own needs first. Ask yourself questions like What do I need? What am I really feeling about marriage? If you don't know how you feel, or you've dismissed how you really feel, your partner will also find it easy to dismiss how you feel"
(Mary Hutchings, Relate Counsellor)

- **Embrace Transition**

"We as humans are so ready to get to the end result that we lose the beauty and the enjoyment of the process. Don't think about it as waiting time, but a process of transition. Try to be more present and notice what's happening in the transition towards marriage. Who are you becoming?"
(Caitlan Siegenthaler, IFS Therapist & Podcaster)

How to Reframe Your Goals

- **Make A Roadmap**

"If you find yourself waiting for a proposal, don't keep it to yourself. Ask your partner why it's not happening, without an argument. Their answers may be surprising. Maybe it's too much pressure to do things a certain way, or maybe it's finances... you can't know, and you can't make a plan about how to overcome the roadblocks and how to get there until you know where you stand"
  (Georgie Davis, Wedding Planner)

- **Play The Long Game**

"If you're lucky, you have a lifetime to look forward to with your partner. In the grand scheme of things, waiting an extra few months, or years, to make sure you're making the right choice, won't matter as much as you think"
  (Kate Berski, Author)

- **Think Marriage Not Wedding**

"Make sure you're planning a marriage and not just a wedding. Set aside the party planning, glamorous dresses, shiny rings and Instagram stories. You can do all of that. But first be sure you'd still choose to marry this person even without the wedding bells and whistles"
  (Kate Berski, Author)

- **Be Prepared**

"Make sure you are in a good place as a couple – it's a strain having a wedding, a lot of conversation about planning and family politics, so knowing you can manage that is step one"
  (Georgie Davis, Wedding Planner)

- **Consider Alternatives**

"Remember, you don't have to do anything that's not right for you. Marriage is not a must; weddings don't have to cost the earth. Give yourself permission to run your relationship your way"
  (Kate Berski, Author)

How To Celebrate The Small Wins

- **Be Positively Pre-Married**

"When I was 28 everyone would ask me how I could be almost 30 and not have a husband. I was like, 'What do you mean? I love my life, I have great friends, I love my job, I travel all the time!"
(Laurie Jennings, GM, Good Housekeeping Institute)

- **Celebrate The Wait**

"Imagine you'd actually married the first person you thought about marrying. Or married your current partner the first moment it crossed your mind. Would that have been the right decision at that time? Don't fall into the trap of marrying in haste and repenting at leisure"
(Kate Berski, Author)

- **Choose Your Partner**

"Don't give your partner the leftovers after giving other people your best all day. Allocate half an hour each day to sit down and really talk about your day - no phones, no TV, no kids around. Practice really listening and reflecting on what your partner says"
(Mary Hutchings, Relate Counsellor)

MINDHACKER QUESTIONS

- Which part of getting engaged do I fantasise about most – the feeling of commitment and contentment or the wedding looks, the celebrations and the Instagram likes?

- What will happen if I do get engaged/married by the time I turn 30? What will happen if I don't? How does each outcome change my life?

TURNING 30 GOALS - REGROUP

Take a look back at your original list of Turning 30 Goals – did you write a marriage goal on there? How high up your list is it sitting? Which words did you use to express it?

Now you've learned more about the external influences that might have shaped your expectations around engagement and marriage, does getting married still feel like a top priority at this time in your life?

If yes, that's great. Now you know for sure that this is a genuine life goal. Does it feel any more or less important on your life list? Would you now articulate it any differently? For example, if your original goal was 'Have a ring on my finger by the time I turn 30,' your new goal might be 'Get married to the right person when the time is right.'

Before moving on, take a minute to re-write your marriage goal, in your own words, on the 'NEW GOALS' list at the back of this book, or wherever you're taking your notes. We aren't writing your annual work KPI's here, so no deadlines needed. And when you're ready to move forward, add a 'BABY GOALS' list too. Jot down two or three simple things you can do on a regular basis that will put you on the path to marital bliss when it feels right for you and your partner. Remember, keep your commitments small, achievable and within your control. While 'issue a marriage ultimatum' might not be the one, 'discuss barriers to engagement with my partner' feels a lot more realistic, and helpful.

So You Don't Have Friends

"True friendship is when you walk into their house and your Wi-Fi connects automatically"
Unknown

Friendship Anxiety Is Real

I've always been a social creature and count myself lucky to have a close group of girlfriends around most of the time. Nonetheless, I can point to a good handful of moments in my life when I've felt genuinely friendless. The first, at university, when it transpired that my closest mates would disappear with their boyfriends every weekend, leaving my single self to twiddle my thumbs 'til Monday. The second, third and fourth times all stemmed from my own geographical mobility.

In my 20s, I relocated three times - to London at 22, Amsterdam at 26, and Sydney at 29 – 'starting over' each time fuelled by new girl nerves.

My first international move was prompted in part by my own failure to launch. At 26, having spent the last few years career-cruising, financially flat-lining and romantically stagnant, it suddenly felt like I'd missed the memo that we were all 'doing big things' now. My closest friends started bagging big ticket items with which to propel their lives forward – like serious relationships, and flat deposits. All while I'd been busy perfecting my recipe for pasta bake (which by my own admission, is excellent). After my boss at the time rejected my plea for a pay rise, I'd decided it was time to up my game. And after job-hunting for a couple of months in London, an opportunity arose at an agency in The Netherlands. Not having a better plan, I thought 'What's the worst that could happen?'

The early months were a struggle though. Whilst Amsterdam is undeniably beautiful, I loved life on a bike and my job was delightful, it quickly transpired that making friends wasn't going to be as easy as I'd imagined. I remember in the early days asking a male co-worker about the social scene at the office. With classically Dutch directness, he smiled at me and said 'Kate, we are your colleagues, we are not your friends.' Back in London, I'd made several mates at after-work drinks, so this felt like a bit of a blow. In hindsight, I realise I spent far too long stewing on my disappointment, whilst sitting on the sofa hoping my new BFFs would barrel through the door at any moment. They did not. So, after a couple of months, I decided to take matters into my own hands.

Having always simply befriended whomever I was studying/working alongside up to this point, this was my first experience of consciously *trying* to make new friends. And it was fraught with all of the false starts, awkwardness, disappointments and cringe moments you get with romantic dating, only with a lot less snogging. I started out with classic networking techniques – attending events and asking friends from back home to 'set me up.' Cue, the guy who invited me round to do an Ikea flat pack on the first friend date, the girl whose social scene involved dancing naked in the moonlight with relative strangers (no judgment by the way if that's your thing) and the monosyllabic German with whom it was impossible to carry on a fluid conversation, because she disappeared to the ladies every five minutes to 'powder her nose.' Again, each to their own lifestyle, but compatibility is key when it comes to forging new friendships.

Eventually, after about six months, I'd managed to assemble my new tribe. I'd met each girlfriend individually – one from an expat group, one through work, one was a friend of my flatmate and another a girlfriend of a friend in London. Since we'd clicked instantly, I just knew they'd gel together as well. And I was more than willing to be the social glue.

Luckily it didn't take many bottles of cheap white wine before we'd become fast friends. My efforts were successful, and the experience completely changed my mindset on friendship. It taught me that as an adult, friendships don't just fall into your lap. Making friends over the age of 25 requires serious commitment and conscious effort. And it's worth it. The self-styled *'Dammers in Distress,'* as we have henceforth been known, were the undisputed highlight of my expat experience.

I met Laney somewhat reluctantly after a co-worker introduced us. 'She's a new client, and I really think you'll hit it off.' For context, when you work in an Ad agency, socialising with clients is part of the job, and not a part I'd ever particularly enjoyed. Somehow the idea of 'relaxing' over a few drinks, while simultaneously trying to impress them with your wit and wisdom, and not saying anything stupid, felt like spinning too many plates to my over-thinking 20-something self. So, I didn't expect to enjoy this cringey client set-up one jot. BOY was I wrong. I knew within about two minutes that she was awesome. My intentions of being on best behaviour went out the window after the first sip of Sauvignon Blanc, as it became abundantly clear we were going to bypass professionalism and skip straight to friendship. A warm-hearted Scot with a wicked sense of humour and a boujis side to match my own, she felt like a little piece of home. Yes, I thought, she's a keeper.

It turns out, my need to make friends wherever I go isn't just about having fun, it's a survival instinct. Scientific and Psychological research studies have found that having close friendships increases our overall life satisfaction, decreases our risk of depression and reduces mortality rates for a range of chronic diseases. Conversely, friendlessness increases our chances of premature death almost two-fold and is more damaging to our health than smoking twenty cigarettes a day.

My own research reveals a strong correlation between social ties and attitudes towards ageing. 74% of the young women I surveyed who are happy in their friendship group also feel positive about turning 30, compared to only 11% of those who feel dissatisfied with their current friendships. Strong friendships, I found, were a better predictor of positive ageing than even romantic relationships.

While the body of evidence linking friendship to *'well-gevity'* grows, actual rates of friendship appear to be falling dramatically. A 2021 survey by Gallup and the Survey Centre on American Life found that 12% of Americans claim to have no close friends, rising from just 3% in 1990. A YouGov study in the UK found that 7% of Britons don't have anyone in their life they call a close friend.

Despite close friendships being essential to our survival, and sanity, it seems that the world in which we live is conspiring against us when it comes to meeting and keeping our besties close. Especially when it comes to our turbulent 20s. In a decade of constant change, conflicting priorities and swelling responsibilities, female friendships are often the first casualty, as more pressing priorities take over.

Friendship Anxiety: It's NOT You

It's precisely because friendship is such a fundamental human need, that not having friends, or drifting apart from the ones we do have, can cause us so much anxiety. Especially when the lives we live create barriers to friendship, and the media we consume makes us feel like we're the only ones feeling lonely or lacking in the social department. Some of the biggest factors influencing 20-something friendships, and our feelings about them, include:

1. Growing Apart

2. Dates Before Mates

3. #Squadgoals

4. Fake Friends

5. Organic Aspirations

Growing Apart

Loneliness shows up strongly in transitional times – and our 20s are amongst the most transitional of all. This is the decade in which same-age peers start to follow wildly different life paths. Within a single friendship group, you suddenly find PhD students and world travellers, corporate fast-trackers and struggling artists, single girls and married mothers, homeowners and couch surfers. With such disparate priorities, responsibilities and circumstances at play, it's not hard to see why historic relationships come under strain.

"I'm 28 and live in London, but I grew up in Merseyside. I'm single, but in my girl group of 5 from home, the other 4 are all engaged. I've always been quite career-focused, only ever had long-distance relationships and feel far too young to consider settling! The others are homeowners or in the process of buying whereas I have zero savings and spend any spare penny after rent on travelling. We're still friends but our lives are so different"
(Bethan Jenkins, Journalist)

Coach Carrie Eaton explains that late 20s lifestyle divergence often leads to the end of old friendships, a process which she sees as inevitable and potentially necessary:

"In our 20s we don't always carry over those same friendships that we've had in high school or college. They don't necessarily serve us in the same way they did or help us move forward into the future. In this life stage, you're learning about what no longer works for you, naturally you're going to experience more of those Friendship Breakups"
(Carrie Eaton, Friendship Coach)

Navigating A Friendship Break-Up:

"I was really close with a woman in college. We lived together and spent almost every day together at college. Afterwards, she went down more of the party route, she was pursuing a lot of different relationships with men. I respected that it was the way she wanted to live, but I knew that being her friend was no longer serving me. I was starting to feel really drained, and inauthentic. I started changing my own behaviour just to make hanging out with her a little bit more tolerable. In the end, I had to be honest with myself, and with her, that I didn't want to live that type of lifestyle. It was uncomfortable, but we are okay with each other now, we check in sometimes but it's no longer a close relationship"
(Carrie Eaton, Friendship Coach)

My research suggests friendships fall down the priority ladder as the decade wears on. While 50% of 20-year-olds say friendship is a top priority in life, only 33% of 29-year-olds feel the same. Women in their early 20s tend to socialise most often, with 42% seeing friends daily, compared to 28% of 26 to 29-year-olds. But social disconnection can happen at any age. Overall, nearly 50% of 20-somethings feel they are 'growing apart' from their friends, and 58% say their social life is not as fulfilling as it used to be.

And herein lies the problem.

While it's tempting to focus on the big-ticket items in our 20s; Marriage, kids, careers, homes, de-prioritising friendship can come at the expense of our mental health.

"In our 20s we start prioritising building a career or a family or both. Schedules get much busier and these big things take priority over little things like regular catchups with the girls. Essentially, we de-prioritise connection. That's a problem because less social connection means a decrease in support, which reduces life satisfaction and increases the likelihood of mental health challenges"
    (Carrie Eaton, Friendship Coach)

The demotion of friendship by young adults, whether intentional or not, worries me greatly, especially as someone who has relied heavily on the support of close friends in turbulent times. Like the year I became a mother. A transition which, contrary to what the books told me, felt to me wholly unnatural and entirely unreasonable. I remember one particularly painful morning a few months port-partum - chronically sleep-deprived, overwhelmed and close to breaking point, I was walking the rainy streets, pushing the buggy, and bawling my eyes out. Even in that sorry state, I knew how fortunate I was to be able to pick up the phone to my best friend (who is also a therapist as luck would have it) and feel able to share my greatest fears, my darkest thoughts, and be genuinely heard, and supported. Even now on a good day, I always leave my catch-ups with Michelle feeling lighter. Because a good friend with whom you can be exactly yourself, ugly crying and all, is quite literally worth her weight in gold. Close friends help us survive and thrive. This is why I believe investing in friendship should be a top priority for all women, wherever our lives should take us.

Dates Before Mates

Between the ages of eleven and sixteen, I attended a highly academic all-girls high school. So naturally, my first experiences of real friendship were with women. To this day I remain a girls' girl to my core, which I believe is proof positive of how formative teenage friendships can be. In fact, the only time I thought I'd made a close male friend, I ended up married to him. So, there you go.

It's fair to say that my teenage friendship group was not wildly successful with the opposite sex, despite our best intentions at the much-anticipated termly 'mixers' with the local boy's school. Most of the group didn't really get going until university, myself excluded – as my dry spell seemed to roll right through until my late 20s. My best school friend, however, proved more successful in the romance department – finishing up university with a serious boyfriend attached. I'm ashamed to say I didn't take this development very well. I was flat-out envious if I'm honest. I also assumed (wrongly) that she was now far too busy being *'boyfed'* up to hang out with me and was probably looking down on my sad single status from her position of romantic superiority. So, I jumped the gun and ghosted her myself. To her credit, she forgave my poor friendship form and kept in touch. And when I eventually agreed to meet her boyfriend, I had to grudgingly admit that he was alright actually.

While my experience of 'bros before hoes' might have been largely in my head, for many women it becomes all too real, especially when the mid-20s hit. A 2022 study by UK dating site Match found that 26 is the average age at which women meet their life partners. And my data indicates that 26-year-olds are also least satisfied with the state of their friendships. Journalist Alyssa believes this is no coincidence:

"Guys can start to come in the way of friendship in your late 20s. Your friends start to get into serious relationships and they're just not as available to hang out anymore. You don't want to be the needy friend, but it's sad when things change"
 (Alyssa Montagna, Hearst Magazines)

Relationship status divides 20-somethings like nothing else. Not least because more of our friends will meet their person in this decade than any other. And when you're the single girl in a group of mates caught up in their cosy 'love bubbles,' you can quickly find yourself out in the cold.

Unsurprisingly, single and childfree women consistently prioritise social connections more highly than those in relationships. In my survey, 43% of childfree women and 47% of single women named friendship as a top 5 priority, compared to just 26% of mothers and 33% of couples. This is just one of the reasons why I'm now grateful for my 'grindingly single' years – I believe the space this gave me to focus on my friendships made our bonds even stronger. And whilst I have no empirical data on this, my hunch is that women who have long periods of being single, or who settle down at a later age, are more likely to have a close circle of friends around them for life.

#SQUADGOALS

Thanks in no small part to Taylor Swift et al, friendship is finally having its media moment. On Superbowl Sunday 2024, headlines historically reserved for romantic partnerships were overtaken by BFFs Taylor Swift and Blake Lively hugging it out in the stands. Don't get me wrong, I am absolutely here for positive, supportive representations of female friendship. Lord knows I've watched enough episodes of Real Housewives to wonder what went wrong. But I'm also increasingly aware of how media representations of female friendship can impact the expectations of regular people.

Famous friendships can set a high bar which can't always be met in real life (and probably isn't true to the behind-the-scenes reality either). As we scroll through Instagram images of gorgeous girl squads frolicking on a Malibu beach wearing string bikinis and matching smiles, can make us worry that we don't have those kinds of friends, or wonder whether our own group is having that much fun. Much like romantic relationships, when we only see the highlights reels, it can be tempting to assume that other people's friends are always around; That friendships should be smooth sailing and conflict-free; That you must entertain your mates with endless wisecracks to stay relevant; Or that you have to look a certain way to be accepted by a group.

"If you are already feeling a challenge in making friendships, already experiencing loneliness, it can be easy to romanticise what you see externally. Social media is a lens that influences our perception of what reality should look like. Real friendships aren't always going to be this sunny, beautiful, perfect thing"
(Carrie Eaton, Friendship Coach)

When it comes down to it, friendship is all about a sense of belonging. And loneliness often stems from a feeling that we don't belong. Psychologist Vassia Sarantopoulou observed some of the most common factors that can make us feel like outsiders:

"Loneliness often starts with an event - for example, a breakup with a partner or moving to a new city or country where they don't speak the language. Their support system is suddenly taken away. Sometimes people experience discrimination which leads to a feeling of being an outcast. Or they'll suffer childhood trauma causing them to hold people at arm's length. Anything that makes people feel that they don't belong in their environment can create loneliness"
(Vassia Sarantopoulou, Psychologist)

My conversation with Vassia really hit home. In terms of my own experience as an alienated expat, living in a country where I didn't speak the language. And also, in terms of my new family. I currently live in the UK with my Polish husband and our four-year-old daughter. Soon after she was born, desperate for some more support, we moved his parents in around the corner. Neither of them speaks English, so whilst they're both friendly and sociable people, they've struggled to connect with others or make friends within our community. Having been in similar situations myself, I can imagine how isolating this experience must be for them. I really need to cut them a bit more slack.

The challenge with 'in-crowds' is that they necessarily create an 'out-crowd.' And anyone who's ever moved cities, started a new job or rocked up alone to an event will be all too familiar with the awkwardness of being the new girl, or experienced that deep-rooted fear of rejection. Coach Carrie explained how this fear can backfire if left unchecked:

"When we are in a situation where other people have their solidified

friend groups, it's much harder to integrate into that. We become a little bit more self-conscious, we worry about being accepted or not fitting in. And so those feelings can hold us back, causing us to withdraw from or not participate in social situations"
(Carrie Eaton, Friendship Coach)

The best solution I've found for being an outsider, is to band together with other outsiders. When you move abroad, integration might be the ultimate goal, but other expats are always the lowest-hanging fruit. When you're new at work, find the next newest person. Their own experiences of settling in and navigating new systems will still be fresh, and they're likely to be a lot more empathetic, not to mention helpful.

Fake Friends

The nature of my work means I often get messages from people who are struggling with their mental health. One that really sticks in my mind was from a young woman who admitted she felt very sad, and incredibly lonely. She wanted to connect with me because she believed the key to making herself happy would be to get more Instagram followers, and she wanted advice on how to do that. In the gentlest way possible I told her that she might be looking in the wrong place. While online friendships can be a helpful source of support, it's real-life connections that really matter when it comes to improving mental health.

It's easy to see the source of her confusion though. We live in an era of external validation. I mean, did it ever really happen if it didn't get 500 hearts on Instagram?? With so many of us living for likes and freaking out over followers, it's easy to blur the lines between real friends, and virtual ones.

A friends' teenage daughter recently described Gen Z as 'a sad generation posting happy pictures,' and I could have cried at her level of insight. Psychologist Vassia explained to me that social media creates an illusion of being connected, but these virtual connections can fail to meet our need for genuine human connection:

"We are suffering, because everybody's pretending that they are connected, that they are doing great and that they have plenty of friends. We live in this technologically connected era. Everybody has followers, likes and connections. But these connections are not real. The opposite of loneliness is a meaningful fulfilling, authentic connection where you can be yourself, you can allow yourself to feel embraced and accepted as you are without needing to change yourself. People don't show their true selves online, and they can be ashamed to admit that they might have 1,000 'friends' but they're still feeling lonely"
(Vassia Sarantopoulou, Psychologist)

Another reason, Vassia explains, why online (and even offline) friendships can fail to fill the connection void is because they're one-directional:

"When the focus is one-way connections instead of two-way, when you are just giving and giving and getting nothing in return it can leave you feeling depleted. But when we allow ourselves to take something, this is when we create the two-way connection, that is the balanced and equal relationship that we want to build that will defeat loneliness"
(Vassia Sarantopoulou, Psychologist)

Psychotherapist and Relationship Guru Esther Perel coined the term 'Artificial Intimacy' to explain how technology is depriving us of genuine human connection. Our mobile phones, it seems, are the ultimate false friend. We've become so attached to our devices that they're often the last thing we look at in the evening and the first thing we embrace in the morning. We carry them close for comfort, we experience separation anxiety when they're not around… And because our devices offer a quick dose of apparent connection and validation, we can fail to invest in our less convenient, messier IRL friendships. Even when we are physically there – habitually and often unconsciously 'phubbing' (phone snubbing) our real friends and family as we scroll instead of staying in the moment.

For today's 20-somethings, online relationships are clearly taking precedence over IRL friendships. My research shows that whilst 91% of women in their 20s use social media daily, only 34% connect with friends in the real world.

Psychologist Vassia worries that the societal focus on the performative aspects of friendship (such as posting #squadgoals pics or seeking validation in our social stats) could be undermining our ability to build authentic, and healthy, connections in the long run:

"Our society focuses on results, there's a pressure to perform rather than represent the real effort of the journey that we're on with other people. This leads us sometimes to create and allow relationships that are not fulfilling, just because we feel we have to be seen to have these relationships in our lives. That ends in us being fake or pretending within these relationships. We ended up not knowing how to create authentic connections with others"
(Vassia Sarantopoulou, Psychologist)

If I can offer any guidance here to help find authentic friendships it would be this – focus more on how your social life feels and less on how it looks. In my mind, true friendship is a feeling, and not a tangible, measurable outcome. Like so many things in life, it's quality and not quantity that truly matters. Remember – your happiness really does have very little to do with your social media stats. And mental pictures can mean more than Instagram pics. Often, it's when we're having the most fun that we flat-out forget to take a single photo.

Organic Aspirations

Perhaps the biggest misconception about making friends is that it should be an organic process. Whilst the world has embraced dating, both online and off, as a conscious mode of finding romantic love, few of us apply the same rigour to meeting platonic friends. The media perpetuates the myth of organic friendship by representing close bonds fully formed, with BFFS entering the scene as if by magic, rarely offering insights into the journey to friendship.

Our own past experience can mislead us too. As a child, our relationships are fluid, malleable, and seemingly automatic. We are channelled through the education system in a consistent cohort, thrown together with the same group over long periods of time until eventually someone sticks.

I have no memory of consciously 'making friends' as a kid. I was well into my 20s before it dawned on me that making connections as an adult might require a higher level of effort. Fortunately, my financial insecurity came to my rescue. The economic necessity of flat sharing when I first moved to London and Amsterdam respectively brought with it the colonels of connection which, in both instances, led me down the road to meeting my kind of people. But once we're past the flat-sharing, pre-married phase (if that's the way life goes) things can get even more challenging. Mexican American Opera Singer Tricia, who relocated to the UK, described the turning point in her friendship journey:

"When I moved here, I was just working, working, working, working. And then all of a sudden, I just felt this wave of loneliness come over me. Because the only person I knew here was my husband. And I was like, Okay, we need to fix this. If I wallow in this it's not gonna be good for anyone. I'm gonna want to move back. No, there's nothing positive that's going to come from me just being here sitting around and waiting to meet people... So, I let myself feel it. And then I was like, hey, it's time to go out and meet people, and I put in the work..."
  (Tricia Rosas, Opera Singer and Content Creator)

Friendship Coach Carrie suggests many of us want to believe in the organic friendship myth because we ultimately fear rejection. It feels safer to sit in our loneliness than to risk putting ourselves out there and be disappointed:

"There's a level of discomfort when you're starting over, when you're trying to put yourself out there and introduce yourself to someone. It can be really scary, so it feels safer to wait for them to come to you. It goes back to that fear of rejection or desire for belonging"
  (Carrie Eaton, Friendship Coach)

According to the experts, the real danger of sitting in loneliness is that we start to create false narratives that can sabotage both our progress and our sense of self:

"When people are lonely the negative self-talk can start to emerge, they may believe that there's something wrong with them, that they won't be accepted as they are and they need to change something

about themselves. I find that lonely people are often struggling with their own identity, it goes together"
  (Vassia Sarantopoulou, Psychologist)

If you're hard relating to any of these feelings, I want to reassure you that it probably won't last. Because loneliness, like all feelings, is usually temporary. So, if you're feeling friendless at the moment, especially if you've just gone through a major life change, make this your mantra, "it's not me, it's my situation".

Lonely At 30: Am I Normal?

The Myth: SOCIAL BUTTERFLY. You'll reach peak popularity in your 20s. By 30 you'll have a close-knit circle of besties and a satisfying social life.

The Reality: SOCIALLY CHALLENGED. 13% of women in their 20s rarely or never have any social contact, and only 22% are very satisfied with the state of their friendships.

Lonely And Anxious? Get Unstuck In 4 Steps

How To Stop Looking OUT

- **Don't Measure Friendship**

"Stop measuring social success in followers, likes and comments. Nurturing a few close friendships in real life will make you far happier than attracting a community of thousands online"
  (Kate Berski, Author)

- **Drop The Deadlines**

"Don't tell yourself it's too late or you're too old to make new friends. This is never true. In reality, these false narratives cover fear of rejection"
  (Carrie Eaton, Friendship Coach)

- **Don't Force Relationships**

"People change and relationships change. Don't force a relationship just because it worked for you in the past. If you can't radically accept someone for where they're at right now and who they've grown into, it might be time to move on from that relationship"
    (Carrie Eaton, Friendship Coach)

- **Don't Take Rejection Personally**

"If interactions don't go how you planned, try not to take it personally. It usually says more about them than it does about you. They may not be in a space to communicate with a stranger that day for many reasons. Don't let that stop you from trying with someone else. Move on from the interaction and give yourself props for practising putting yourself out there"
    (Carrie Eaton, Friendship Coach)

- **Focus On Feelings**

"Focus less on how your friendships look on social media, and more on how it feels to be in them"
    (Kate Berski, Author)

How To Start Looking IN

- **Be In Your Feelings**

"The first step to feeling less alone is to embrace loneliness. It's a normal, healthy human feeling. Its function is to pinpoint what's missing so we can do something to change our situation. Just don't sit too long in that feeling"
    (Vassia Sarantopoulou, Psychologist)

- **Know Your Values**

"Look inward and define your core values and the qualities you therefore want from friends. Write it down if it helps. It's important because your values translate into your expectations. For example, if you value

trust, you'll expect your friends to keep your vulnerable conversations confidential. If you value time, you will expect regular contact. Friendships get tricky when you're misaligned"
  (Carrie Eaton, Friendship Coach)

- **Reverse Negative Self-Talk**

"Start recognising your negative thinking. When you say things to yourself about social situations such as they're not gonna like me, I will feel embarrassed or awkward, I don't belong here... These types of thoughts can prevent you from reaching out and meeting new people. So just notice the negative self-talk and start reversing it"
  (Vassia Sarantopoulou, Psychologist)

- **Find Your Friendship Triggers**

"If you're having conflict with friends, pay attention to what triggers you. It might not mean your friend is doing something wrong. It could mean something is coming up from your childhood, how you were treated by a caregiver for example. If you were abandoned by a parent, that can come out later as fear of rejection, or possessiveness"
  (Carrie Eaton, Friendship Coach)

- **Trust Your Emotions**

"Pay attention to the way people make you feel. Do you feel safe, strong and more confident with them by your side? Do you walk away from an interaction feeling supported, and energised or do you feel drained? Use that as a guide for which friendships to invest in"
  (Carrie Eaton, Friendship Coach)

How To REFRAME Your Goals

- **Be Patient**

"Accept that building quality relationships is going to take time. Give yourself a lot of grace and love through the process. You might not meet somebody you click with right away"
  (Carrie Eaton, Friendship Coach)

- **Age Up**

"When we're younger, it can feel like everyone is too busy and wrapped up in themselves to really look at you and listen. You can find that in an older friend. And since we feel negative emotions less strongly as we age, inter-generational friendships can bring balance and perspective"
 (Michelle Hawkins-Collins, The Wisdom Space)

- **Go Global**

"Don't surround yourself just with people that look and think like you. Know that the world is a much bigger place. Be proactive and invest in growing different networks without agenda"
 (Karina Valencia, COO Wheely)

- **Become A Local**

"Find your regular spots - grocers, bookshops, cafes... go there regularly and you'll start to bump into the same people, it's natural that over time you'll get talking"
 (Patricia Parisienne, Travel Influencer & Opera Singer)

- **Start Small**

"If you live in an apartment building, or if you go to a gym, start by saying Hi to people you come across regularly. When they become more familiar you can ask their name or tell them you're new to the area. You don't have to launch right into inviting them for coffee"
 (Carrie Eaton, Friendship Coach)

- **Ask, Don't Tell**

"Stop trying to be interesting and be interested instead. Making connections is about asking questions and being curious about people. So, if in doubt, just ask people about themselves"
 (Patricia Parisienne, Travel Influencer & Opera Singer)

- **Give People A Chance**

"Don't expect to find your best friend instantly. Keep in mind that everybody has been hurt by relationships, everybody is tiptoeing around others until they feel safe. Give people a second chance so they start feeling safe, opening up and being more authentic"
(Vassia Sarantopoulou, Psychologist)

- **Be Present**

"Nothing beats IRL connections, put the phone down and meet people face to face whenever you can. And if you can't, even a voice note feels more personal than a text"
(Patricia Parisienne, Travel Influencer & Opera Singer)

How To CELEBRATE The Small Wins

- **Celebrate Quality**

"Don't put so much emphasis on quantity - the number of friends or the number of interactions... it's quality relationships that contribute most to your well-being. If you have two or three close friends in your corner, you're in a great place"
(Carrie Eaton, Friendship Coach)

- **Cherish Your Ride-Or-Die**

"If you have one person in your life you can call in the middle of the night if you're really struggling, one person you can talk to openly without fear of being judged, you have a good friend"
(Carrie Eaton, Friendship Coach)

- **Build Yourself Up**

"Practice friendship mantras that boost your self-confidence like 'I am kind' and 'I am loyal.' Build your resilience with mantras like 'I am comfortable being uncomfortable' and 'I can do hard things'"
(Carrie Eaton, Friendship Coach)

- **Do What You Love**

"Join groups and clubs but do things you genuinely enjoy already rather than trying new things, so you'll feel like you belong straight away. You'll already have something to talk about, that's how you find your tribe"
  (Vassia Sarantopoulou, Psychologist)

The conversations I've had in the making of this chapter, with both experts and everyday people, have reminded me just how strongly I feel about this topic. It is my belief that society has wildly underestimated, and under-supported friendship for far too long. Our online infrastructure is robbing young people of the essential friendship skills they need to live longer, healthier and happier lives.

The under-representation and trivialisation of friendship as a topic has encouraged us to relegate unromantic love to the optional extras column in our life lists. My own data suggests fewer than 1 in 5 20-somethings are actively prioritising this part of life.

And yet, things are starting to change. I'm encouraged by the experts who are publicising the life-enhancing value of friendship and supporting the social media generation to get social in the real world. If I leave you with one piece of advice it's this – make the effort. While our 20s are characterised by turbulence, and transience, the friendships forged during these trying times are often all the stronger for it. Lovers may come and go, but a true friend can be forever.

MINDHACKER QUESTION

- Which would be worse when pursuing new friendships – trying and failing or failing to try? To what extent is fear of rejection holding me back from making connections?

TURNING 30 GOALS - REGROUP

Take a look back at your original list of Turning 30 Goals – did you write a friendship or social life goal on there? How high up your list is it sitting? What words did you use to express it?

Now you've learned more about the factors that may have shaped your expectations or approach to friendship, does investing in friendship feel like a top priority for you right now? Does it feel any more or less important on your life list? Would you now articulate it any differently? Before moving on, take a minute to review your friendship goal on the 'NEW GOALS' list at the back of this book, or wherever you're taking your notes.

And if you're ready, jot down a few 'BABY GOALS' too. What are two or three things you can do easily, or commit to doing regularly, that will put you on the path to finding your tribe? For example 'Write a list of my friendship values.' or 'Invite one new person to coffee this month.' Remember – don't put pressure on yourself and be patient. You can't hurry love, even the platonic kind.

So You Don't Have Bank

"All I ask is the chance to prove that money can't make me happy"
   (Spike Milligan)

Let's start this chapter with some radical candour. I am NOT, by any measure, a financial wizard. I'm not even particularly good with money. I've always been a bit boujis, and never let my income hinder my aspirations, meaning I lived most of my early adult life in my overdraft.

At university, I would work every day over the summer just to get back to net £zero, and I once ate packet bread sauce for three meals in a row while I waited patiently for payday. I haven't looked at Christmas dinner quite the same way since. So, if you're reading this hoping for savvy saving tips or titillating tax advice (said nobody ever), you might be sadly disappointed.

Here's what I do know.

Broke can be temporary.

And a decade, or two, can make all the difference to your bank balance. It did for me. At 29, I had £minus money in the bank. At 34, I co-founded a haircare business, Curlsmith, with my husband, which paid me precisely £zero for the following three years. At 39, I became a financial success story, when the business was acquired by an American corporation. I share this not to make you hate me, but to make the point that where you are right now is not where you have to stay.

Despite what Instagram would have you believe, there is no 'deadline' for getting your financial act together, and true financial security is not gained by curbing your Costa Coffee habit. It starts with understanding, and potentially radically rethinking your money mindset. And that, friend, is what I can promise from this chapter. Thanks to great expert advice and as always, real facts without the fluff.

Financial Anxiety Is Real

When I first set out to write 30-Phobia, financial fears were not on the agenda. But the beauty of this project is that you, my wonderful community, showed me just how big of an oversight this would have been.

One of the reasons I love data is that it cuts through the crap and shows you the reality of a situation. So, when I asked 2,500 Quarter-Lifers from all walks of life about their biggest hopes, dreams and fears for the future, financial anxiety rose to the top of the list. In fact, 55% of 20-29-year-olds are worried about financial insecurity, or not being able to afford a home by the time they turn 30 and 51% rank achieving financial security as a top 5 future life goal.

Finance, in my opinion, represents one of the most gaping expectation gaps of 20-something life. After all, how are we supposed to go out, explore the world, meet all the people and have all the experiences when we haven't got two fivers to rub together?

I found that economic anxiety exists across salary bands, though women earning under £29k / $29k per year feel least financially stable. Only earning more than £100k / $125k a year appears to protect 20-somethings from financial fear – an income level that just 2% of Brits and 5% of Americans actually achieve by age 30. By my deductions then, over 95% of women in their 20s could be grappling with financial insecurity. And financial fears, both present and projected, are strongly correlated with turning 30 anxiety too. Those who feel unsatisfied with their financial set-up now, also have significantly more negative feelings about ageing up.

Financial Anxiety: It's NOT You

The facts are signalling to me that financial health is a generational issue, and not, as numerous media sources might suggest, a problem faced by a minority of less fortunate or 'lazy' individuals.

But how did we get here? And more importantly, short of mass-issuing winning lottery tickets, how do we face up to the financial roadblocks and find our way to financial freedom?

The first step is understanding the context in which both our financial reality and our money mindset has been created. Some of the most significant external influences I've identified include:

1. Relative Poverty

2. Peer Comparison

3. Financial Insecurity

4. Rich-fluencing

5. Tech-motional Spending

6. The Education Gap

Relative Poverty

65% of the women I surveyed feel life is more difficult for them than previous generations. And having examined the financial realities facing today's 20-somethings, I'm inclined to agree. The data reveals that the current generation is quite literally in a poorer position than both their parents and grandparents were at the same age.

To start with, todays Quarter-Lifers earn less. An American study reported that the proportion of adult kids who go on to out-earn their parents has been steadily declining since the 1940s and stood at just 50% at the last count. UK figures in The Guardian newspaper show that 20-somethings currently earn 2% less than the national average. In the USA it's 9%. Meanwhile, retirees' incomes have grown three times faster – meaning working 20-somethings are now significantly poorer than pensioners in real terms. Additionally, the Guardian estimates that 20-somethings' disposable income is around 20% below the national average.

To make things even spicier, the cost of living continues to rise as incomes flatline. Inflation is at its highest level since the 1980s, resulting in higher prices and lower purchasing power.

According to UK Bank TSB, 18-24-year-olds are now 7 x more likely than 66-75-year-olds to take on new debt, and funds are mostly being used to cover basics such as rent, council tax, household bills and groceries. Under 25s are also more likely to struggle with repayments, adding significant stress to this financial burden. As this 27-year-old describes:

"My relationship with money is quite negative. Having spent most of my 20s in my overdraft and struggling to save, I am constantly worrying about not having enough money. With energy prices rising and also rent and everything else, my wage doesn't cover everything anymore and it's impossible to save. The biggest issue is the constant dread of being in my overdraft, living in debt is miserable"
(27yrs, UK, via Imagen Insights platform)

The cost of living appears to be rising in several areas that disproportionately affect young adults. A recent EY study reported a whopping 200% increase in the cost of education since the 1970s. More recently in the UK, the steep increase in university fees has seen young people emerging from higher education with an average debt of over £45,000. Comparatively, my generation of Geriatric Millennials got off incredibly lightly, and even so many of us are still paying off our student loans long into our forties. Reportedly, since 2000, student loan debt in England has risen by an eye-watering 1578%!

The upshot of this is a generation of baby adults born into debt and firmly on the financial back foot. Perhaps more worryingly, this situation is normalising debt from a young age, which could prompt fatalistic attitudes to earning and spending (what's the point in trying?); further beyond means living (who cares about another few thousand on some store cards?!) or crippling financial anxiety.

"I went to Uni a year or two before student loans went up to £9,000. A lot of people my age have now paid off their loans, but those who

went two years later have got over £40k of debt and they're repaying it at a higher rate too. Those numbers are having a big impact on how people are feeling and creating anxiety around money"
(Ellie Austin-Williams, Financial Educator & Author)

When I asked the community on the Gen Z insight platform Imagen, recent university graduates told me that in addition to racking up heavy debts, they feel 'cheated' out of the financial security that further education promised, putting them in an untenable financial position now:

"The current economic state has screwed over graduates who were promised jobs after completing a Masters or PhD, this has put us in even more debt just so the government can profit. It's terrible how they expect graduates to be earning minimum wage yet pay back their loans and commute far away for a grad role and still be able to eat. It's a world in which I won't be able to survive much longer"
(26 yrs, UK, via Imagen Index)

The job market is also undeniably tougher for today's 20-somethings. UK Recruitment firm Reed reported a 40% decrease in graduate-level positions between 2018 and 2023, and according to search engine Adzuna, applications for grad jobs will increase from 36 to 44 per role in 2024 - making even the lowest paying jobs significantly harder to land. Moreover, the financial challenges don't end for those lucky enough to bag these elusive graduate roles, as one American I spoke to explained:

"Rent where I live is around 2,000 USD a month. To live by yourself comfortably you would need a high-paying job, and all the high-paying jobs for bachelor's graduates are not even in the range of $2,000, so young people are forced to live with their parents or house share into their late 30s because it is just impossible to find a job with a high enough pay. Baby Boomers could work a factory job their entire life, live well and get a comfortable retirement. Now we work supposedly good office jobs and still have to apply for governmental assistance. It's just so unfair"
(21 yrs, USA, via Imagen Index)

The real problem with being poor, whether real or relative, is that it delays progress in life. While many have painted Gen Z as 'eternal children,' by choice, unwilling and unable to do the basics of adulthood, I see things differently. The 20-somethings I spoke with were keen to make progress, yet see financial insecurity as THE major barrier to pursuing major milestones such as buying property, or starting a family:

"There's a lot of pressure throughout your 20s to ensure you're comfortable by 30. Seeing people at the age of 30 now with children, mortgages etc is scary because I am not even close. I'm too anxious about my finances and job stability"
(21yrs, UK)

"I'm apprehensive about my financial situation. I worry that it may not get better in the future and will impact my ability to get a home"
(29yrs, UK)

"I don't think it's really possible to be financially secure in your 20s. I'm just trying to look after me, just to cover the basics, and I find that hard sometimes. But trying to live in London and have a child, that seems impossible"
(Bethan Jenkins, 28, Journalist)

Contrary to popular criticism, I have come to view Gen Z's apparent unwillingness to launch, as evidence of increased financial awareness, and responsibility, not eternal immaturity. A perspective with which Financial Wellness experts I spoke with would echo:

"Women now are very aware of the gender pay gap. They know that it starts as soon as you decide you're going to have a family, when women's earnings get stuck while men keep on going. For a lot of young women that is a big question mark or concern, they don't want to lose their financial independence, or earning ability, or feel like they are relying on someone. A lot of women are unsure about whether or when to have children because of the financial implications"
(Ellie Austin-Williams, Financial Educator)

"Young adults know that future financial security won't come from living paycheck to paycheck, but from having some money stored away as an emergency fund and in savings. They know that they also need

to work to make money to live, and when the two things don't seem financially feasible it can keep them stuck"
(Laura Ann Moore, Financial Wellbeing expert)

Peer Pay Gap

It's fair to say that those of us born into the Western World have been dealt more favourable financial cards than many others on this planet. However, while mercifully few of us will ever live in absolute poverty, many 20-somethings do experience being relatively poorer, not just compared to previous generations, but to their same-age peers. And these disparities often come to light in our 20s. It's easy to see why. In my survey, incomes amongst same-age women varied wildly. Annual salaries for 20-somethings span £0 to 100k in the UK and $0 to $300k in the USA, rendering 'average salary' figures somewhat arbitrary, and almost certainly disheartening for lower earners.

"One of the biggest challenges that happens in your 20s is this divergence in financial circumstances, because people are suddenly earning different amounts of money. When you all start out as graduates, you're earning pretty minimal amounts. And then you start to see these big splits - your lawyers and your bankers up here, your arts down there... it can make things very uncomfortable"
(Ellie Austin-Williams, Financial Educator)

Peer pay disparities understandably feed into the negative 'compare and despair mindset.' In my survey, the lowest earners express more negative feelings about turning 30 and greater future finance fears than their higher-banking peers.

Even before we open our pay packets, the truth is we are all dealt different financial cards. Whilst some of our outcomes are more within our control, like the career paths we choose to follow, others are less so. Coming from a family with money can, for instance, allow some young people to stay in further education or work in unpaid internships which could lead to greater opportunities in the future. They can live in expensive cities or get a first foot on the property ladder. Journalist Bethan Rose-Jenkins explains the struggles of starting out in her career without the benefit of family funding:

"It's really difficult to get into a career like magazine journalism, because of the amount of work experience and internships you need to do at first, a lot of it unpaid. I didn't live in the city, so trying to find somewhere to stay was tough. At the start, it definitely cost me money to work. It took me two, two and a half, maybe even three years into actually starting work before I was making more than it cost me to live. I was having to pay to stay somewhere to do free work experience, or couch-surfing just to get by"
  (Bethan Rose-Jenkins, Hearst Magazines)

As well as making us feel financially worse off, peer pay gaps can create significant social strain too. According to a 2016 study we have statistically the most friends at age 25. And as much as we love our girlfriends, female friendships often come with financial expectations. When we reach our 20s, friends start to celebrate mega milestones – buying properties, getting engaged, getting married, having babies... and naturally they want to bring us along for the ride.

According to research by UK loan provider Amigo, UK adults attend an average of 7 'life events' per year and spend a whopping £142k on their friends over their lifetime. And I'd guess that a large proportion of this spending is racked up during wedding season. According to a 2023 report by American Express, the average cost of being a wedding guest is now £1,045 – with gifts, accommodation, childcare and travel being the biggest expenses.

In a survey by Credit Karma, 1 in 3 Millennials and Gen Z said they had a friend who pushed them to overspend. And credit card company Acqua calculated 'social tax' at £800 per year in the UK, with social pressure to spend driven by guilt and fears of letting people down or missing out.

Not only does forced social spending take a painful, and potentially devastating, bite out of already stretched 20-something budgets, but it puts a strain on friendships too, especially when we keep quiet about our financial struggles.

"One of the things that always comes up is people feeling really overstretched because they're trying to keep up with their friend's plans. And your friends probably aren't even thinking about the fact that you

might be earning half what they're earning, people don't tend to operate like that. They'll be picking a restaurant based on what they're comfortable with, not because they're trying to make you overspend"
(Ellie Austin-Williams – Financial Educator)

If you've ever been to dinner and panicked the whole way through about how you're going to pay the bill, I see you girl. In my 20s, I rarely enjoyed eating out because I was so anxious about how I'd pay for it at the end. Someone would inevitably utter the dreaded 'Shall we just split it?' comment right at the end. And that someone would usually be the one who'd ordered three courses plus sides, and cocktails. Meanwhile, I'd selected my main based on price point alone and sipped the salty house white out of austerity. One time a foodie friend took me to dinner at a fancy restaurant for my birthday. It was the kind of place people waited months to get a table and you were never quite sure which bits of the dish in front of you were edible, and which were just window-dressing. Seeing my panicked expression over the menu she gave me a knowing wink 'Don't worry, I know the chef, we'll get mate's rates.' Which didn't make me feel that much better, because even at half price the set menu was over half my monthly rent. Fortunately, it turned out to be a total freebie, but the fear of the unknown cheque rather ruined that particular gastronomic experience for me.

On the opposite extreme, my former London flatmates to this day, a good twenty years later, STILL talk about the time that all of our food and most of our drinks were accidentally comped in a Chinese restaurant. The debate about whether or not to tell the server was furious let me tell you, but even after we came clean, she insisted that no, the £9 bill was fine to be split eight ways. So, we took our full tummies and ran. Even now, it's one of our most celebrated moments in life.

Financial Insecurity

I recently put a personal finance poll out on my Instagram stories – and received over 500 responses in 24 hours. 90% of 20-somethings admitted they are financially 'struggling', or 'just getting by' at the moment. And digging into my survey I see that financial anxiety has a significant impact on overall future outlook. Here are just a few of the responses to the general question 'How do you feel about turning 30?'

"Apprehensive – my financial situation is not where I want it to be"
(28yrs, UK)

"Panicked and anxious because of my financial situation"
(26yrs, USA)

"Afraid of not having enough time to get financially stable, start my career, and be where I want to be physically and mentally"
(24yrs, USA)

"Anxious because I am not where I want to be financially and career-wise"
(25yrs, USA)

"I get more stressed about it day by day because I don't have any money, the cost of living is going up, I have no idea how to make things better"
(24yrs, UK)

In the past, 20-somethings may have been perceived as having a somewhat laissez-faire approach to money. However, living with financial insecurity appears to be fostering a more conservative money mindset. In an EY study, Gen Z respondents were asked what they would do with $100, and most said they would put the greatest proportion into savings. Now, in principle saving is good, but Finance Coach Ellie warns that when this becomes fear of spending, the outcomes are less positive:

"I come across a lot of women who are afraid of spending money because they have learned from a young age that money doesn't grow on trees. They are living in fear that the money will disappear and never come back, so they struggle to spend on things that aren't absolutely essential. Often, they are quite miserable because they have no real quality of life"
(Ellie Austin-Williams, Financial Educator)

For todays 20-somethings, the money milestones appear to have shifted. Where financial success seemed possible for my generation of Geriatric Millennials (whether or not we ever got there), for todays cohort it can feel entirely out of reach. Young adults are now less likely to shoot for financial prosperity because they have yet to even achieve financial security. In a 2007 study by Pew Research, 8 in 10 Millennials stated 'getting rich' as a top 1 or 2 life goal. In a 2023 study by EY, less than 1 in 3 Gen Z respondents felt it was important to 'get rich.' Whilst they did seek increased income, they equated this with greater security, not success. This brings me nicely to my next point...

Rich-Fluencing

When I asked my Instagram community to complete the following sentence 'I will be happy when...' the most common response was 'when I have money!' And I get it. Whilst countless miserable millionaires have shown us that money doesn't buy happiness, in many cases, lack of money can feel like a one-way ticket to unhappiness. This isn't helped by the ubiquitous 'overnight success' stories, 'Get Rich Quick' motivation moguls and tween TikTok trillionaires shoved in our faces every time we go for a casual scroll.

"Today's 20-Somethings have been bombarded by all these messages about unrealistic achievement at such a young age. They see people building careers on the internet from 13 or 14. But they've obviously the outliers, most normal people are not making millions on TikTok age 15"
(Ellie Austin-Williams, Financial Educator)

Now, whilst there's nothing inherently wrong with inspiration, ambition and dreaming big – what concerns me is the effect that constant exposure to #lifegoals can have on the self-worth, and mental health of us mere mortals. When the gap between expectations and reality is as big as 'I plan to be a millionaire by 30,' and 'I'm barely making rent at 28,' it's no surprise that so many of us feel like our finances are falling short. In my study, 64% of women in their 20s agree that 'other people find life easier than me,' and 61% say social media makes them feel worse about themselves. 41% of women feel unsatisfied with their current financial situation, and only 4% describe themselves as 'very satisfied.'

While we don't all have lofty financial goals, I do believe that social media is unnaturally inflating our expectations around money and making us feel less-than in the process, by deliberately selling us a lie. Instagram would have us believe that if we're not selling a company, signing six-figure contracts, being named on the '30 Under 30' lists and flying private by 30 we have categorically failed in life. It's effectively normalised abnormal levels of wealth.

"Aspirational lifestyles are really over-represented on social media, because people don't always want to watch an average person's life, it's just not as interesting, but I think you so easily forget that what you're looking at is not representative of reality"
(Ellie Austin-Williams, Financial Educator)

Which brings me to my real beef. #Lifegoals – as manifested in luxury lifestyle content, 'manifestation', or 'vision boarding.' Now don't get me wrong, I am not anti-ambition, or against goal-setting (more on that later). And I do understand how wildly popular these concepts have become over recent years. Not to mention how much fun you can have selecting dreamy inspo pics, so don't come for me, there are good reasons behind my objections.

Firstly, because social media is inherently visual, the lifestyle content we consume focuses on the physical manifestations of financial success – the fancy cars, lavish homes, slinky designer dresses or luxury hotel rooms we'd buy if only our bank balance agreed. Talk Twenties Founder Gaby worries that this type of content perpetuates a level of materialism that is neither achievable, nor desirable:

"When we look online and see people we look up to driving fast cars and living in these amazing houses we get the message that to be successful and happy we have to have all of those things. And that's complete bullshit. Nobody needs to have all of those material things. It perpetuates this one-dimensional definition of success that is completely unachievable for most people on a normal salary on a normal budget"
(Gaby Mendes, Podcast Host & Founder of Talk Twenties)

Secondly, and somewhat ironically, by showing us what money can buy, influencers are actually showcasing the money they no longer have, and not, as financial well-being expert Laura warns, what they have invested, or saved along the way. A quick scroll of the Daily Mail reveals numerous human-interest stories of wannabe influencers racking up eye-watering debt in the pursuit of actually living the lifestyle they're already (falsely) selling.

Recently social media has seen a backlash against 'fake wealth' influencers, with several high-profile creators being exposed for their fabricated online lifestyles.

Even for creators who have achieved genuine financial success, all is not always what it seems. Having got to know several successful influencers personally, it's clear that even they would not be in a position to afford all of the expensive trips and designer handbags they promote on a daily basis if;

a) the goods themselves weren't #gifted

b) they weren't being paid to sell them!

Put simply – they're not spending their own money! And what's more, the individuals who make making money look the easiest, are usually the ones hustling the hardest.

It's important to stay aware that what we are consuming online isn't social content, it's social selling. Most creators are trying to make a living, and fair play to them. But doing this usually means collaborating with brands who have products to sell. As a former business owner, I also have no problem with the odd #paidAd. However, I believe this kind of marketing should be authentic, and relevant. So, when I became a creator myself by starting the 30-Phobia project, I chose only to collaborate with other authors, educators and creators who share my interest in helping women feel seen, empowered and levelled up. Sadly, this has meant turning down quite a few free skincare products!

I also endeavour to always be helpful. Something which Rich-fluencer content often isn't, because it focuses us on the least helpful type of goals. It showcases Milestone Goals over Process Goals. In other words, showing me a posh watch tells me very little about how I might go about gaining enough funds to actually buy the aforementioned posh watch. Social content rarely sets out the specific, and achievable, steps it would take to get us from where we are now (and bear in mind we are all starting from a different place) to where we want to get to financially.

"A lot of the time we just have these crazy figures in our head – how much we want to earn, how much that dream house costs. But we can't see the journey from where we are now to how we will actually get there. If you're earning 30 grand, and you're looking at flats in London, you're looking at a very big gap, and you're gonna have a big gap for a very long time, you're going to get very frustrated and upset. We need to start getting more specific about what we need to earn, or save, to reach our goals"
  (Ellie Austin-Williams, Financial Educator)

Logically, we already know that we can't get anything just by wanting it really hard and thinking about it a lot. Otherwise, I'd be able to manifest a roast dinner with all the trimmings on my kitchen table every night. Simply showing us the end goal gives us little clue as to how we might actually get there. Which is a recipe for anxiety, frustration, negative comparison, dissatisfaction and discontent.

"Whilst money can help bring you some level of happiness, (once your baseline needs have been met, money can allow you to live a much fuller life), I don't believe you do need money to be happy. When you long for items you do not have, and compare yourself to others, you are missing out on all the beauty in your own life"
  (Laura Ann Moore, Financial Wellbeing Expert)

Tech-Motional Spending

From the misery of living with austerity, to the stress of dealing with debt, there's no doubt that our feelings and our finances go hand in hand. And whilst many of us have experienced first-hand the negative emotional outcomes of financial struggles, we rarely stop to think about the other side of the coin - the emotional and environmental drivers behind our spending behaviour.

The research on this leaves us is no doubt that emotions drive our financial decisions, which in turn dictate our economic, and mental well-being. So, understanding our triggers is paramount. According to money marketplace Lending Tree, 69% of Americans admit to emotional spending, with Millennials (76%) and Gen Z (75%) being the most emotional of all. For 76% of these people, their feelings drive over-spending. The study found that for women in particular, retail therapy is the real deal – with 57% claiming they spend to manage their mood. The top emotional triggers are reportedly stress (50%); happiness (48%); boredom (37%) and sadness (32%). Women are more likely than men to say that emotional spending has impacted their financial well-being.

At this point, I have to come clean and admit that I too am an emotional spender. My trigger? Tiredness. My online scrolling and spending appears directly proportional to the number of hours I've clocked between the sheets the previous night. No surprises then that my splurging has been surging since becoming a mother! Luckily for me, and my bank balance, Net a Porter has a fabulous returns policy.

So why is it, when I like to think of myself as a relatively sensible human adult, do I still find it so challenging to curb my shopping impulse? And how is technology making the struggle ever more real?

Neuroscience provides some answers, in the form of the brain's reward systems. The key culprit is dopamine, a neurotransmitter (chemical messenger) in our brain that is linked to motivation, reward and pleasure. Neuroscientists have found that dopamine levels rise not only when we spend money, but when we anticipate spending money. Like when we add things to our wish list or double tap out those tiny hearts online. That rush we feel when we Apple Pay our way to a new top? Dopamine. And since we are hard-wired to repeat behaviours that bring us pleasure, the emotional spender, aka the shopaholic is born as is the science of so-called Retail Therapy.

"When we impulse spend, we are using it as a coping mechanism to change how we feel. Spending gives us a dopamine rush, so if we are feeling low, stressed, anxious, or any other uncomfortable emotion, our spending habits tend to reflect this"
    (Laura Ann Moore, Financial Wellbeing Expert)

Financial coach Ellie adds that our shopping habits may not be anything to do with the specific items we are buying. Whilst we might believe that we desperately need another black tee, our true motivation is often chemical, not practical:

"One of the things I always say to people who emotionally spend is that firstly, it's entirely normal and easy to do. And secondly, it's not actually about wanting to spend, or wanting that specific item, it's about chasing the dopamine hit. Knowing that, means you can do something about it"
    (Ellie Austin-Williams, Financial Educator & Author)

Unfortunately, retailers and tech giants are all too willing to exploit, and exacerbate, our human predilection for spending. The OG Amazon, with its patented 'Buy Now' button has a lot to answer for. Especially in my household – where barely a day goes by without one of those smiling brown boxes materialising on the doorstep. Half the time it's a surprise even to me what might be waiting inside.

More recently, 'Chinese Amazon' Temu, has enjoyed bombastic growth in the Western world thanks to tantalisingly low prices combined with a 'gamified' shopper experience. With a dynamic display of colourful visuals and a never-ending, ever-escalating reel of time-limited offers with tempting calls to action, the App taps directly into our chemical reward centres. Arguably, Temu has more in common with online gambling than online shopping. I became so overwhelmed by the constant barrage of Chinese tat being flogged in my direction that I deleted the App within 24 hours of downloading it.

Another example is the global Buy Now Pay Later market - now worth over $500 billion, with 360 million users worldwide, 16% of whom are aged 18-34. One young woman described her fear that technologies like Klarna were fuelling impulse spending and enticing young people into debt:

"I feel wary of buy now pay later, as I'm aware of the dangers of overstretching my financial capability, and things add up really quickly if I use it for too many things"
    (22yrs, USA, via Imagen Insights Platform)

And lest we forget social media, an online world which 91% of Quarter-Lifers frequent on a daily basis. It's fair to say TikTok has come a long way since the silly dances we all enjoyed during lockdown. The Chinese social media giant now self-describes as a direct sales platform. Commentators have warned that the 'shopper-tainment model,' with its highly addictive algorithm and never-ending scroll of hyper-personalised content, could be driving young adults into debt. With over half of 18-24-year-olds taking on new debt in the past 12 months, this feels like a very real concern.

Whilst the reward systems in our brain may be ancient, it's clear that our shopping addictions are being super-charged by emerging technologies which make it easier and quicker to act on our emotions. After all, if the only way to scratch my shopping itch was to get off the sofa, change out of my PJs and schlep into town, during actual opening hours, I'm pretty sure my wallet might be feeling decidedly fatter right now.

Education Gap

In my survey of women aged 20-29, 48% say they worry about future financial insecurity. Yet, fewer than half of these are taking active steps to improve their finances. What this tells me is not that 20-somethings are lazy, but that they're stuck. Unsure, unclear, and crucially, uneducated on how to achieve their financial goals. And this uncertainty is breeding financial anxiety. In a 2022 EY study for example, 39% of the Gen Z respondents said they feel very or extremely worried about making the wrong choices with their money.

"Britain has one of the lowest rates of financial literacy compared to similarly advanced economies. Lack of financial education can cause both worries and concerns and leave people questioning what they should be doing with their money"
(Laura Ann Moore, Financial Wellbeing Expert)

Much like the pay gap, there are gender differences in financial education too. Recent studies have found that Gen Z, and in particular women demonstrate low levels of financial literacy – meaning they have limited understanding of and competence demonstrating key financial skills such as budgeting, saving and investing. Financial Educator Ellie told me she believes men and women are being socialised differently when it comes to managing money. She's observed that women have historically been pushed towards frugality, while men are encouraged to maximise their earning potential – suggesting disparities in financial education are actively fuelling the gender pay gap. Which is exactly why she supports women in levelling up their finance skills:

"Educating yourself is one of the most important things you can do as a woman, because without knowledge you are basically stabbing around in the dark trying to find solutions or answers. In reality, the rules or the guidelines around how to make better financial decisions are not that hard. They're just not communicated to us. They're not taught to us. That's where I can help"
(Ellie Austin-Williams, Financial Educator & Author)

It's likely that the multiple, and often contradictory messages young people receive about money is contributing to their growing financial anxiety, and confusion. They struggle to strike a balance between spending, experiencing and living life now versus holding back, saving and planning for the future.

"My relationship with money is a work in progress. I'm always trying to find that balance between saving for the future (to buy a house and live comfortably) and living my best life. Social media has a huge influence in it though I'm not gonna lie. Seeing people my age travelling or flaunting the latest tech makes me want to do the same. But then again there's this constant buzz about the importance of investing and saving, especially with the economy being so unpredictable. My parents always emphasise saving, but it's hard when you're bombarded with trends and the pressure to keep up with things. Plus, the whole concept of financial independence is a big goal. So yeah, it's complicated but I'm learning to navigate it day by day"
(22 years, USA, via Imagen Insights Platform)

The great news is that many of todays 20-somethings are motivated to learn, actively seeking advice on personal finance. My conversations with women in media show that young people are turning to more accessible, less traditional sources to educate themselves:

"On the Talk Twenties podcast our finance episodes do really well. A lot of our listeners are anxious about money. They are doing the adding up at the end of the month and realising it doesn't calculate. You have to pay for rent, and you have to pay for bills and all these things from a starting salary, yet starting salaries haven't gone up in line with the cost of living. They want to know how to save, how to make more money, how to find additional incomes and how to manage their budgets, so they turn to us for information"
(Gaby Mendes, Podcast Host & Founder of Talk Twenties)

"Women in their 20s are really focused on finance. Articles about how they spend their money, how much you should be earning, how to ask for a pay rise, they all do really well"
(Alyssa Montagna – Hearst Magazines)

"Bored of the same old money tips written by middle-aged men in suits, I started This Girl Talks Money on Instagram to open up the conversation around earning, spending, saving and managing money"
(Ellie Austin-Williams, Financial Educator & Author)

One area of financial education that is often neglected, and was certainly news to me until recently, is the importance of source of funds. Now, you would be forgiven for thinking that money is money, and all types of income are born equal. But you'd be wrong. In his latest book, The Algebra of Wealth, Serial Author and NYU Professor Scott Galloway identifies the one thing that distinguishes 'those who are wealthy from those who are yet to be.' He calls it Earning Versus Owning. Put simply, business owners pay significantly less tax than employees. For salaried employees (approximately 71% of you), tax is taken automatically before the money hits their account. Business owners on the other hand (about 5% of 20-somethings), pay tax on any dividends they take (small sums of money drawn from company profits) as well as capital gains (typically larger sums from selling shares or selling their company). For Owners, there are various fancy ways of circumventing, deferring and massaging if, what and when tax is paid.

There are other benefits to being an Owner too. The first is that your earnings are directly proportional to your effort – the more successful you are, the more you make. Seems fair. But even more important is passive income – that is, the ability to make money even when you're not working. Imagine making bank while you sleep - what a win!

"Financial independence isn't about having a big salary. It's when you have enough money in investments and through passive income that you no longer have to swap your time for money - it takes a lot more time and effort to get there but it's very rewarding!"
(Laura Ann Moore, Financial Wellbeing Expert)

Having tried and tested almost every way of working myself, I can tell you that my financial situation only shifted dramatically (in both good and bad directions I should note) when I became a business owner. To help you understand, I'm going to take you on a tumultuous financial journey spanning 2 decades. Strap in.

Between the ages of 21 and 32, I was very much an Earner. As a creative agency employee, my starting salary was £17,000. This crept up as I rose through the ranks and switched jobs a couple of times over the next 10 years.

By the end of my Earning career, I was bringing in £70,000 annually, which is certainly not too shabby. It also made me a high-rate taxpayer, and my monthly pay packet remained the same regardless of how many hours I'd been working or how much business I'd been winning for my company.

At 32, I became a (very) Small Business Owner. I set up a limited company and started consulting for a number of different clients. I was fortunate to have built a good reputation and network by that time (major benefits of being an employee first!) so winning work was surprisingly simple. In my first year, I worked half the hours and more than doubled my income, benefitting from a solid day rate and preferential tax rules at the time.

Any spare time was spent on my side hustle, the haircare brand Curlsmith, founded with my husband who ran the business full time. And since we weren't making money for quite some years, I wasn't able to draw any income in return for my efforts. For all intents and purposes, 'Business Baby' (as my friends referred to it) was a very stressful, time-consuming and expensive hobby.

But everything changed when I had a baby at 36. The financial fallout was devastating. As a self-employed Consultant, I was only earning when I was working. So now, with a newborn at home and a global lockdown hitting a few months into my maternity leave, I had no access to external childcare and no way of actively making money. I'd even stupidly failed to apply for statutory maternity pay (a paltry amount anyway) mistakenly believing that I'd be able to continue my consulting business in some way with my tiny plus-one in tow. After that, my bank balance went from Hero to Zero overnight, and I became financially dependent on my partner for the first time.

Friend, it did not feel good.

Luckily it was around that time when our haircare business started to take off. My husband was finally able to pay himself a big enough salary to support the three of us. This was fortunate because as a partnered woman the lovely chaps at Universal Credit had absolutely no interest in helping a sister out!

When I was eventually able to return to work, I found my former schedule was wildly incompatible with my babies,' so I decided to commit to the family business full-time, becoming a salaried employee once more. Now, here I'll point out that there's a bit of a misconception in start-ups that the Founders make the most money. In reality, they often pay themselves less than their staff (or not at all when times are tight), plough any profits back into the business, and only make a mint if and when the business sells.

An event that we were fortunate to experience in 2022.

Having scrimped and struggled for years, we exited the company, aged 39, as millionaires.

The point of sharing all this is not to inspire negative comparison or to suggest that everyone can and should risk it all on building a business. After all, most businesses do fail and believe me, even in a successful business there are more than a few hardships and hairy moments along the way. And there's no accounting for luck and timing of course. What I do hope my story shows is that owning can be more lucrative than earning, and that for some, the less conventional path can be the quickest route to financial freedom.

Broke At 30: Am I Normal?

If you are in your 20s and feeling less than fluid, it may help to know you're not alone.

The Myth: BALLING AT 30. Failing to meet your financial goals by 30 means you're financially doomed for life.

The Reality: BROKE AT 30. Based on my Nationally Representative Sample (2023), the average annual salary for 20-somethings is £28,900 in the UK and $42,975 in the USA. But this belies the true spread. 27% of those surveyed earn below £20k in the UK and below $30k in the USA, and only 2% of Brits and 5% of Americans earn over £100k / $100k in their 20s.

The good news is that earning trends up through the decade, so whilst the average income for 20-year-olds is £21k in the UK and $31K in the USA, by age 29 the averages increase to £36k and $52k respectively. 52% of women in their 20s say their income is behind where they expected it to be at this age. Suffice it to say, whatever your individual circumstances, failing to meet your financial expectations in your 20s makes you NORMAL, and most probably an ambitious individual with unlimited future earning potential.

Financial Insecurity In Your 20s:

"I had a kind of crisis at 25. I just had to rip everything up and start again, I realised the job I was in just wasn't turning out how I thought it would, and it was just destroying my confidence, so I needed to quit. At the same time, I knew I was in a terrible relationship, which was eroding my confidence, and also draining my bank account. We were living together, so I ended up borrowing money from my mum so I could move out. It was all like going back to square one, and I didn't have any clue what I was going to do for a while.

That's when I started my business, This Girl Talks Money. But at

the start, I put a load of pressure on myself to achieve financially. I wanted to earn X amount of money by 30 and buy property. Now I know that the deadline was arbitrary, there was no real reason for it. I shouldn't have been comparing my new income to what my situation would have been if I'd stayed in my job because it was totally incomparable. I was starting a business from zero. The important thing is that I got out of a situation that wasn't working for me, and I was on the right path at last. Being financially insecure in your 20s isn't always a bad thing, it often means you're trying to find your path, or investing in your future"
(Ellie Austin-Williams, Financial Educator & Author)

Money Worries? Get Unstuck In 4 Steps

OK, so we have established that being financially insecure in our 20s is absolutely normal, and most likely temporary. We also know that not making bank gives us major anxiety. In the absence of a winning lottery ticket, what then, can we do to feel less anxious and more in control of the contents of our bank accounts?

I consulted money mindset experts to bring you specific advice on overcoming money fears and improving your future financial security, and I've added some of my own tips too.

How To Stop Looking OUT

- **Drop Financial 'Shoulds'**

"We are so exposed to other people's ideas of what success or financial fulfilment looks like that it's easy to lose track of what you actually want and need. So, take a bit of time out to unpack that - ask yourself, am I pursuing this financial goal or this item because I want it or because I think I should want it? That goes for everything - the house, the car, the clothes, the three-month travelling sabbatical. You've got to figure out whether it's you or whether it's the voices you're hearing that are telling you that that's what you should want"
(Ellie Austin-Williams, Financial Educator & Author)

- **Stop Comparing And Despairing**

"We are all dealt different financial cards. So, if you find yourself comparing your situation to a friend, talk to them about it. Let's say they've bought a house and that seems unachievable to you. Try to understand how they did it, and you'll probably find that they've not done it all on their own. You're not starting from the same place as them so you're not comparing like with like. Stop looking at the cards that other people have been dealt and wishing that you had those. Because it doesn't serve you, it won't get you anywhere"
 (Ellie Austin-Williams, Financial Educator & Author)

- **Turn Envy Around**

"If you find yourself comparing your financial situation with others, first ask yourself why. What are you saying to yourself? Sometimes jealousy is okay because it highlights to us what we really want in life and what we should aim for. But do not make someone else's success mean something negative about you. All this does is keep you stuck!"
 (Laura Ann Moore, Money Mindset Expert)

- **Remember Social Media Is Fake**

"Recognise that wealth is silent. When you see people on social media you do not know how much they have saved or invested, you just see what they have spent and what they no longer have. Remind yourself of this regularly, because on social media what you see is not always the reality"
 (Laura Ann Moore, Money Mindset Expert)

- **Be Transparent**

"Instead of resenting or avoiding friends who push you to overspend, communicate with them. Tell them about your budget, it's Ok to say you'd love to go out, but you can only really afford to spend £30. Great friends will understand and make the effort to choose somewhere that you can afford. You just can't expect people to read your mind"
 (Ellie Austin-Williams, Financial Educator & Author)

- **Push Back On Time Pressure**

"Try not to stress about the fact that you're not earning as much as quickly as you want to. Because you are still early in your career, you're still learning skills and you really do have time to increase your income. Allow yourself that space to learn and to grow so you can step up to better-paid roles over the years"
(Ellie Austin-Williams, Financial Educator & Author)

- **Don't Believe In Miracles**

"Sometimes people think there is a secret sauce, a special recipe, one specific way to build wealth. But it really is an amalgamation of good financial habits that helps you reach a place of financial security and independence"
(Laura Ann Moore, Money Mindset Expert)

- **F*ck Tradition**

"Further education and climbing the corporate ladder may be well-trodden roads to financial security – but there are other paths to financial success. Don't fall victim to 'sunk costs' by getting stuck in a corporate role that doesn't offer fulfilment or fair pay. Be brave and explore alternative paths, you may find it pays dividends down the line"
(Kate Berski, Author)

How To Start Looking IN

- **Get Financial Clarity**

"Get crystal clear on your financial situation. How much are you earning? What are your expenses? How much do you have in savings? How much debt do you have? Write down those figures. From there, you're in a position to start a new conversation about where you want to be. Once you know where you are, and you know where you want to be, then you can start figuring out how to get from A to B"
(Ellie Austin-Williams, Financial Educator & Author)

- **Take Charge**

"A lot of people struggle to reach a place of financial security because they're letting their money make all the decisions. But put yourself back in the driving seat by keeping a journal. Knowing exactly where your money goes, understand your spending triggers, and proactively plan for what's to come"
    (Laura Ann Moore, Financial Wellbeing Expert)

- **Know Your Triggers**

"If you're prone to over-spending, start taking notice of when you're doing it and why it's happening. Identify the triggers that set you off, and when you feel that way again, try to replace that spending behaviour with something else. So instead of clicking 'buy,' watch YouTube for 10 minutes, walk around the block, or buy yourself something that's £2 instead of £20. You may not be able to just stop behaving in a way that you have been behaving for years overnight, but you can reduce the financial consequences"
    (Ellie Austin-Williams, Financial Educator & Author)

- **Challenge Your Limiting Beliefs**

"Work on improving your relationship with money - confidence comes with knowledge plus taking action. Challenge the language you use and the beliefs you have about how money works in the world, because how you think and feel about money is what your reality will be with money!"
    (Laura Ann Moore, Financial Wellbeing Expert)

- **Learn Deferred Gratification**

"When my toddler wants something in a shop, I take a photo of it and add it to a 'wish list' album on my phone. If she hasn't forgotten about it by her next birthday (she usually has!) then she can have it. Try using a similar 'cooling-off' technique to help curb impulse spending by taking screen grabs of items you're checking out online"
    (Kate Berski, Author)

How To REFRAME Your Goals

- **Know It's Temporary**

"The truth is, most people are broke in their 20s, and many become more financially secure with time. Understand that short-term financial insecurity can be the key to long-term financial security. Investing time and money in education, re-training, work experience or starting your own company now can unlock significant future earning potential"
   (Kate Berski, Author)

- **Reframe Your Financial Identity**

 "If you see yourself as a saver and you struggle to enjoy spending your money, you might want to reframe your relationship to spending and to money itself. A lot of the time our relationship with money is a reflection of the relationship we have with ourselves. Why do you feel so guilty spending on yourself? Do you feel you are not worthy of these things? Journal on where the guilt comes from, make a 'guilt-free' spending pot and every month put money towards it and permit yourself to spend it completely guilt-free"
   (Laura Ann Moore, Financial Wellbeing Expert)

- **Don't Defer Happiness**

"Stop saying 'I'll be happy when I'm rich, or when I have X amount of money.' You will never be happy if you're living in the future, find ways to be happy right now"
   (Gaby Mendes, Founder and Podcast Host, TalkTwenties)

- **Plot The Path**

"When you have a specific goal in mind, like buying a house, a car or having a baby, plan ahead for that. Work out how much that's going to cost and break down how you'll get there into manageable steps. Figure out exactly what you need to be earning, and how much you need to be saving. But be realistic. If you're earning 30 grand and looking at flats in London, you've got a big gap, and you'll have that gap for a long time. You're going to get frustrated, so you need to manage your ex-

pectations. Put numbers on things, break it down and work out what that looks like over the course of a year or five years. Be clear on how much you realistically need to be setting aside to get to your goals"
   (Ellie Austin-Williams, Financial Educator & Author)

- **Aim For Emotional Neutrality**

"The ultimate goal with money is to reach a point of emotional neutrality. Not feeling any real emotional attachment to money is a good thing. Try to see it as a tool, which you can use to create the life that you want to live. It's not about discarding all emotion and just throwing money away, but equally, it's not about holding on to it really tightly because you value it too much"
   (Ellie Austin-Williams, Financial Educator & Author)

- **Prioritise Income Over Saving**

"I don't like frugality, it's like you're trying to shrink as much as possible, minimising your life. There might be times you need to do it, but I don't think it's a healthy way to live full-time. The most powerful thing you can actually do is increase what you're earning. So, if you can get a grasp on your expenses, and know what you need to spend to maintain a certain standard of living, you can then focus on how to actually bring in more, and that might be through work opportunities, switching careers, and investments. There's always going to be a limit to how much you can cut back, but there's no limit to how much you can increase"
   (Ellie Austin-Williams, Financial Educator & Author)

- **Flip Your Finances**

"Stop waiting until the end of the month to put money into savings or investments. Make a spending plan that prioritises your long-term financial goals – then spend what is left over. And learn about investing ASAP - no one got rich from just saving. The sooner you start the better, because the most important thing when it comes to growing your money is how long you are investing for. You don't have to be rich to get started, you can start investing on the stock market from as little as £5 a month"
   (Laura Ann Moore, Financial Wellbeing Expert)

- **Cultivate an OWNER Mindset**

"Think about how you can become a small business owner, or start to generate passive income on the side (even if it's small). Maybe it's time to monetise your hobby. Over time, this income stream will enable you to earn more without working more hours. It could also allow you to quit your day job and pursue your passion at the same time"
   (Kate Berski, Author)

How To CELEBRATE The Small Wins

- **Celebrate What You Do Have**

"We're hard-wired to focus on the negative, so we are very good at seeing what we don't have, and not very good at seeing what we do. The irony is, while you're busy being envious of other people, other people are probably looking at aspects of your life enviously. Try to be grateful for the things you have, and celebrate the progress you've made, and recognise that other people may not have it as easy as you imagine"
   (Ellie Austin-Williams, Financial Educator & Author)

- **Practise Gratitude**

"Be especially grateful for the things that money really cannot buy... a loving partner, a family that loves you, friendships that make you feel seen and heard, your health. It is proven that when you focus on the good in your life, there is more good to focus on"
   (Laura Ann Moore, Financial Wellbeing Expert)

MINDHACKER QUESTIONS

- Who in my life has already achieved the kind of financial freedom I aspire to? (Have a chat with them)

- Where did they start?

- What steps did they take?

- What skills did they acquire?

- What changes did they make?

- What did it feel like when they got there?

- What progress have I already made towards achieving my financial goals?

TURNING 30 GOALS - REGROUP

Take a look back at your original list of Turning 30 Goals – did you write a financial goal on there? How high up your list is it sitting? What words did you use to express it?

Now you've learned more about the environmental factors that might have shaped your financial circumstances, and your expectations, would you frame that goal any differently? Does the goal (or the deadline) still feel realistic, and achievable, taking into account where you are right now? Would you now express that goal any differently?

Take a minute to re-write your financial goal if required, in the 'NEW GOALS' list at the back of this book, or wherever you're taking your notes. Now add to your 'BABY GOALS' column.

Take some time to think about the achievable next steps that could help inch you towards that goal. You will probably find it helpful at this point to create a separate spreadsheet detailing your current incomings and outgoings and breaking down your future financial goal into achievable chunks to work out how, and how long, it may take you to get there. Remember – you don't have to have it all figured out by 30, your current situation won't last forever and financial security can come in jumps, not just increments. Getting to financial freedom takes time – but luckily there is no stopwatch on success and no limit to your potential future income. You got this!

So You Don't Have A Place

"When you realise you should have bought a house in 1998 instead of wasting time learning how to walk"
  (Anon)

Property Anxiety Is Real

For many Quarter-Lifers, nothing feels more 'failure to launch' than going back to live with your parents or rinsing 90% of your income on rent and being forced to flat-share when you're so over communal bathroom vibes. And yet, thanks to myriad factors beyond our control (more on that later) property ownership feels like a pipe dream for many of today's 20-somethings.

For the average cash-strapped Quarter-Lifer, housing options are limited – ranging from the deeply un-aspirational to the uncertain, insecure and downright unsanitary. Here are just a few of the less-than-desirable living situations my survey respondents find themselves in:

"I'm still living at home. How do I know if I'll be financially stable enough to not live with my parents at 30? I can't see how anything will change by then..."
  (21yrs, USA)

"We desperately want a family home, but me and my husband still can't afford to buy a house. We are currently living with my parents, paying off debts and trying to save a deposit. It's hard and not easy and none of us are happy"
  (28yrs, UK)

"I am almost 30 years old, married and I have 3 kids. I am nowhere where I thought I would be. I just lost my home, and my relationship

is on the rocks"
(29yrs, USA)

Clearly, housing uncertainty adds considerable stress to a life stage already characterised by multiple moving parts. It's also a far cry from how we expected to be living in the run-up to 30. Many of us grew up simply assuming that we would have our own place long before 30. And my data demonstrates that this remains an important life goal for a huge proportion of Quarter-Lifers. 47% of my non-owners selected homeownership as a top turning 30 goal. Other studies have put a figure as high as 97%. But they're not there yet.

57% of the aspiring owners I asked say they feel behind on their goal of buying property, and 41% worry that they'll never be able to achieve it. And therein lies the problem. Quarter-Lifers are coming up against some very real barriers to securing their own place. And when their experienced reality falls short of their expectations, they're left feeling disappointed, disillusioned, and even desperate, as their candid comments reveal:

"I feel anxious about not having my own house at age 30, what if I don't make it to that goal?!"
(26yrs, USA)

"I feel like there are things I am supposed to have achieved by the age of 30 which are unrealistic at this point in my life, like owning property"
(27yrs, UK)

"This is a thoroughly depressing survey. I feel regretful that I have not achieved things for example, house ownership by the time I am 30"
(29yrs, UK)

"I worry that my financial situation won't get better in the future, and it will impact my ability to get a home"
(29yrs, UK)

Homeownership appears to be one of the biggest Expectation Gaps of Quarter-Life. Arguably, having a home of your own by 30 shouldn't be a lot to ask. After all, our parents seemed to manage OK. So why are so many young adults struggling to get started? Why does home ownership feel so impossibly out of reach? And how can aspiring owners start to close the gap, and get themselves in a better position to realise their dream?

I am here to show you that it is possible to own a home, wherever you're starting from. And I have a wealth of juicy expert tips coming down the pipe on how to make it happen. But first, let's get a sense check.

Whatever your living situation right now, I need you to know that you are not alone, you are not failing, and you're not wrong, it really does suck to be a 20-something navigating today's property landscape.

No Place At 30: Am I Normal?

The Myth: EVERYONE ELSE HAS THEIR OWN PLACE AT 30. Still living at home, flat sharing or renting instead of owning means you're falling behind or failing to launch.

The Reality: THE MAJORITY (70%) OF UNDER 30s ARE NOT HOMEOWNERS. 53% of 20-somethings are renting. 31% of women aged 20-29 (and 51% of 20-year-olds) still live with their parents. Londoners, singles and those of Asian descent are more likely to reside in their family home. The latest figures show that the average age of a first-time buyer in England is now 34 (35 in the USA) and nearly 70% of first-timers are over 35, so not being a property owner by 30 makes you absolutely normal.

Property Anxiety: It's NOT You

My first challenge is where does our desire to own bricks and mortar, and the associated anxiety about not achieving this goal by 30 actually come from? Moreover, can we really blame our property-challenged status on a penchant for flat whites? Let's start by examining the environment which has spawned, and spurned, our real estate expectations.

1. Uncertainty Aversion

2. Property Porn

3. Individualistic Ideals

4. Mad Math

5. The Wage Gap

Uncertainty Aversion

I've said it before and I'll say it again. Uncertainty equals Anxiety. And for most people, their 20s are THE Era of Uncertainty. Every Quarter-Lifer I've come across is grappling with one or more of life's big question marks.

When will I find my person?

Will I ever have babies?

How do I find a job I actually like?

Will I ever get out of my overdraft?

When on earth will I be able to afford a place of my own?!!

Even writing this list is giving me anxiety.

So, if you're in your 20s and feeling overwhelmed, stressed out or in full-blown crisis, know that this is an entirely normal and rational reaction to your current circumstances.

The thing is, despite any aspirations we may have to 'go with the flow' and 'live in the moment,' human beings are actually hardwired to hate uncertainty. And for good reason. Out in the wild, uncertainty could be a signal of imminent, life-threatening danger. Far better, our brain reasons, to anticipate and prepare for the 'worst case' scenario rather than risk getting snaffled by a sabre tooth tiger. Which is why we evolved to favour the known over the unknown. So strong is this inbuilt bias, Psychologists have found, that most of us would choose certain negative outcomes over uncertain ambiguous outcomes. In one study, respondents overwhelmingly chose to receive a painful electric shock right now instead of the threat of a potential electric shock in the future.

What, I hear you ask, could electric shocks possibly have to do with the pressure to buy property?

Well, historically owning bricks and mortar has been seen as the ultimate certainty. A sure-fire investment, a reliable living situation with zero threat of being chucked out, or priced out, by an unruly landlord, a safe place to shield us from the stresses of the outside world, a solid foundation for adult life. Put simply, property ownership meets a fundamental human need for safety. And at a time of life when many things feel uncertain, living in a world that feels decidedly unsettled, even unsafe, I'm not at all surprised to see 20-somethings drawn to the promised security of home ownership. Especially those who grew up with housing insecurity, like prolific Property Investor and Coach Barbara Escolme:

"Growing up, my earliest memory was being repossessed. I grew up in rented accommodation, I didn't come from a wealthy family. There was no 'Bank of Mum and Dad.' So it was important to me to own my own first home as soon as possible. So when I went to university, I also did a call centre job on Saturdays and Sundays so I could use my student loan as a deposit for my first home. Owning a home was a big deal for me, a goal that nobody else had achieved in my family"
   (Barbara Escolme, Property Investor & Coach)

Barbara believes that the promotion of home ownership and the demonisation of renting by the media, has contributed to the property pressure felt by young adults:

"The media does demonise renting, they call it dead money, even though there is also a lot of dead money in owning – like interest-only mortgages. There are a lot of articles and stats out there about how great property is for making money, how house prices grow, amazing before and afters. Property is a popular topic, but the messages

are often confusing – one minute they're talking about a house price crash, and the next it's about how prices have grown by 2% in the last month"
(Barbara Escolme, Property Investor & Coach)

In her 2024 book, Dr Eliza Filby describes the property prognosis for Gen Z as an 'Inherictocracy.' Which brings me to the part when I check my own property privilege. I was one of the lucky ones. I became a homeowner myself just before I turned 30. And like almost every young owner I know, especially those living in big cities, my flat deposit was entirely drawn from the Bank of Mum and Dad.

At the time, that poky, over-priced, dank-smelling ground floor flat in Ealing was all I'd ever wanted in life. And I'll always be grateful for that massive leg up the ladder. But it also came with an unexpected price. The week before I got my keys, my flatmate told me to go out and buy myself a whole new outfit, shoes and handbag included. Baffled, I asked her why? "Because you won't be spending money on anything but that flat for the next five years." And she wasn't wrong.

Properties, especially those in need of renovation like mine, are a bona fide money pit. And with every home improvement, new problems are uncovered. Like the actual TREE my (now) father-in-law found growing under our wonky bathroom floor, or the wet mould that would seep through the bedroom wall after every coat of paint like something from a Japanese film noir.

Of course, the boiler did conk out two months after we sealed the deal, the roof did fall into disrepair when I was at the tail-end of my overdraft, and the gas company did hike their prices just as I dared to dream about holidays.

When it happens for you, you'll most likely be looking around for an adult, only to realise that you, in fact, are the adult. And nobody is coming to save you. Unless you're lucky enough to have an incredibly handy father-in-law who just so happens to be a builder and a dad who is a dab hand with ancient plumbing. Again, checking my familial privilege.

I don't wish to appear ungrateful. I am fully aware of my good fortune in this department. I simply mean to point out that property ownership may not be the first-class ticket to emotional and financial stability that you imagine. Believe me, I cried for hours the day the £4k bill for my portion of fixing the communal roof came through. And several friends have come a cropper of late with interest rate rises rendering their formerly affordable mortgages untenable. My hope is that pointing out the pitfalls may go a small way toward assuaging the property pressure if ownership feels out of reach for you right now.

When you do get your own place, and you will, maybe, just maybe, you'll look back fondly at these carefree days of living at home, renting a room, or even couch-surfing. And remember when your time, your money and your topics of conversation, were entirely your own. Please note - you will become a home furnishing bore when you get your place, and you will spend your weekends painting the bathroom wall instead of painting the town red... don't say I didn't warn you.

My hope is that instead of focusing on the instability of your current living situation, you can learn to embrace the opportunities it presents. The freedom, the flexibility, the excitement. Your 20s are the time to explore the options before committing to putting down roots.

So, move a lot, move around your city, and the world, live with different people and 'try on' different lifestyles to find the one that fits. There's plenty of time for paint swatches in the future.

Property Porn

Hands up if you've ever binged Selling Sunset, Buying Beverley Hills, Million Dollar Listing or all of the above? As if our innate desire to acquire property wasn't enough, the content we consume can ramp it up tenfold. The last few years have seen a new wave of uber-aspirational 'property porn' streaming into our living rooms, getting us salivating over unbelievable homes affordable only to the wealthiest 1%. It's a far cry from the more 'accessible' home-improvement shows I watched as a kid. Like Changing Rooms, in which the rooms of regular people were turned upside down in a weekend by flamboyant interior design personalities, often constructed entirely out of flimsy MDF you just knew would fall to pieces the minute the cameras stopped rolling.

Oh no, these days it's not enough to simply set foot on the property ladder, the goal is to acquire an Instagrammable property – replete with hardwood floors, Italian marble worktops and an infinity pool out-back. On social media it can seem like everyone else is living in an impossibly photogenic, not to mention well-organised, home. That they probably built from scratch with their bare hands, helped by a smooth-chested model boyfriend. And whilst most of us can acknowledge that expecting to actually live in one of these dream homes by age 25 is unrealistic, it's hard not to compare our own dreary, dated and cramped interiors against them. We feel like we're failing at life when our home doesn't exactly match up.

I remember returning to our home in London from our honeymoon in 2016 – we hadn't spent much money on the wedding but we'd gone big on the holiday, with a two-week tour around the States. Ending up in Vegas, we still had bright lights and sequins in our eyes when we stepped into our dimly lit ground-floor flat. It was as much of an anti-climax as the day we moved in only to find the previous owner had stripped out every fixture and fitting, right down to the toilet seat, yet had failed to run a hoover across the ancient carpet, thickened with years of black dust. We'd been perfectly content before – it was the contrast that killed it.

As the homes we see on screen become ever more fabulous, the property expectation gap gets ever wider. I spoke with Property Investing Coach Caroline Tolman about how social media is not only fake, but when it comes to property, it belies the inequalities that would help explain why our 'peers' are in such an apparently superior position to us:

"They say comparison is the thief of joy, which is why Instagram makes us feel so bad. It's just this window into everyone else's perfect life. What it doesn't show is that everyone comes from different backgrounds and starts from a different place. When it comes to property ownership, the position that you're in is not the same as anyone else's so it really can't be compared"
  (Caroline Tolman, Property Investor & Mentor)

Individualistic Ideals

Like many 20-somethings, I ended up living communally by default and not by choice. After finishing University with barely a penny to my name, I spent a year working an office job and living at home with my parents, before making the move to London to start my career in Advertising. Naturally, not being a nepo baby or knowing a single living soul in the Big City I had one option – gumtree.com. I'd also fallen for the 'immediate start' trick at my new job, allowing myself just one paltry weekend to secure a room in a house full of strangers.

Cue a mad Sunday dash around London in my dad's car, viewing accommodations boasting what can only be described as the 'squatter' aesthetic. I was too afraid to even get out of the car at one particularly 'stabby' looking spot in Whitechapel, and I remember nervously eyeing another room above a chip shop sporting dubiously stained net curtains.

Only one place on my list turned out to be remotely normal – nice even, nestled handily between Highbury & Islington and Holloway Road in North London. As a bonus, its' residents were a group of bright, smiley and chatty 20-somethings. This is it! I thought. I had found my place. There were just two problems.

Problem 1: The Interview. This bunch weren't about to take in any warm body who could pay the rent, they were friends, and they were looking for a good fit. They were selective. Luckily for me, I managed to pull off an affable yet responsible vibe and was offered the room.

Which brought me to **Problem 2**: The room. Which could generously be described as a broom cupboard. Forget about swinging a cat – there wasn't room to open a wardrobe door and enter the room at the same time. It was also located on the ground floor inches from the front door – meaning I'd be rudely awoken by the wall next to my head shuddering violently if anyone returned home after bedtime. Of course, I took it. And it turned out to be the best moving decision I ever made. Those housemates, not to mention their friends and partners by extension, became my urban family and lifelong friends to this day. Had I been flush enough to realise my dream of living alone in my 20s, I am a hundred percent sure I wouldn't have been as happy.

Now I DO live alone (if you don't count my husband, my four-year-old and my in-laws).

And yet, every couple of months my friend Zoe (one of the aforementioned OG housemates) sends a link to our WhatsApp group to some sort of cavernous castle in Scotland or idyllic farmstead in Somerset, which could be ours for a temptingly low price (split 12 ways). She's long been a proponent for what she calls 'The Commune Dream.' Envisioning a world in which friends live alongside friends, sharing cooking, childcare and unlimited crates of wine for the rest of our days.

And, I have to admit she's on to something. Because, as Coach Laura Guckian points out to me, 'The Village is gone.' More of us are moving away from our families and support networks for work, and data shows that the most educated amongst us are often the most isolated. The cost of living continues to rise, while the number of people living in single-person households, and therefore shouldering the financial burden alone, has increased from 8% to nearly 28% since 1940. In co-habiting couples and families, it is still women who shoulder the burden of domestic labour and take on the bigger 'mental load' (the many invisible tasks involved in running a household like meal planning, buying birthday gifts, staying in contact with family, bag packing, managing children's schedules and more). All of this can leave us feeling overwhelmed, under-supported and under-appreciated.

Today, with so many of us living in isolated bubbles, it's easy to see why loneliness has become a global epidemic. The latest figures suggest 60% of adults now experience loneliness, an increase of over 30% in 20 years. 18-22 year-olds have been identified as the loneliest age group, and lack of social connection has been linked to a range of devastating mental and physical health outcomes (for more on this see Chapter 4).

Given all of the above, it's not hard to see the appeal of the Commune Dream – an alternative way of living in which extended 'family' members each contribute equally, and responsibilities, labour and finances are shared across the group. This set-up would also deliver on our innate need for 'community,' and close human connection. When I put a poll out on my Instagram stories recently, 80% of voters said they'd consider buying with friends, indicating a staggering level of interest in alternative ways of living.

Recent years have seen a new wave of 'Intentional Communities' popping up, to provide a more economically equal, environmentally sustainable and dare I say, aspirational way of life. And I have to tell you I've been tempted. But on closer inspection, I usually find they're too far from the shops, or the airport, for my tastes. So, I guess I'm missing the point.

Despite the arguments in its favour, co-living remains outside the consideration set of regular people and is often laughed off as 'hippie' or 'cultish.' In Individualistic Western societies, self-ownership maintains the aspirational top spot. Not to mention the only option supported by our legal and financial infrastructure. Last time I checked there was no platonic multi-person 'co-ownership' box to check on the form for buying a house.

When it comes down to it, most of us, myself included, are material girls living in a material world. Owning property is still the ultimate baby adult status symbol. Not to mention an incredible achievement that should not be downplayed. But next time you find yourself fielding comments about why you really should get on the property ladder, think on this; Home ownership is not a fundamental survival need, it's a social construct. That is, an idea that has been created, validated and normalised by our society to such an extent that it has become an unquestioned expectation. Not reaching this expected milestone is often perceived as failure, and not the functional outcome of the environment in which we find ourselves.

Mad Math

Turns out there's a lot of bad advice out there on how to get on the property ladder. Most of it concerns victim-blaming unsuspecting young coffee drinkers. It doesn't take a degree in finance to understand that nobody ever saved up a house deposit by simply swerving Starbucks for a few months. Financial Wellbeing Coach Laura sets the record straight on the Mad Math equations that have become so insta-popular in the past few years:

"I hate this idea of 'stop buying oat milk lattes and avocado on toast and you will be able to afford to buy a home'. Firstly, 37% of first-time buyers in the UK have had help from 'the bank of mum and dad' (aka been lent money). The average first-time deposit in the UK is £53,414. If a latte is £4 and avocado on toast is £11 which is a total of £15 spent. If you were spending this at the weekend so £30 a week, by stopping you are only saving yourself £1,560 - only 2% of the required deposit needed"
    (Laura Ann Moore, Finance Coach)

Bad advice isn't just maddening, it's contributing to the unhappiness of aspiring property owners. Adding to our list of failures, serving up scant simple pleasures (a nice coffee, a crisp new book, a cheeky cocktail with brunch...) with a side of guilt. Moreover, as we saw in Chapter 5 (So you don't have BANK) there is a finite limit to how much you can cut back. Living like a monk indefinitely might help us save money but it won't make us into wealthy landowners either and it certainly won't save our sanity. Quarter-Life is stressful enough as it is, so I'm an advocate for quality of life over extreme austerity. Girl, I give you full permission to buy yourself the damn latte!

The Wage Gap

Many of the Quarter-Lifers I speak to feel like they have been sold a lie. Brought up to believe that if they worked hard, got a decent education and beat the competition to a cosy corporate job, property ownership would naturally follow. But this, they tell me, has not been the case.

"I have a good job. I work for the biggest-selling magazine in the country and I'm one of the editors there, but I can still just about afford a flat share in London"
    (Bethan Jenkins, 28, Journalist)

"I'm anxious because I don't own a home and am not financially secure, despite having a Masters degree"
    (29yrs, USA)

Gen Z, it appears, are in the worst position to buy property of any generation to date. Boomers like my parents were afforded relatively cheap house prices but were hit with eye-wateringly high interest rates in the 1980s. Millennials like me had to stump up steep deposits for our first homes, however, we did enjoy very low interest rates until the recent rises. While Gen Z have inherited the worst of both worlds, with already unaffordable homes garnished with increasingly inaccessible interest rates. When I consulted the experts, they had great empathy:

"For 20-somethings it is more expensive to exist than ever before, especially in comparison to previous generations; wages have not increased in accordance with the cost of living. We are told to go and get a degree, get a job, buy a house and yet having a degree no longer secures you a job and it's so much harder to get on the property ladder. Housing has become exponentially higher than your average wage compared to the past..."
(Laura Ann Moore, Money Mindset Expert)

"The 90s was the most affordable decade, so when our parents were buying. The average price then was around four times their income, whereas now you need up to nine times your income to afford the average house price in the UK of £264,000. So, there's a massive struggle to actually get on the ladder, topped off with inflation, high interest rates, and lack of supply. We've got a housing shortage in the UK. We're not building enough homes, and rents have increased, so when people are renting, they're unable to save for a deposit at the same time"
(Caroline Tolman, Property Investor & Mentor)

As Caroline mentions, the affordability data makes depressing reading. In 2022, the average home price across the UK topped 8 times the average annual income, up from 4 times the typical salary in the late 1990s. In the USA, price-to-income ratios are 6:1 on average and 8:1 in bigger cities. These figures are the highest since records began in the 1970s. And recent world events have made things worse. The price-to-income ratio has risen by 2 points since 2019, thanks to what I'll call 'Pandemic Lift.' Remember that time when we spent 24/7 tearing our hair out at home for months on end, emerging from lockdown with a newfound intolerance for our own living space? Well, all the frantic moving and shaking that followed (for those who could afford it) hiked the prices up for everyone. Soaring interest rates then sealed the fates of many aspiring owners, as housing affordability, and hopes sank to new lows. As their comments reveal:

"I am way behind where I expected to be, and not as financially stable as I would like. I have school debt and will never own a house in this economy"
(29yrs, USA)

"The dream of homeownership is going down the drain. We normal day-to-day workers have difficulties saving enough to own a house. This forces many of us to turn to credit, which can lead to even more problems"
(25yrs, USA, via Imagen Insights' Index)

Despite being aware that the inter-generational disparities are largely beyond their control, some 20-somethings can't help but compare where they are in life with where their parents were at the same age. Unsurprisingly, the comparison isn't favourable:

"My parents were married, owned their home and had savings and a nice car by 30. At 26, I'm single, I still rent, have little savings and drive an old car"
(26yrs, USA)

Wages might not be the only gap we need to worry about either. While the gender pay gap is well-documented, I was shocked to find in my research that a gender mortgage gap exists too, and I suppose the two go hand in hand. 2022-23 figures show that 65% of first-time mortgages are offered to individuals using the title 'Mr.'

It's not all doom and gloom though. While many still do feel property pressure acutely, a new wave of Quarter-Lifers are embracing mortgage freedom and investing in memories instead. A recent study by Insure & Go Australia found that 71% of under 30s would rather spend their money on travel than property in the next 12 months. And with the market as it is right now, who can blame them?

Journalist Bethan is with them. She tells me she's let go of her aspirations to own, in favour of enjoying life right now with the little money she does have. As a firm believer in following your own path, instead of the expected route, it's an attitude I can't help but admire:

"I'm not thinking of buying at all. I'm renting a flat, I've got about 20 quid to last me this month, absolutely no savings. I'll probably never buy a house, but I'm not bothered. Now all of my money goes on travelling. And I'm fine with that"
    (Bethan Jenkins, 28, Journalist)

No Property? No Problem

OK, so we have established that NOT being on the property ladder by 30 is absolutely normal, nay understandable, BUT not having the certainty of a home base can also give us major anxiety for entirely relatable reasons. So, what do you do if owning your own bricks and mortar is still firmly on the life list? My experts are here to help you get unstuck in four simple steps.

How To STOP Looking Out

- **Drop The 30 Deadline**

"Stop pressuring yourself to purchase by 30 or beating yourself up for being behind. The average age for first-time buyers in the UK is 34. You have plenty of time"
    (Caroline Tolman, Property Investor & Mentor)

- **Stop Comparing**

"Understand that everyone starts from a different place and has access to different resources, so don't compare your position to others. Focus instead on understanding your own position, maximising your own knowledge..."
    (Caroline Tolman, Property Investor & Mentor)

- **Challenge Societal Scaremongering**

"Like me, you may need to unlearn a fear of debt instilled in you from

society, or your own parents. Embracing good debt actually improves your position as a future property owner. To secure a mortgage you need to demonstrate you're a good borrower – so applying for credit and managing it well goes in your favour. Get comfortable with being in debt"
 (Caroline Tolman, Property Investor & Mentor)

- **Remove Property Pressure**

"Let go of the idea that buying a house is the ONLY good investment and way to reach financial independence. It's a myth. Our parents and grandparents had access to affordable housing, but we have access to the stock market and the ability to make money from anywhere in the world! Luckily, we have low barriers to entry for the stock market. You can get started investing on the stock with as little as £5 a month"
 (Laura Ann Moore, Finance Coach)

- **Stop Seeking Instant Gratification**

"Detach yourself from the 'Instagram' mindset that makes you think you should have your dream house right now. Understand it's going to take time, patience and work to get where you want to be"
 (Caroline Tolman, Property Investor & Mentor)

- **Don't Keep Up Appearances**

"Don't be tempted to shoot for a shiny new build that makes you look successful on social media. New homes are priced high and can lose value fast, like buying a new car. Instead, look to invest in a lower priced 'fixer upper' you can add value to over time and grow your investment"
 (Caroline Tolman, Property Investor & Mentor)

How To START Looking In

- **Know What You Want**

"Get clear on what you genuinely want, what will make you happy, what matters to you. Identify your non-negotiables. And buying may

not be right for you at the moment. It might be that being in a particular location or living a certain kind of lifestyle, even if you're renting, might be more important to you right now than becoming a homeowner"
(Barbara Escolme, Property Investor & Mentor)

- **Check Your Credit**

"A good credit score is essential to get a mortgage, yet a lot of people don't know what their credit score is. Understand and get on top of your debts now, starting by signing up to a credit score website to find out where you're at. A small thing, like a missed payment on a store card, could be the only thing standing between you and your future mortgage"
(Caroline Tolman, Property Investor & Mentor)

- **Educate Yourself**

"Before you make any decisions, get educated. Don't just approach your bank, speak to a whole-market mortgage broker who can educate you about all the different products that are available to you as a first-time buyer. Speak to people you know who have bought or invested in property before to learn how they got started"
(Barbara Escolme, Property Investor & Mentor)

How To REFRAME Your Goals

- **Be Intentional**

"Instead of just scrolling Rightmove, proactively register your interest with a range of estate agents and let them know what you're looking for. The simple act of stating your intention will make it more likely to happen. And you could get first dibs on great properties even before they hit the market"
(Barbara Escolme, Property Investor & Mentor)

- **Prioritise Earning Over Saving**

"Spending less and cutting back so that you can save money is one

strategy but there are only so many cutbacks you can make. And you cannot budget your way out of a low income and into a mortgage. Looking for ways to make more money is always a great option"
(Laura Ann Moore, Finance Coach)

- **Don't Be A Wage Slave**

"Think beyond your main job and salary to raise a deposit or secure a mortgage offer. Think about additional income streams, other ways you can trade your time for money to boost your income"
(Caroline Tolman, Property Investor & Mentor)

- **Embrace Growth Over Austerity**

"No one has ever saved their way to wealth. That is just not what happens. You have to get comfortable with considered risk, and taking on debt as a way to grow your passive income"
(Caroline Tolman, Property Investor & Mentor)

- **Use Your Head**

"Many property investors buy to let, not to live, and actually live in rented accommodation themselves. If you consider your first property as an investment, not a home, you will buy with your head, not your heart"
(Barbara Escolme, Property Investor & Mentor)

- **Plot The Path**

"Speak to a Mortgage Broker to plot your path to property ownership. Most will do a review for you, and check affordability for no cost. They will help you get clear on where you stand now, and the steps you need to take to reach your property goal - what you can afford, how much you'll need for a deposit, how much you need to save and when you will be in a position to go ahead and buy a property"
(Caroline Tolman, Property Investor & Mentor)

- **Embrace The Process**

"You're either doing something that gets you closer towards your

goals, or you're doing nothing and you're moving further away. So, write a list of small and manageable tasks you can do to move you closer towards your goal of property ownership – for example, checking your credit score, speaking to a mortgage broker, meeting a property investor for coffee, selling off unwanted items, exploring an alternative income stream etc. Do one small thing every day"
(Caroline Tolman, Property Investor & Mentor)

How To CELEBRATE The Wins

- **Enjoy Mortgage Freedom**

"Write a list of Pros for not having a home of your own. There are many positives to your situation – including the freedom to live and move whenever and wherever you want, the flexibility to change your mind, opportunities to save money by living with others, the peace of mind that you won't be hit my interest rate hikes, and the opportunity to spend your money on fun experiences"
(Kate Berski, Author)

- **Try Before You Buy**

"Renting allows you to test out living in an area and see whether it's the right place to invest, before you commit to a mortgage or get bogged down by maintaining a home"
(Caroline Tolman, Property Investor & Mentor)

- **Tap Into Your Power**

"Find the power in your situation. If you are a first-time buyer, you have access to preferential products and rates. If you're renting or living with your parents, you can move faster because you're not in a chain, and you have the flexibility to use strategies that somebody who's tied to a house can't do, like flipping your primary residence, or buying with the plan to rent out the other rooms and have other people pay for you to live in your home. You also might already know people who can help you – people in your network who are tradesmen for example"
(Barbara Escolme, Property Investor & Coach)

- **Celebrate Your Progress**

"Every time you complete a task that moves you closer towards your goal of buying a place, write it down. Read the list back every so often to remind yourself how far you've come and how productive you can be"
(Caroline Tolman, Property Investor & Mentor)

MINDHACKER QUESTIONS

- How many of my close friends have already got their own place?

- To what extent am I motivated by feeling left behind?

- What have I already done to move myself closer to my property goal?

TURNING 30 GOALS - REGROUP

Take a look back at your original list of Turning 30 Goals – did you write a home ownership goal on there? How high up your list is it sitting? Which words did you use to express it?

Now you've learned more about the external influences that might have shaped your real estate expectations, does it still feel like a realistic priority or goal for you right now? Does it feel any more or less important? Would you now articulate it any differently?

Can you add any behavioural commitments or process goals to help you on your way to homeownership? For example, if your original goal was 'Buy a flat by the time I turn 30,' or 'save £50,000 for a deposit,' your new goal might be 'Apply for five jobs that would give me a £10k pay increase in the next year' or 'Start saving £200 a month.' And if it makes you feel any better, I'll leave you with this. I never regretted a home I didn't buy.

So You Don't Have Immortality

"The older you get, the better you get, unless you are a banana"
(Betty White)

Ageing Anxiety Is Real

"There are two kinds of women" starts Hearst Journalist Alyssa Montagna as we sit down to chat. *"The ones who are terrified about ageing and will do anything to stop it – like getting preventative Botox in their 20s – and the women who embrace ageing positively..."*

Which category, I pondered, do I fit into? Well, both as it turns out.

And the wild part is that the older I get (I'm 39 at the time of writing), the more I seem to gravitate towards Team Positive.

In my 20s, I'd assumed the opposite would be true – my ageing fears growing exponentially with every fine line written on my face.

Gerascophobia, aka fear of ageing, seems to be an affliction suffered by the shockingly young. When I started the 30-Phobia project, I had expected my core audience to be the almost 30s (after all, 29 was the year in which I experienced my own Quarter-Life Crisis). In reality, what I found were 30-phobic women (and men) as young as 18 and 19 sliding into my DMS sharing their panics about losing their looks, falling behind their friends, and running out of time to do all the things they wanted to do. It made me sad, and it made me want to learn more about what, exactly, these young people were so afraid of, and moreover, what was making them feel this way.

When it comes to phobias, fear of ageing is perhaps the oldest one in the book. Especially in its original form – fear of dying, which most humans would agree is a pretty legit reason to feel anxious. And yet, as global life expectancy has dramatically increased (babies born in 1900 could expect to live to age 32, compared to 70+ in 2021 fear of ageing does not appear to have halved to follow suit. If anything, we are all more youth-obsessed than ever.

Fear Of Aging: Am I Normal?

If you're freaking out at the prospect of ageing up, it may help to know you're not alone.

The Myth: EVERYONE ELSE IS HANDLING AGING BETTER THAN ME, probably because they've all got their sh*t together and I haven't

The Reality: IT'S PERFECTLY NORMAL TO BE ANXIOUS ABOUT AGING AND TO STILL BE FIGURING IT ALL OUT BY 30. 95% of women in their 20s report age-related fears, and only 1% feel they have nothing left to achieve at 29.

Ageing Anxiety: It's NOT You

The factors influencing the way we perceive ageing (both our own and other people's) are many and powerful. And here are just some of the external factors affecting Quarter-Lifers in particular:

1. Arrested Development

2. External Valuation

3. The 30 Deadline

4. Competitive Comparison

Arrested Development

When it comes to the parental lottery, I've always felt like one of life's winners. For starters, my mum and dad are both still alive, and relatively healthy in their seventies. They're also two of my most favourite people, with whom I would choose to spend time, regardless of any familial obligation. But whilst we remain close, I'm also aware that at age 39 I'm no longer reliant on them – for financial, practical or emotional support. I could not have said the same in my 20s, or most of my 30s for that matter.

Aside from the university years (when, admittedly I still popped home regularly for clean washing, a home-cooked meal and a night off the Smirnoff Ice), I lived at home until I was 22, when I made the move to the big city for work. Even then, whilst I was physically separated from my parents, they were still regularly bailing me out when my starting salary couldn't cover my London rent, and on the end of the blower when I found myself sobbing in the office toilets again. As the decade developed, my salary crept up, but The Bank of Mum and Dad was still very much open for business, as was 'Dad Cabs' every time I decided to move to a new flat, or a new country, which happened surprisingly often.

Given my own experience, it isn't a surprise to me that today's 20-somethings are equally dependent on parental support to survive. According to PEW research, 70% of 18-29 year-olds are still financially dependent on their parents, and only 39% of 21-year-olds are working full time, compared with 64% in 1980. My survey shows that 51% of 20-year-olds are still living at home with their parents, declining to 19% by age 29.

Census data shows that today's 20-somethings are reaching several traditional life milestones, such as gaining full-time employment, getting married and having children significantly later than their predecessors – which effectively extends their period of 'dependence' into adulthood.

My hunch, having spoken with countless frustrated Quarter-Lifers, is that much of this delayed independence is purely practical (read financial – see Chapter 5). I've yet to meet a young woman who aspires to remain romance-free, house-sharing with her parents and living on pocket money for the rest of her life, so articles that put Quarter-Life 'arrested development' down to a lack of ambition or desire to 'grow up' really grind my gears.

Parental support goes beyond the practical though. 50% of 20-somethings are in daily contact with parents, and 68% say they're the number one source of support in life. This is true for both the single and partnered.

Whilst family ties are invaluable, if not essential, for young adults' survival these days, this situation clearly breeds anxiety too. Nearly half of the Quarter-Lifers I spoke to say their parents getting older or dying is their biggest fear about getting older – and significantly scarier than facing their own mortality.

"I feel sad about turning 30 - less for me but more because my parents are ageing too, and I worry about them getting ill or dying"
   (UK, 29yrs)

"Getting older just makes me nervous. More problems can come with getting older. I have older parents and the older I get the more I realize how old they're getting and I start thinking the worst when it comes to them dying soon"
   (USA, 26yrs)

"I'm 27 and it terrifies me that I'm approaching 30! I think it's the realisation that I'm actually getting older, which means people around me are too, like my parents"
   (UK, 27yrs, via TikTok)

Herein lies the tension for 20-somethings – on the one hand, they know they are still heavily reliant on family for their basic needs – but on the other hand, they're increasingly aware of their parents' mortality, and fear the consequences of the emotional and practical ties being cut. Thus, as they age-up themselves, the pressure to become independent from their parents intensifies, adding another layer of fear to the inevitable tragedy of losing Mum and Dad.

Having often assumed my parents would keep going forever, life has a way of reminding me that nature is finite. Over Winter I spent a few months in Miami with my partner and child – such is the luxury of working for oneself, and largely online. When my husband had to travel for work, my dad offered to come out and help with the childcare. But two days before he was due to take off, he broke his hip and had to have an emergency replacement. He'd kill me if I didn't mention that 'the fall' that instigated this was off his bicycle, and not off a kitchen chair – which would almost definitely make him sound like 'an old bloke.' Fortunately, the operation was a great success, and he was back on his bike a few weeks later, but it reminded me that I can no longer take my parents help, or their presence, for granted.

When it comes to arrested development, one thing does appear to cut the proverbial cord quicker, and it involves attaching another one. Mothers tend to feel less dependent on their own parents, and significantly more reliant on themselves, and their romantic partners than child-free women. This makes a beautiful kind of sense to my primary school teacher Mum, who has long asserted that the best way to make a wayward kid more responsible is to give them more responsibility.

External Valuation

Growing up, I always considered myself average-looking, erring on the 'scrubs up alright on the night.' And nowadays I view my 'accessible' looks as somewhat of a super-power. Faced with a busy train platform or crowded street, it's often my face that the bewildered tourist makes a beeline for. I never fell foul to 'pretty privilege,' which can drive a wedge between women or call workplace motives into question. I didn't have to trade on my looks, so I was free to develop a well-rounded character instead. I can safely say that my current strong self-esteem, success in life, and valued relationships, are built on internal qualities – like being naturally ambitious, empathetic, hard-working and inquisitive. And the older I've got, the more I've felt able to celebrate such inner qualities over my outward appearance.

Not so in my 20s, when I was my own biggest critic – body-shaming and beating myself up for not being beautiful enough from the age of approximately 14. The other day I came across a photo of me at 22. What I saw was a young, energetic, healthily shaped and enviably smooth-skinned young woman. It was like looking into the real-life TikTok 'teen filter,' and it made me sad just the same way. Back then I never appreciated what I had, focusing only on what I had not. If you'd asked me to describe myself at 22, I'd have said I was a little bit fat (I wasn't). I'd tell you I had severe acne, when my pimples could be put down to period spots and a poor skincare regime. I'd tell you I couldn't possibly be as pretty as my friends because they all had boyfriends, and I didn't. Honestly, what I wouldn't give to go back and give 20-something me a big hug and a solid slice of cake!

It seems the external experience is much the same for today's 20-somethings. In my survey, Quarter-Lifers admitted that they're more afraid of how ageing will change their outer appearance, than their inner health. 38% fear weight gain, 32% looking older, 22% wrinkles, 15% greying hair and 15% reduced sex appeal. And this fear of looking older starts shockingly young. I've had comments on my TikTok videos from girls as young as 19 saying they're already afraid they're 'passing their prime."

Which is a prime example of the insidious influence of social media – in which almost every face we see has been subjected to endless preening, editing and filtering, to the extent that we probably wouldn't recognise certain influencers should we walk past them in the street. When falsified images are habitually passed off as 'real', our expectations of beauty, and ageing, undoubtedly become skewed. And when we habitually compare our own unfiltered reality with the edited externals of others, we can't fail to feel deeply dissatisfied, and inadequate. The thing about social media is that it is an innately visual platform. The more we like what we see, the more likes the content gets. According to analysts, Instagram has an 'algorithmic bias' towards attractive women, which only encourages and perpetuates the superficiality of content. Recent trends like 'guess my age' actively encourage users to judge others' appearances under the guise of 'fun.' As a creator myself, I struggle to understand what good could possibly come of this.

Even so-called 'positive ageing inspo' can perpetuate the pressure to stay young forever. My normal 40-ish physique pales in comparison to Jane Fonda's well-preserved 86-year-old frame, or J Los' impossibly toned 54-year-old abs. And those 'before and afters' in which a 42-year-old celebrity appears identical to her 22-year-old self? I find them quite the opposite of inspirational. Back in the day women were urged to 'stop the clock' on ageing, and that was bad enough. Now we are apparently supposed to age in reverse?!! Filters and Photoshop notwithstanding, few of us mere mortals have access to the elite teams of doctors, trainers, nutritionists and make-up artists afforded to the rich and famous. Female youth and beauty standards, in my humble opinion, have gone from the unattainable to the impossible.

Science has also fuelled the expectation of eternal youth. Back in 2014, the best my 29-year-old self could hope for was a jar of Olay. And the cosmetics industry has a lot to answer for when it comes to pedalling the anti-ageing narrative. But it's the growing adoption of more invasive age-preventative treatments that worries me more, as 'tweakments' like Botox and Fillers have hit the mainstream – capturing the hearts of ever-younger consumers.

According to the American Society of Plastic Surgeons, the use of injectables increased by 75% amongst UNDER 19s between 2019 and 2022, and by 71% in those aged 20 to 29. The debate rages as to whether Gen Z are actually ageing faster than Millennials as a result of over-zealous interventions. But my take on all of this is more pragmatic – if it aint broke, why fix it?!

Of course, it can be argued that a woman's appearance is hers to do with as she wishes. And I'm not claiming to be a low-maintenance girly myself – I wear make-up daily, get my nails done regularly, spend far too much on fancy SPFs, and I am partial to eyelash extensions. I've also worked for many of the world's biggest beauty brands as a consultant, and founded a beauty company myself, so I'm very much pro self-care and pampering. However, what I take issue with is society's insistence on judging women and how we age ONLY according to our external qualities and not our internal characters. I discussed the consequences of this external valuation with Entrepreneur Lindsay Kane:

"For a long time, people would tell me you got good genes, you're pretty and you've got nice hair, so you'll be alright, you'll get a successful husband. All the compliments I got were about external stuff. And as women that is put on us a lot. The problem is, that when people repeatedly emphasise your external qualities, it actually dismisses your true value. Not to mention putting huge pressure on you to stay looking young. If your confidence and self-esteem are tied to your looks, if you get into a relationship where your appearance is your biggest asset, then it's inevitable that you'll fear ageing. There's a danger in

placing your self-worth in the external because the external is always going to change"

(Lindsay Kane, Founder of Jolt)

Despite the valiant efforts of positive ageing advocates, the truth is, that we still live in a society that fetishises female youth and vilifies female ageing (like it's not an inevitable part of life!) Even now, the women who dare to show their true selves are trolled mercilessly. At 63, actress Andy McDowell was shamed for sporting her salt-and-pepper hair at Cannes. In 2018, 50-something Julia Roberts faced vitriol about her ageing appearance after snapping a candid pic with niece Emma Roberts. Whilst I'm sure the majority of us appreciate big-name stars keeping it real, I worry that the small minority of trolls will make them think twice next time. The beauty bullies are ruining age positivity for everyone.

In Chapter 9, we will talk more about The Happiness Myth – the societal misconception that our 20s are 'the best days of our life,' and the false assumption that we get more miserable with age. In reality, the data shows that women not only feel happier overall with age, but they feel happier with their appearance too. In fact, according to a 2021 study published in the Journal of Body Image, women aged 19-24 are least happy with their bodies, and women over 60 enjoy the greatest body satisfaction.

"In my 20s I panicked about getting older, I would look at older ladies and think how they must hate being like that, it made me feel anxious. And it is completely normal to feel like that. Because you're afraid of what you don't know. But when you get there, you just get on with it. And all the real benefits of age come to the fore"

(Sally Bee, Broadcaster & Author)

If you're in your 20s right now, and feeling anxious about ageing, I implore you to pause for a second. Don't waste as much time and energy obsessing over your outsides as I did. Step away from content that causes you to compare and despair. And most importantly, start celebrating your beautiful and enduring inner qualities. It's on the inside that your true value as a woman lies. And what's more, you have so much to look forward to - knowledge, experience, competence, wisdom, accomplishment, contentment. Put it this way and the prospect of ageing up doesn't seem quite so shabby.

The 30 Deadline

For many Quarter-Lifers, 30-Phobia is less a fear of wrinkles, and more a fear of not getting their ducks in a row by 30.

57% agree that the closer they get to 30, the more they feel like they're running out of time to achieve their life goals. A 2022 survey by UK relationship charity Relate supports this assertion, reporting that "milestone anxiety" is an increasingly important topic in therapy sessions. Interestingly, women of 20 are just as likely to feel this way as women of 29, indicating an entire decade dominated by turning 30 panic. As evidenced by a quick scroll of my TikTok comments:

"I'm 23 and terrified of turning 30 – I'm worried I won't achieve things by the time I'm 30"

"I've been terrified since about 23. I'm 29 in November and I'm absolutely feeling sick about turning 30 next year. I'm just not where I thought I'd be at this age"

"I'm 29 and in a horrible birthday phobic spiral, I am in constant anxiety mode at the moment. I never worried at 21 or 22, but when I hit 27 I started to get real anxiety about it as though I hadn't achieved much by this age"

After many conversations with struggling 20-somethings, and the experts who support them, I have concluded that almost all turning 30 anxiety comes down to one thing – expectations. More specifically, The Expectation Gap – when our experienced reality fails to match up to our long-held expectations of what life at this age would look like, we feel like we are falling behind, or even failing at life.

I blame the training. From a wildly early age, women appear to be programmed with a set of identikit life goals which go something like this: get a degree from a good university; find my dream job; meet 'the one;' save money; get married; buy a house and have a couple of cute kids. We usually expect to complete this list by a socially approved age, like 30, or 35 if we're feeling free-spirited. Failure to tick even one of these boxes by the assumed deadline can result in undue stress, anxiety, and overwhelm.

My issue with all of this is that so many women, myself included, will pursue the expected path to the point of panic, without ever pausing to question whether it is the kind of life we actually want or need. We don't think to challenge whether achieving these goals, or pursuing them at this time in life, will make us happy. The ultimate irony is that often when we do finally achieve our dreams, they can fail to live up to expectations too! Psychologists call this The Arrival Fallacy – the deeply held belief that when we achieve certain goals, we will be eternally happy. Which is about as realistic an expectation as eternal youth!

The question I'm often asked in interviews is Why? Who made up the 30 deadline? Why do we place so many expectations on this particular milestone age? And why does it mess with our mental health for more than a decade? The most obvious explanation, says Michelle Hawkins-Collins, is historical life expectancy:

"Fear of turning 30 is a legacy from when we didn't live as long. When you tip towards 30, your productive years decline. And when your productive years decline you become aware of your own mortality. It brings forth all these questions you haven't dealt with earlier in your life when you've been in growth. Suddenly you hit your 30s and bits of your body biologically stop growing and start to shift into a diminishing state. So, I think that's potentially why people get anxious. Plus, you have just the societal and cultural trends around these arbitrary chronological milestones, when there's so much variety within a single age group. It's bonkers really"
    (Michelle Hawkins-Collins, Gerontologist & Founder of The Wisdom Space)

Psychologists Tonya Kelly and Erica Martin bring a Developmental lens to the societal pressure so many of us feel in the countdown to our milestone birthday:

"Throughout your 20s, there is leeway to be a 'kid' and to still be figuring it out – by 30, however, adulthood expects that you have it fig-

ured out or you are well on your way. It's no different than the pressure to meet developmental milestones in infancy to walk and talk by a certain age. By 30, the 'developmental markers' are – do you have a career? Are you in a relationship? Do you own a house? Not only are there unspoken societal expectations, but there is overt pressure when these questions are embedded in small talk conversations to get to know someone"

(Tonya Kelly, MSW, RSW and Dr. Erica Martin, Ph.D. C. Psych. Founders of Core Therapy Centre)

The Quarter-Lifers I've met seem to fall into two camps – The Panickers ("*I should have it all already!*") and The Phobics ("*Marriage and babies? I'm still a baby myself!*") 'Baby Adults' indeed seems to be the truest term to describe today's 20-somethings - barely out of school, living on parental life-support, brains not fully developed, identities a work-in-progress. It's not hard to see why Milestone Anxiety runs rampant during this decade.

In my view, Quarter-Lifers should cut themselves some major slack over the 30 deadline. It's outdated, arbitrary and ultimately unhelpful. After all, psychological research shows us that Milestone Goals (like '*I need to meet someone by 30*') are significantly less achievable than Process Goals (for example '*I will attend one social event a week to meet new people*'). Put simply, panicking is pointless, because it won't change a thing.

Competitive Comparison

How old are your closest friends? I'd hazard a guess that most of them are around the same age as you. It's inevitable, given that many friendships are formed during times when we are deliberately stratified by age, like school, university or graduate programmes. Work friends can be more age-diverse, and yet we still tend to gravitate towards co-workers at a similar stage of their careers which often means age proximity. According to the Snapchat Friendship Report 2019, the average age at which we meet our best friends is 21, meaning our 20s are a peak friendship-forming decade.

And there's good reason why 'birds of a feather flock together.' When your friends are going through the same experiences and challenges as you at the same time, it's eminently validating and comforting. We are more likely to share common interests, attitudes, goals and even language with our same-age peers. Such friendships make us feel less alone, and this is never more important than in our turbulent 20s.

But there are downsides to mixing exclusively with same-age peers. Notably, it promotes direct comparison and competition. 20-something friendships can feel like a race to reach all the milestones – in which some contenders are forced to watch others cross the finish line while you're still stuck on the starting blocks. My survey showed that 64% of young women feel that life comes easier to other people. And 24-year-old me can relate. I acutely recall the feeling of rising panic, the sense of falling behind as my peer group all pursued pay rises, partners and property ownership at the same time. Positioning myself in 'last place', I felt embarrassed, unworthy and envious of their successes.

"It's so unfair", the childish voice would whine inside my head, "why does she get to have a boyfriend and not me?"

"Because you're not as good as her" replied my inner critic helpfully.

And so went the internal spiral of doom. In hindsight I can see I was neglecting a few key truths here:

- Comparing positions is irrelevant, because we are all starting from a different place

- There is no such thing as ahead or behind, because we are all running our own race

- You can't covet the outcome without seeing the process, and you can never truly know what another person has gone through to get where they are

If you're stuck in a negative cycle of peer comparison, the simplest solution is to get older friends. Seriously. You'll be less tempted to 'compete' with women from different generations. And there is a growing body of evidence supporting the added value of 'age-gap' friendships. According to an American study, only 37% of adults have a close friend 15 plus years their senior. Yet the benefits appear to be significant. Inter-generational friendships, the experts say, can bring new energy, ideas, experiences and opportunities into the lives of both parties. They can bring greater understanding, empathy and respect for other generations. And for Quarter-Lifers in particular, older friends can provide valuable perspective, life experience and hard-won wisdom.

I spoke to former Gerontologist Michelle Hawkins-Collins, who proactively built an inter-generational community in the UK, about the positive benefits of age-gap friendships, especially when it comes to fostering positive attitudes about ageing:

"Our members range from 20s through to mid-90s. The older ones get a lot of energy and new perspectives from the younger people – they get an opportunity to discuss topics that society often deems irrelevant to old people, like sex and relationships. All the generations bring a different time perspective. Those in their 20s and 30s particularly love having older people who really have the time to listen, because they don't get that from their friends who are all too busy with their own lives... The older members can address bigger topics like ageing and death and because they have a lot of life experience, and tend to experience negative emotions less strongly, they help remove the fear for the younger members"
  (Michelle Hawkins-Collins, Gerontologist & Founder of The Wisdom Space)

This is something I've discovered for myself. I recently attended a boot camp in which all of the other attendees were more than 10 years my senior – and what struck me was just how bloody refreshing the conversation was. Having broken free from life's 'rush hour' there was far less talk of work stress, money troubles and bringing up babies, and much more chat about interests, entrepreneurial endeavours and travel. I can certainly see how such company would be a welcome break for any woman taking a less traditional path or feeling the pressure to keep up with her same-age friends.

I'm afraid there's a much sadder side to comparing lives with same-age friends. And that's when it comes to the end of life. Now at 40, I honestly feel in the prime of my life. And my friends appear to be healthy, happy and thriving too. I thought I'd have decades before I had to face my own mortality. I was wrong.

Shortly after I started writing this book, a good friend broke the news that she'd been diagnosed with breast cancer, and that the prognosis wasn't good. It turns out there are as many strains of breast cancer as there are boobs that battle it, and her version was amongst the most aggressive. I was floored. Here was a woman who was otherwise fit, healthy and full of life. She's the same age as me, and in the same life-stage - building a career and raising a young family. I was terrified for my friend, and so sorry for the struggle she was facing. But the similarities between us meant I also couldn't help but imagine myself in her shoes. The thought of leaving my husband and young daughter at this moment was utterly unthinkable. But unthinkable tragedies happen every day, and by the time this book reached the editing stage, my beautiful friend had passed. Her loss has devastated our friendship group and left a gaping hole in a young family. The heartbreak and the unfairness of it all is palpable, and I'm still struggling to believe she's really gone. But if her untimely death has taught me anything it's this – life is more fragile than it looks. And even doing all the 'right' things is no guarantee of survival. So, let's stop letting our fears hold us back. Let's stop putting happiness on hold. Let's start living life our way. Starting today.

Positive Ageing - Sally Bee, Aged 54

"At 36 I had three heart attacks, and I nearly died with a husband and 3 young kids. So from that moment forward, I looked at ageing, and life, differently. My motto became 'Every day above ground is a great day'. For me, it's a privilege to get to get older, because I wasn't maybe meant to. I do absolutely everything I can to keep feeling and looking young, and my main priority is to live in the present moment, to be present with people. At the end of my life, that is what I will miss, I won't miss the worry and the anxiety, I will miss precious moments with the people I love"

(Sally Bee, Broadcaster & Author)

Anxious About Ageing? Get Unstuck In 4 Steps
How To STOP Looking Out

- **Drop The 30 Deadline**

"Milestone Birthdays are fake deadlines. Nothing will change if you reach your life goals at 30, 40 or later because you have your whole life to get there, and to change your mind. Remember that 30 is the start-line, not the finish line"
  (Kate Berski, Author)

- **Don't Believe The Lies**

"Don't believe the lies society tells you about ageing – you will become happier, more interesting and more comfortable in your own skin with every passing year. Your best days are yet to come"
  (Kate Berski, Author)

- **Be Unfiltered**

"Know that what you see on social media is filtered. Don't compare your real face to a fake face. And stop using filters on yourself – using them and knowing that's not how you really look actually damages the way you feel about yourself"
  (Lindsay Kane, Founder of Jolt)

- **Stop People Pleasing**

"When you're younger, looking good is influenced by how you think others perceive you. But later you realise the only thing that matters is your opinion of yourself. So do that now. Dress for yourself, have that haircut that you love, and don't worry about what anyone else thinks"
  (Sally Bee, Broadcaster & Author)

- **Rebel Against 'Shoulds'**

"Stop telling yourself what you should be doing or how you should be behaving by this time. Be a rebel, challenge the expectations, do things because you want to do them, do more of what you like and

never stop learning who you are..."
(Lindsay Kane, Founder of Jolt)

- **Give Less F*cks**

"Stop caring so much what other people think. There are billions of people in the world, and there's not one person that is liked by everyone, so don't try to be liked. As long as you're a good person, you're empathetic and compassionate, you've got integrity, that's enough"
(Lindsay Kane, Founder of Jolt)

- **Don't Fall For 'Anti-Ageing' Marketing**

"SPF is the ONLY proven anti-ageing skincare ingredient. Sunscreen is the one skincare product that is backed by overwhelming evidence that it actually works. So use SPF every day"
(Dr Federica Amati, Medical Scientist & Head Nutritionist at Zoe)

How To START Looking In

- **Focus On Feelings Not Looks**

"Instead of basing your self-worth on external things like how you look, focus on how you feel instead. Invest more energy into your internal life – mental health, growth, a healthy lifestyle, and a positive mindset. Negativity and moaning are ageing. Feeling good is really the secret to staying young"
(Lindsay Kane, Founder of Jolt)

- **Make An Impact**

"First impressions count, but not in the way you think. You will be remembered for how good you make people feel, not for how good you look"
(Kate Berski, Author)

- **Eat Yourself Young**

"Healthy ageing starts with your diet. So, avoid ultra-processed foods

and increase your intake of polyphenol-rich foods like berries, nuts and beans. These reduce inflammation in the skin, improve hydration and minimise the visible signs of ageing. Eat more fermented foods like sourdough bread, kimchi and sauerkraut – they're rich in probiotics which promote a healthy gut microbiome and protect the skin"
(Dr Federica Amati, Medical Scientist & Head Nutritionist at Zoe)

How To REFRAME Turning 30

- **Level Up**

"Instead of telling yourself you're one year older, tell yourself, and everyone else, you're levelling up. Don't dread your birthday. It's a badge of honour to be able to live another year and expand your experience, whatever that looks like"
(Carrie Eaton, Friendship Coach)

- **Find An Older Friend**

"Invest in age-gap friendships – benefits include learning from one another's experiences, developing empathy for people of different ages and potentially having a different perspective on life, and ageing..."
(Dr. Angharad Rudkin, Chartered Psychologist)

- **Step Into Your Power**

"Instead of dreading your birthday, look forward to the next decade. Your 30s are one of the best decades of your life, because you will be at your most competent, with the most energy with the most opportunities ahead of you. Get ready to step into your power"
(Michelle Hawkins-Collins, Gerontologist & Founder of The Wisdom Space)

How To CELEBRATE The Small Wins

- **Check Your Privilege**

"Remind yourself that ageing is a privilege – and only the lucky ones

get to die old. Try to appreciate your body for the youth, health and strength it has today, instead of beating up on it all the time"
(Kate Berski, Author)

- **Choose Happy**

"Life is too long to wait for joy, and too short to de-prioritise pleasure. Stop putting happiness on hold, grab every moment of joy, indulge in all the small pleasures, celebrate the glimmers in everyday"
(Kate Berski, Author)

- **Take A Today Selfie**

"You will never be younger than you are right now, and sometime in the not-too-distant future you will look back and wish you looked exactly as you do today. So snap a selfie, just for you, and never forget how beautiful you really are"
(Kate Berski, Author)

- **Embrace Nature**

"Get outside and move. Instead of going to a HIIT class and sitting down for the rest of the day, embrace natural movement like walking. Spend time in nature – it's been proven to reduce anxiety and improve your mood"
(Dr Federica Amati, Medical Scientist & Head Nutritionist at Zoe)

- **Celebrate Your Virtues**

"Write a list of 5-10 of your best qualities. Don't include anything about your looks or material successes. Focus on your inner characteristics. This might not come naturally at first, so ask a friend for inspiration if you struggle"
(Kate Berski, author)

- **Celebrate Your Mistakes**

"Your mistakes made you who you are today. Celebrate the fact you survived, and you are where you are now. So many people are so keen to only celebrate and shout about their achievements. But shouting

about the things you've gone through, the things that have been difficult, creates connection, and respect"
(Sally Bee, Broadcaster & Author)

- **Keep A Hype File**

"Every time someone compliments you or you get some positive feedback, don't dismiss it! Screenshot it, type it in your notes, and save it on your phone. Look at your hype file whenever you have a wobble"
(Gaby Mendes, Founder of TalkTwenties)

MINDHACKER QUESTIONS

- Imagine you are gone and someone close to you is sharing your eulogy.

- What do I want them to be saying about me? How do I want to be remembered? For which moments? For which qualities or values? How does this change the things I'm doing or worrying about right now?

- How can I cultivate a sense of gratitude for where I am in your life right now?

TURNING 30 GOALS · REGROUP

Take a look back at your original list of Turning 30 Goals – did you include any goals about maintaining or changing your appearance? Or achieving certain milestones by your milestone birthday? How high up your original list are they sitting? What words did you use to express your wishes?

Now you've learned more about the external influences that might have shaped your expectations around ageing, does this change anything? Would you now de-prioritise, or re-articulate any of your stated goals? Would you shift, or remove any age-related deadlines?

Do you have any new goals about ageing well or feeling better about ageing? Add them to your 'BABY GOALS' column. Think about some regular practices or daily habits you can commit to that could help you feel good, and maintain a youthful mindset, both now and in the future. Make sure they're enjoyable and achievable. Going for a daily walk for example, rather than pressuring yourself to hit the gym at 5am every morning! Remember – for the lucky ones, life is too long not to enjoy yourself!

So You Don't Have Kids

"Biological Clock? I don't even own a watch"
(Sarah Mlynowski)

Fertility Pressure Is Real

When it comes to life goals, and milestone anxieties, it doesn't get more real than female fertility. It also rarely gets more emotive. Of all the TikToks I posted during my writing journey, the comments sections never got more heated than when talking about babies. The reality of having them, or not having them. The choice to become a parent, the choice not to, having that choice taken away due to circumstances beyond your control. It still shocks me just how invested, passionate, judgemental or wilfully ignorant human beings can be when it comes to the life choices of complete strangers.

What makes female fertility such a hot 20-something topic is that, unlike almost any other life goal, there is an expiration date on having babies. And to make things even more spicy, we don't get to know our own personal shelf life until the whole factory is forcibly closed for business.

Unlike many of the other milestone anxieties in this book, the pressure to procreate isn't simply a social construct, but a biological reality too. This is why there are plenty of highly credible books, studies, articles and more, created by medical professionals to educate us on the biological realities of female fertility, and infertility. This is not one of those books.

With that said, I am choosing to tread very lightly when it comes to the scientific data around female fertility. I will also say up-front that I fully acknowledge and respect all perspectives on if, how, when, why and why not to have babies. Being childfree, whether by choice or circumstance, is just as valid a life path as parenthood, and in my opinion does not deserve the trolling it so often attracts, both online and IRL.

The thing about procreation, whichever side of the fence you sit on, is that it is one of the only genuinely finite decisions we ever make in life. Having a baby can never be undone, redone or necessarily done later. You can get out of almost any other questionable life choice, with the right lawyer. But once you become a parent, regardless of the outcome of that child, and I would include those who sadly experience baby loss here, you will always be a parent.

Given the finite and highly emotive nature of reproductive decisions, I was initially surprised to find family planning so low on the agenda of today's 20-somethings. 42% of childfree women in my Turning 30 survey state having children as an immediate life goal (a priority within this decade). Given that 82% of women in the UK and 85% in the USA do ultimately have children by age 50, we might assume that given a longer timeline, a few more women would make that choice too.

Digging into the comments sections helps explain young women's lack of immediacy. Far from rejecting the idea of motherhood, for many women in their 20s, the prospect of parenthood seems incongruent with their current practical or emotional position. They view having children as contingent on 'sorting out' several other aspects of their lives first. My survey data shows that single women and non-homeowners are more likely to feel behind on their goal of having children, which adds weight to the 'ducks in a row' argument:

"I just feel like I'm nowhere I should be in life, no stable relationship, no savings, no kids etc, I feel behind but also at the same time not ready for any of this stuff"
  (27yrs, UK)

"I'm 27 and I'm always feeling scared that I haven't got married or had kids yet. I'm in a healthy relationship but I'm still figuring out my own life, let alone trying to bring a new one in..."
  (27yrs, via TikTok)

The data reveals a stark gap between where women expected to be at this age compared to their experienced reality. 43% of childless women (who want children) say they expected to have kids by their current age, and 31% worry that they never will. Their explanations reveal not a lack of desire to have children, but a lack of certainty. Many feel overwhelmed by their current life situation, and even events in the world at large, all of which holds them back from even considering starting a family:

"I always thought that I'd have my life together, married, kids with the job of my dreams by 30, but the way things are now, I'm aware this simply might not happen"
(20yrs, UK)

"I always wanted children, but now I'm unsure. I've been with an unsure partner for 10 years now and the state of the world, especially climate change and the cost of living, has made me really scared I'll make the wrong decision either way. I've no idea if I'm even fertile. I'm trying to progress a career, renovate a property, stay on top of the housework and life admin and socialising. It all feels like way too much but my body clock ticking just gets louder..."
(20-something, via TikTok)

Fertility Pressure: It's NOT You

If you're feeling pressured, panicked, confused or indecisive about having kids, you are not alone. I'm about to break down some of the biggest external influences that could be making you feel these types of ways.

From a young age, women are subjected to powerful societal and cultural expectations that influence them to (want to) become mothers, and make them feel less than if, for whatever reason, it doesn't happen. Some of the biggest pressure points I've identified include:

1. #Whenning

2. Fertility Fearmongering

3. The Relationship Gap

4. Financial Infertility

5. Positive Pressure

#Whenning

When are you having a baby?

When are you going to start trying?

When are you going to freeze your eggs?

When are you having another…?

It's only in the writing of this book that I've realised just how much 'whenning' us girls have to put up with. The language we use around female fertility is often inherently assumptive – piling unconscious pressure on women and pushing them down the path of least resistance, motherhood.

So insidious is this societal 'whenning' that even the most pro-choice amongst us can slip up. A while back I shared some fertility stats on social media – and followers quite rightly picked up on my unconscious linguistic bias. At one point I said, 'If you don't have kids YET.'

My first job out of Uni was in Market Research, which might help explain the data geekery that forms the backbone of this book. Back in the early 000s, researchers would use the term 'DINKY' to describe childless couples – Dual Income No Kids Yet. I'm assured that the industry has since dropped the 'Y,' but nonetheless, if even our most objective analysts are 'whenning' all over us, it just goes to show how deeply embedded this societal pressure has become.

Any discussion around female fertility will inevitably throw up the age-old arguments

'Having babies is a woman's only purpose in life' and *'Childless*

women are selfish.'

Funnily enough, these opinions invariably come from men, for whom the physical, emotional, practical and even financial consequences of having kids still pale into insignificance compared to what we women are facing.

It's a fact that individuals born as biological females are currently the only type of people who can birth a human child. But it's the suggestion that motherhood is our only viable life choice, and our sole source of value to the world that really gets my goat. And don't even get me started on the mental load. Just recently, I was recording a podcast with a male host, who stated that it was only natural that women should do the lion's share of the childcare because they're just inherently more nurturing. In my opinion, aside from the biological birthing of offspring, any person of any gender can be equally equipped to care for a baby.

But I digress.

My main beef is that by presenting childbearing as the only acceptable path, what message do we send to women who are not able to have a child, often through no fault of their own? What are we saying to childfree women, whether through choice or circumstance? Even as a mother myself, with myriad accomplishments, interests and goals outside of parenting, I find this mindset reductionist and offensive, so I can only imagine how unedifying these arguments must be for my childfree contemporaries. Dating Coach Dani called this out during our conversation:

"Why is it that society doesn't like women getting older? It's to do with reproduction, like you are only valuable or attractive when you're reproducing, of reproductive age. There's this pressure that you've gotta be married and be having kids by 30. But it's just socially constructed. It's incredible that it's so pervasive"
(Dani Weiss, Dating Coach)

However we feel right now, many of us women grow up with the unquestioned assumption that we will have kids someday, and so far, the statistics show that the majority of women go on to do just that.

To state the obvious, both men and women are intrinsically motivated to procreate, to ensure the survival of the species. But what interests me is how much of the decision to start a family is truly a personal choice, how much is down to societal conditioning, and how we are supposed to know the difference!

"Many of us are living our life by the 'should' rulebook... We go through life blindly, you go to school, you go to college, you get the job, you find a partner, you buy the house, you have kids. But few of us have the opportunity to step back and think, 'What do I actually need and want? How do I do it? How do I block out all that external noise and pressure so I can get clarity?' The problem with not having clarity on what we want, and need is that whenever we're not living our life in line with societal expectations (like not having a partner or a baby), we feel like we're doing something wrong"
(Laura Guckian, Founder Mind Mommy Coaching)

Laura raises an important point about just how difficult society makes it to take an 'alternative' life path, and how hard it seems to be for others to understand when our lives don't quite look like theirs. As this Quarter-Lifer in my survey explains:

"I feel like everything's telling me I'm running out of time, that all my best years where I could achieve something are behind me. I feel like people look at me in pity if they find out I'm not married, I'm not planning to have kids"
(27yrs, UK)

Fertility Fearmongering

"Time is running out!"

"Use 'em or lose 'em!"

"Don't fall off the fertility cliff"

"Vaccine X or Product Y causes infertility"!...

However unhelpful these scaremongering headlines may be, they are rooted in one inescapable medical truth – female fertility is finite. This is probably why society feels justified in subjecting women to fertility pressure practically from birth – dangling the good ol' 'biological clock' above us like the sword of Damocles as we go about our business.

"Fertility has medical limits of course, but I do think there's a societal component to it. There are plenty of women who do have babies in their 30s and 40s, yet we put all this pressure on specific ages like 30, when you may have an extra 10 years. It's that extra societal pressure on top of the biological clock that gets to women"
　(Dani Weiss, Dating Coach)

The irony of this looming threat is that the term 'biological clock' has itself been wildly misappropriated. The scientific term simply refers to the circadian rhythms that govern human sleep-wake cycles. And if that's not a great factoid to bamboozle anyone directing irritating 'tick tock...' comments at you over Christmas lunch, I don't know what is.

"Is my biological clock ticking Barbara? Why yes, it is getting rather close to nap time!"

Jokes aside, the natural decline in female fertility over time is well documented, as are the data suggesting negative health outcomes with both advanced maternal and paternal age. And in reality, female fertility is widely variable, almost like a lottery system, in which don't get to see your numbers 'til you enter the draw. And what's more, regardless of your age, stage, relationship status, dietary preferences or current bank balance, there are absolutely no guarantees when it comes to creating human life.

Perhaps all these unknowns explain in part why many young women take a 'cross that bridge when I come to it' approach to reproductive health. In my Turning 30 survey, 77% of women said they aren't worried about declining fertility, and only 10% ranked it in their Top 3 concerns about getting older. Interestingly, there is no clear correlation between proximity to 30 and increasing fertility fear – which instead appears to peak around age 26.

But the pressure is still there.

Talking with women reveals a very real pressure to factor babies into the life plan. Many 20-somethings view motherhood as the ultimate end goal – which can trigger a high-pressure 'backward maths' much like the famous 'Rachel's 30th Birthday' scene from the 90s TV show 'Friends'. 28-year-old Magazine Journalist Alyssa explains:

"A friend told me about the fertility cliff at 35, so now I have that rooted in my mind. Then I start thinking OK so I need to get pregnant by 34, so I need to meet someone by 30 so I can get married and spend some time as a couple before we have kids, then I think I'm 28 now so I'm really running out of time... I can really start to spiral"
(Alyssa Montagna, Journalist)

Which brings me very neatly to my next point.

The Relationship Gap

58% of single women in my survey, say they feel behind on their goal of having children. That's compared to 26% of women in relationships. Since most view a stable relationship as the precursor for starting a family, it's arguably not a lack of desire or ability to procreate that's holding women back from prioritising parenthood, but the lack of satisfactory partners. For most women I spoke to, not being in a relationship, or being in the wrong one, was the number one barrier to having children:

"My biggest fear is not finding someone and missing my opportunity to have kids"
(26yrs, via TikTok)

"I haven't found my king yet so no baby, I don't think I'll ever have one"
(30yrs via Tiktok)

"I'm anxious because I don't have a spouse, and my biggest dream is to get married and have kids"
(24yrs, USA)

While 30 was rarely seen as the cut-off point for kids, many women do feel under pressure to lock down a relationship by their milestone birthday:

"I feel like I'm in a sinking relationship and in order to have kids and get married I would have to have a better relationship before I'm 30"
   (25yrs, USA)

"My career is going really well, and I feel like I've ticked that box. But I want to be married and have kids and I'm 28 and still single, so that's not going to happen before I'm 30"
   (Alyssa Montagna, Hearst Magazines)

"I don't have a partner at the moment, and I would love to have kids and be married someday but I am worried that my window is closing which makes me really sad. I don't want to admit I am getting close to 30"
   (28yrs, UK)

"I recently had who I considered to be my soulmate break up with me which has put me back on my family goals, put me back financially and put me back on my house goal too. I've had to take on another job, so I don't get evicted. All my friends are now married with kids and I'm nowhere near"
   (29yrs, UK)

What strikes me in researching this topic is the extent to which society overlooks the contextual or situational side of female infertility. Much sympathy is, rightfully, afforded to infertile couples, yet the same is not true for women whose romantic situation during their fertile years prevents them from having children organically.

I found countless medical studies documenting the prevalence, causes and experiences of biological infertility – yet none that examined the social causes. So, if we're looking to explain the global fertility gap, isn't the relationship drought the most obvious start-point?

From where I'm sitting, we can no longer afford to overlook single women. According to recent data, almost half (45%) of women of childbearing age will be single by 2030, the highest figures ever recorded. And whilst we can do most things in life alone, when it comes to this particular topic, it really does take two to tango baby.

Financial Infertility

If you were reading the previous section screaming 'Just do it on your own!' inside your head, you wouldn't be the first. Advice like 'Just get IVF' or 'Just adopt' is often levelled at single women who yearn to become mothers. And an increasing number of women are choosing solo parenting. However, it's not as simple as it seems.

For starters, In the UK, the NHS make it very difficult, bordering on impossible, for single women – and many partnered women for that matter - to access fertility treatments such as IUI (Intrauterine Insemination) and IVF (In Vitro Fertilisation). Criteria vary wildly by geographical area and personal circumstance. Women may be denied treatment if their partner has a child, if they're unable to prove they've been 'trying' for a couple of years, if they're over 40 or if they suffer from conditions including endometriosis or unexplained infertility. Forgive my ignorance, but surely that rules out quite a lot of candidates?

This young woman explains her situation:

"I'm single and haven't been able to find a relationship, but I want kids. Everyone says just do it on your own but it's not that simple. I don't have a stable income or housing and the financial situation in the UK is unstable, it wouldn't be a responsible thing to do. And single women are not entitled to IVF on the NHS"
   (20-something via TikTok)

Even if a single woman manages to run the gauntlet, few can afford to support a child on a solo income. According to ONS data from 2022, a single parent working full time would have to spend 51% of their take-home pay on childcare alone, and up to 74% for Londoners. Bills and other essential living costs are not included. And that's based on the median annual full-time salary of £33,000, so if your pay packet falls short of that, you're basically screwed.

Financial infertility is not just the preserve of single women either. The financial barriers to parenthood can seem insurmountable even for women who don't face significant challenges in their relationship status or biology. This came up frequently in my, on and offline conversations with 20-somethings:

"Financial stability stops me from having kids, which I would love. The cost of living is so high, I don't want to struggle financially"
   (20-something via TikTok)

"I don't want to be financially dependent on my partner, especially in a cost-of-living crisis"
   (20-something via TikTok)

"Even if I wanted a kid there's absolutely no way to ever do it. I have a really good job as an Editor, but I couldn't support a child in London. I don't think any of my friends, even the ones who are in Finance jobs could afford it"
   (Bethan Jenkins, Features Editor Good Housekeeping Magazine)

Women who choose to delay having children are often accused of being 'selfish,' but my impression is that they're far from it. It seems counter-intuitive to me that choosing not to use up government resources on antenatal services, maternity pay, education and healthcare – and choosing instead to continue working and paying taxes to benefit those who do is the selfish option.

Moreover, many women see delaying or even avoiding having children as the more responsible life choice. I have certainly observed that those who are childfree by choice have often spent considerable time weighing up the holistic impact of bringing a child into their life, and the world as a whole.

Don't get me wrong, I'm not anti-kids. I do believe in representing and respecting all possible life choices. I say that as a mother myself. However, my husband and I did think long and hard about whether that was the right path for us. The day we got married we were both a hard NO. We were more interested in starting a business than a family. And the horrifying descriptions of childbirth and sleep deprivation from our closest friends did nothing to raise our enthusiasm. Until... I hit 35 and something just, changed. Whilst we still didn't see ourselves as 'baby people,' we realised we couldn't imagine not having a child at all. What had not been a priority at all throughout my 20s and early 30s suddenly rose to the top of my To Do list. And while it was certainly not a good time – we were flat broke, living in a tiny flat and busy as hell getting our start-up off the ground – there probably wasn't going to be a better time.

Naturally, we assumed it would take ages once we'd made the decision, given my 'geriatric' age, and all the scary headlines. But I fell pregnant faster than expected. I had my daughter just before I turned 36. I understand I'm fortunate that I had good fertility in my mid-30s, but I always knew that even if parenthood didn't happen, I was enough. We were enough. Our lives were enough. Waiting doesn't work for everyone, but I don't for a second regret putting it off until I was mentally ready for the responsibility.

According to the Office of National Statistics though, I was late to the parenting game. Even though the average age for a woman in the UK to have her first child has been creeping up since the 70s. It's currently at nearly 31 years old. In the USA, women have historically cracked on sooner, but the median age of first-time mothers just hit 30.

So, I might have been a little late to the party, but I'm by no means unusual. In my circle of girlfriends, very few bit the baby bullet until their mid-30s, and several more are as yet undecided in their late 30s.

Financial insecurity most definitely has a part to play in these delaying tactics. Now, I don't want to get into Boomer-bashing, especially as the current generation of Grandparents are basically propping up the UK economy right now by providing £7.3bn of free childcare.

However, I do need to make the point that previous generations enjoyed certain economic perks that the current cohort does not - free university education, education grants, lower property prices relative to salaries and limited debt – all of which gave them a firmer foundation on which to build a family life. 65% of the women in my survey agreed that 'life is more difficult for people my age than previous generations.'

Far from its popularised 'carefree' reputation, our 20s can feel like a pressure cooker for many of us. Held to traditional standards yet lured by modern dreams of financial independence and under pressure to prioritise multiple and often contradictory life goals at the same time.

"So now women can do it all... you need to go to university and get a degree, buy the house, and have the kids but at the same time, you've got to have enough money to do all that, because you can't rely on the guy. So, you've got to do well in your career, but you'll need to take time out of that career to have the kids. So, it's kind of like an impossible dream, really. In reality, there are very few years in which to do it all"
   (Bethan Jenkins, Editor Good Housekeeping)

For myriad reasons, today's women are decidedly less settled and sorted at age 30 than previous generations. Yet they're still expected, or expecting, to live to the same timelines. It's little wonder why many 20-somethings feel like they're constantly failing or falling behind in life. And yet, the myth that 'you can have it all' lives on, often without the crucial caveat – 'just not all at the same time.'

Positive Pressure

To throw in an uncharacteristically positive note, I must add that a great deal of the fertility pressure women experience does come from a good place. The cliches are all true – if you have a child you will experience a love like nothing you have ever felt before, even if it takes a minute. That child will be the best thing that ever happens to you and the centre of your entire world. Becoming a mother will fundamentally change you, the way you see the world and the way you live in it – whether you like it or not. And once you have crossed over that bridge you will never be able to imagine going back. And it's all of this knowledge that sits behind those well-meaning, albeit intrusive enquiries about your lady parts and what you plan on doing with them. As Motherhood Mentor Bindi put it:

"Most people experience such huge love for their children they want their friends and relatives to feel it too"
   (Bindi Gauntlett, The Guilt-Free Mum)

While pressure from co-workers or distant aunties at your cousins wedding might constitute irritating small talk, pressure from your parents, or in-laws carries significantly more weight. Essentially, the grandparents are co-conspirators in the whole operation. If you play your cards right, they'll be the ones, along with you and your partner, who will be hands-on involved in bringing up your child. And often their impatience stems from their desire to support you, combined with an awareness of their own mortality. Put bluntly, the earlier you have kids the more help you can hope to get!

"Grandparents want to enjoy grandchildren while they are young and fit. Whilst in the 1980s most grandparents were in their 50s, more often they are now in their seventies, so they have fewer healthy years left"
   (Bindi Gauntlett, The Guilt-Free Mum)

I can clearly remember conversations in which my mum would subtly try to talk me round. Her most memorable argument, bar the promise of extensive babysitting, was 'Maybe you could just manage one?' Like she was offering me an extra sausage or something! My Polish mother-in-law took a blunter approach. Undeterred by a lack of spoken English, she still managed to learn the word 'Baby?' and would cast the word hopefully at me each year over Christmas lunch. She was usually met with a look of abject horror.

In the end, the odds tipped in the Grandparents favour, and we decided for ourselves to give parenting a go. But we also made them all very happy in the process. My in-laws, famously nonplussed by bombshells including 'We're getting married!' 'We bought a house!', and 'We sold our company!' were beside themselves with joy when we told them we were expecting. And now as proud parents to a pudgy little chipolata, especially having come out the other side of the clueless and sleepless years, we finally get what all the fuss was about.

Childfree At 30: Am I Normal?

If you're stressing about whether or not to have children, it may help to know that whatever your situation, you're entirely normal.

The Myth: BABIES BY 30. Most people make babies, or at least make the decision, by age 30

The Reality: MAYBE BABY AT 30. Just under a third (28%) of the 20-something women we surveyed have children (23% in the UK and 32% in the USA). At age 29, 43% of the women have children, meaning being child-free at 30 still puts you in the majority.

Confused About Parenthood? Get Unstuck In 4 Steps

With so much advice and so many conflicting opinions flying about, it's no surprise to me that many 20-somethings feel confused about the prospect of parenthood. Is it right for me? Do I really want kids, or is it something I feel I should do? Is my time running out? Could I do it alone? Is my partner going to be a good co-parent? Will I regret it if I do? Will I regret it if I don't?

While I can't help you with the getting pregnant part, I can help you get clear on whether or not motherhood is a priority for you right now. You might want to make some notes as you go, or talk this through with a trusted friend, because these decisions can be complicated.

How To Stop Looking Out

- **Drop The 'Shoulds'**

"There are no 'shoulds' in motherhood. But the challenge is we don't know what to do if we don't follow the shoulds. Next time you hear yourself saying (or thinking) "I should do X, Y, Z," tune into it. 99% of the time, 'shoulds' are driven by external societal pressures, or ingrained beliefs about how things are supposed to be done. That is very different to things you internally need or want. Can you rephrase it into "I need..." or "I want..." If not, it's not a priority for you right now"
      (Laura Guckian, Founder Mind Mommy Coaching)

- **Manage Your Expectations**

"Remember that there are no guarantees in life. There may never be a perfect time to start a family, you may never feel like you have all your

ducks in a row. You may never find the perfect partner/house/job that you imagined, but that doesn't have to mean you can't have children. You may never feel the pull of parenthood and that's OK too. If you decide to try for a baby, you won't know if you can conceive naturally, how long it will take and what your fertility journey will look like until you start. So be open-minded, try to let go of expectations and be open to alternative paths"
    (Kate Berski, Author)

- **Know Your Boundaries**

"You don't have to share your fertility journey with everyone. Think about what you need – is it emotional support? Expert advice? Who are the people that can give that to you? Also, think about what you don't need. You can choose only to share with a select few people. You can avoid looking at certain triggering things on social media"
    (Laura Guckian, Founder Mind Mommy Coaching)

- **Ignore Outside Opinions**

"The only opinions that matter when it comes to family planning are yours and your partners. Unless someone is going to be responsible for raising your future child, they don't get a say"
    (Kate Berski, Author)

- **Prep Your Pushback**

You have every right to push back when people ask probing questions about your intimate biology, so rehearse a quick answer that works for you. For example:

- 'That's not a priority for me right now'

- 'It isn't in the 5-year plan... and that's as far as I've got'

- 'It's really not a topic for discussion'

- 'I'm interested to know why you are asking me?'

- 'I would love a baby and will let you know when it's happening...'

- 'Thanks for asking, are you planning on having more?'
- 'When are you having your second?'

- **Forget Yes Or No**

"If you're still in your 20s, time is on your side. Your only job is to decide if parenthood is a priority for you right now. Taking the option off the table for a couple of years doesn't stop you from picking it up again in the future, but it will take the pressure off your current situation. It's not a no, it's a not now"
  (Kate Berski, Author)

How To Start Looking In

- **Find Your Why**

"Ask yourself, what is it about motherhood that I feel attracted to? Is it that you want to bring this person into the world to love and nurture them? Maybe you didn't get the childhood you wanted, and you want to undo the bad by doing it differently? What's really driving you? Try to be really, really honest"
  (Laura Guckian, Founder Mind Mommy Coaching)

- **Check Your Capacity**

"Be honest with yourself. Do you have the spare capacity for an all-encompassing relationship with another (small) person right now? How would you feel putting someone else first all the time?"
  (Bindi Gauntlett, Motherhood Mentor)

- **Rule Out Idealism**

"Are you addicted to the idea of having a baby, or have you really thought through the reality? Is it easy to forget the idea, or change your mind? Really think about it... then sleep on your decision for a few days"
  (Bindi Gauntlett, Motherhood Mentor)

How To Reframe Your Goals

- **Entertain Alternatives**

"If you're panicking about becoming a parent, stop asking 'what if I don't have kids?' instead, say 'even if I don't have kids...' and explore what life could look like for you. It will open up more positive possibilities"
   (Sally Bee, Broadcaster and Author)

- **Do An Impact Assessment**

"Think about how your life will change when you become a Mum. Look at all aspects of it - how will your relationship with your partner change, how will it impact your career, how will it impact your finances, your friendships, and your personal time...? Once you have an idea of the impact it may have it will help you figure out if it's the right time. Maybe your relationship with your partner is not where it needs to be right now to deal with that big change of becoming parents. Maybe you're not in a financial position. Maybe you're really investing in your career. Maybe you don't have the support around you right now that you would need. You have to be really, really honest with yourself now, because the reality is, having a baby will completely change your life"
   (Laura Guckian, Founder Mind Mommy Coaching)

- **Lean On 'Big Sisters'**

"Instead of going to Google, or Instagram, find mentors within your circle who you really trust and respect. Ideally, women of different generations, who are further along on their parenting journey and are the kind of parents you aspire to be. Ask them what they would have said to themselves at your age. Listen to their experiences – they'll be able to give you a balanced insight and help you see the big picture"
   (Bindi Gauntlett, Motherhood Mentor)

- **Plan, Don't Assume**

"Plan ahead as much as possible. If you're employed, understand what you're entitled to, and know the maternity policy and shared parental leave policy. Talk to your partner in advance about how you'll

share the finances, and the leave, about how you'll both maintain your careers. Often the assumption is that the mother will take all the parental leave, but this might not make sense practically, or financially. Understand that if you take time off, you are losing out on pension contributions, so your partner needs to understand that, potentially even top up your contributions while you're on leave looking after the child which is both of yours. Save all the money you can in advance, because there's likely going to be a financial hit. Start researching the cost of childcare and explore different options like help from family or part-time work"

(Ellie Austin-Williams, Financial Educator)

- **Project Into The Future**

"Don't just think about what having a baby would mean for life now. Imagine the next 20 years of your life (with and without children). If you were 50, looking back to now, would you want to be taking a child to primary school, interacting with your adult children or enjoying the other hobbies, work and social life that fill your days?"

(Bindi Gauntlett, Motherhood Mentor)

How To Celebrate The Small Wins

- **Be Enough**

"If parenthood is not for you, or not for you right now, remind yourself that you are already a whole person with a full life, and you don't need a child to complete you. You are already enough. don't let anyone try to convince you otherwise"

(Kate Berski - Author)

- **Live It Up Child-Free**

"If kids are in your future plans, actively enjoy a child-free life while it lasts. Go on a pre-pregnancy 'babymoon'. Do ALL the things that will be trickier with a tiddler in tow. Long haul flights, cobble-stoned city breaks, sightseeing without step-free access, hiking holidays and camping trips, fancy-pants restaurants, late nights and lazy Sunday mornings, and sleep – oh sleep it up baby and tell me all about it in

the morning. That is my kind of dirty talk"
(Kate Berski, Author)

MINDHACKER QUESTIONS

- Do I want or need to have a baby soon to feel personally fulfilled and content? Or is it something I feel I should want, or should do, because of other people's life choices or societal expectations?

- What are the positive PULL factors that draw me towards having a baby (the needs it will meet in me and how it will benefit my life)? What about the PUSH factors (am I trying to prove something, right any wrongs, or heal any hurts?)

TURNING 30 GOALS · REGROUP

Take a look back at your original list of Turning 30 Goals – did you write starting a family as a goal? How high up your list is it sitting? What words did you use to express it?

Now you've learned more about the external influences that might have shaped your expectations, explored your own motivations and considered the impact having a baby would have on your life, does it still feel like a top priority for you right now?

If yes, that's great. Now you know for sure that this is a genuine life goal. Does it feel any more or less important on your life list? Would you now articulate it any differently? For example, if your original goal was 'Get pregnant by the time I turn 30,' your new goal might be 'Start a family when it feels right to me and my partner.' Write it on your NEW GOALS list.

If you feel ready to move forward with family planning, add a 'BABY GOALS' list (no pun intended). Jot down two or three simple things you can commit to doing that will put you on the path to making the decision, or making a baby, when the time is right. I don't believe in putting deadlines on end goals, but timings can be helpful when it comes to process goals – so while the goal to 'get pregnant before my birthday,' might be outside of your control, making a five year financial plan with your partner could be a sensible first step. Remember – this is a huge and life-changing decision, and you are perfectly entitled to change your mind, and change it again, a million times in the future.

So You Don't Have Calm

"The 20s? My title for that period of my life would be, 'It was the Worst of Times, it was the Worst of Times...' Did I mention it was the hardest time of my life?"
(Lisa Kudrow)

This chapter was never meant to be here. Mental health was not in my original plan for 30-phobic topics. Truthfully, it's because I was afraid to go there. I was worried about sharing too much of myself and feeling exposed. Whilst behind closed doors I'm frequently an emotional wreck. 'Work me' is often more considered, detached, and scientific. But when my Editor suggested I share a little more of my heart, I knew the book would be all the better for it.

I was also afraid to tackle such a sensitive, complex and 'hot' topic. Especially since I am an informed layperson and not a certified mental health professional. However, after receiving countless concerning messages via social media, I knew for sure I had to do the brave thing.

Each time I get a DM from a young person clearly struggling with their mental health, I have mixed emotions. I feel honoured that they feel comfortable being vulnerable with me. I feel sad, that another human is suffering. I feel angry, that we as a society, are failing to support young people to such an extent that they are forced to reach out to relative strangers for help. And I feel afraid, that I could do or say the 'wrong' thing and cause a vulnerable person additional harm. Further, I am terrified that there are others out there posing as 'experts' who do not have the best interests of young people at heart, or who could be actively looking to exploit them.

So, whilst I'll never promise quick fixes to complex mental health challenges, what I can do is create a safe space in which we can share our honest feelings, worries and anxieties, without fear of judgement.

That being said, let me start by being vulnerable. Right now, I am fortunate to be enjoying a period of excellent mental health. I feel strong, capable and resilient, and I find moments of joy in every day. But I have certainly not always felt this way, and I'm aware that I probably won't feel this way forever. As I continue my journey through life, just like you, I can't possibly know what's around the corner, or how I'll respond to it. If my previous bouts of poor mental health have taught me anything, it's that all feelings (good and bad) are transient, and that staying on top of my triggers is the best way to manage my emotional wellbeing.

Everyone will have their own unique triggers of course, and I encourage you to take a moment to consider your own before moving on. To help explain what I mean though, allow me to walk you through a few of my personal mental health 'red flags'.

#1 - **Uncertainty:**

In my early 20s, my life frequently felt all 'up in the air,' like I was never walking on solid ground. And when things felt especially uncertain, a bout of anxiety usually followed. As it did in my late 20s, when I became increasingly concerned that my noncommittal boyfriend was wasting 'my best years.' As birthdays and mini breaks passed without event, and my diary filled up with wedding invitations, my future fears tipped into panic.

By the end of the decade, as you know, the future of my relationship was hanging in the balance – will I move back to London to settle down or stay in Sydney to start a whole new single life? On the surface, I seemed fine, puffy under-eyes aside. But the body always keeps score. And since my anxiety always shows up on my skin, I enjoyed several attractive flare-ups of eczema, and cold sores. Not to mention insomnia. I'd lie awake for hours running through the 'what ifs?' and crying uncontrollably in a state of pre-emptive heartbreak. My physical symptoms were only alleviated when I'd reached an emotional resolution. I headed home without a ring on my finger, but wearing a firm promise for the future.

#2 - **Over-Working:**

I've always loved to work, but in my 20s and early 30s, I didn't always know when to stop. It didn't help that as an agency employee, the job was never done. I had to constantly balance winning new work with ongoing workstreams, managing multiple projects and personalities with overlapping agendas.

My main job was to keep my clients happy, which could be very tricky given the subjective nature of creative work. I often found myself working late into the night making endless rounds of amends to work I already thought was great. And then there was the travel. I regularly began my workday at 4am in order to get to the airport, to travel to a meeting in Germany, which meant I didn't roll home until 11pm!

I was my own worst enemy too.

Once, already at maximum capacity I agreed to 'help out' a co-worker by taking on her research trip to the States. Five days later, I'd clocked sixty office hours and four consecutive nights of client entertaining, with jet lag.

On the plane home, I broke down – sobbing unselfconsciously for a full eight hours. And I couldn't stop crying all weekend. On Saturday I couldn't get out of bed, on Sunday I stayed slumped in front of the TV in my pyjamas. That was my first memory of burnout. I knew then that it was up to me to put boundaries in place. After all, my team weren't mind readers, and if I kept saying 'yes', the work would keep coming. Instead of doing the smart thing and discussing this with my bosses, I quit. Taking my burnout, and my bad habits along with me.

#3 - **Misalignment:**

The term 'out of the frying pan and into the fire' could have been invented for 20-something job hoppers. Much like leaving a romantic relationship, we often wrongly assume that moving on will allow us to keep all the good bits of the previous situation and add the icing on the cake. Sadly, this is rarely the case. I had taken for granted the culture of mutual respect, integrity and support in my previous workplace. In contrast, my next job felt like stepping into a vipers' nest.

On day one, my team leader filled me in on all the failings of his team. Foolishly misinterpreting this as 'trust' I found out the hard way, that if someone is talking ill of others behind their back, the chances are they're doing the same about you. And worse, this rotten apple had ruined the whole barrel – fostering a culture of mistrust, self-interest and backstabbing. I was frequently gaslit by my boss – who'd privately offer to take something off my plate and then publicly chastise me for not doing it. And in 1-on-1 sessions he'd criticise my capabilities, my personal style, and my 'boring' personality.

Miserable and crippled by an inhuman workload and the toxic culture that flew in the face of my principles, I quickly became overwhelmed. Emotionally exhausted and paralysed with stress, my brain seemed to shut down. My memory was shot, and I started dropping balls. This culminated in mistakes like the time I left my laptop at Starbucks the night before a huge client meeting and begged my boyfriend to drive me into central London at 10pm to get it back. I burned out again. Uncontrollable crying, sleepless nights, anxiety through the roof.

In hindsight, I can see I was set up to fail. At the time I just felt like I was failing at everything. I started to question my capabilities, and my chosen career path. I couldn't understand why my tried and tested approach of being honest, collaborative and diligent, wasn't working here.

Now I know exactly why. The values of the organisation were fundamentally misaligned with my own. And misalignment, I now understand, is a common trigger for burnout.

This time my decision to jump ship before I sank along with it was the right one. And it took a three-day hiking trip with my dad, a psychologist, to set my head straight. Fortunately, I was able to return to my former role, negotiating a part-time contract without issue. And I slowly worked my way back to confidence. Looking back, I wish I'd got clear on my values, and my boundaries much sooner. It would have saved me a whole lot of heartache.

#4 – **Hormones:**

I'm conscious that this last one feeds into the cliches about PMT, but

I know I'm not the only woman whose mood fluctuates wildly with her cycle. Embarrassingly, it's taken me almost two decades to figure out that my regular bouts of low mood, tearfulness and seething anger almost always occur exactly three days before my period. Now when I'm feeling this way I check my cycle app and bingo – it turns out it's not my husband, it's my hormones. Fortunately, my mood is almost always lifted when the bleeding starts.

But on one occasion, the solution wasn't quite so simple. When my daughter was born in 2019, at first, I felt numb. I was exhausted after a traumatic three-day labour, and I assumed this was why I never felt the instant rush of love or enjoyed the cosy 'baby bubble' that other mothers described. She was a troubled sleeper, and so was I. Even when given the opportunity – I'd lie in bed, depleted but too wired with anxiety to sleep. Worrying about dropping my baby down the stairs, terrified she'd stop breathing if I took my eyes off her even for a second. Then, becoming overwhelmed by the responsibility of it all, I'd fantasise about running away. I felt like I'd made the biggest mistake of my life. I couldn't find any joy in my new reality, my personality shrivelled practically overnight, and I had no idea what was happening to me.

The UK entered a global lockdown as I was at my lowest ebb. There were no coffee dates with close friends, no baby groups in which to swap war stories, and no relatives popping by to hold the baby. At the time my husband was working around the clock on the family business, which was at a critical juncture. My parents were a huge support in the beginning, but when lockdown hit, much of the day-to-day help came from my Polish father-in-law. He'd moved in with us for what we expected to be a few weeks. And stayed for more than a year. I'll always be grateful for the help he so willingly offered in those early days, but without a common language or very much childcare experience between us, we were mostly flying blind. I felt completely isolated. At one point I did try to seek help – but having rejected medication, I ended up on a waiting list for NHS talk therapy which took six months to come to fruition. By which time I'd started feeling a little better on my own. Even so, it took several more years, and a lot of self-reflection, to fully feel like myself again.

Despite the title, it would be reductionist to put my post-natal depression down to hormones alone. More accurate would be, surging hormones, combined with chronic sleep deprivation, a twenty-four-hour workload, inadequate support and zero social connection. If I was writing a recipe for a mental health meltdown, that would be it. I'm fortunate that my depression lifted with time, and sleep. But I still wish I'd spotted the signs earlier and got some professional support.

If you or someone you're close to, is struggling with their mental health as a new parent, please encourage talking to a professional to get some help.

In sharing my stories I've touched on a few different types of triggers for mental ill health – some of them situational, and some of them chemical. So, before we go on, it feels important to draw a distinction. The terms 'mental illness' and 'mental health' are often used interchangeably. Yet they actually have very different meanings. Mental health simply refers to our current state of emotional well-being. It can be better or worse and fluctuates in much the same way as our physical health does. Every one of us has mental health, but not all of us have a mental illness – that is, a brain-based condition that endures despite our circumstances and impacts our ability to function over a longer period of time.

Those of you who have grown up around family members or close friends with serious mental health conditions, or who struggle with mental illness yourself, will already have an appreciation for this crucial distinction.

For the rest of this chapter, I have chosen to focus on mental health.

Particularly the fluctuating feelings of anxiety that appear to uniquely afflict people in their 20s, their situational triggers and some of the ways we can take better care of our own wellbeing.

I do not mean to discount the importance of genuine brain-based mental illnesses. If you are seriously concerned about your mental state, or if you are worried about harming yourself or others, I must urge you to speak to your doctor, and/or a therapist as soon as possible. You can get through a lot, but friend, suffering in silence is rarely the solution.

Quarter-Life Anxiety Is Real

"20-somethings are snowflakes." In recent years, the word 'snowflake' has come to be a well-used slur against a whole generation of young people. And I don't know about you, but I'm tired of hearing it. Not least because nothing gets my goat more than an unoriginal insult. The term was popularised by the iconic Brad Pitt film Fight Club, and the Tyler Durden line "You are not special. You are not a beautiful and unique snowflake." The inference is that young adults are less resilient and more prone to taking offence than previous generations. Whatever your stance on this, it doesn't seem particularly helpful.

What I find more helpful is to try to understand how today's 20-somethings are really feeling, which is exactly why I asked 2,500 of them to tell me! I also wanted to dig into the possible causes of mental health challenges in young people. After all, no baby is born with depression or anxiety. So, if today's Quarter-Lifers are indeed suffering more than previous generations, something must have made them this way.

In my opinion, one thing this generation does better than previous generations, is being more willing to share their struggles. They are truly changing the conversation around mental health. When I was turning 30 ten years ago, very few of my peers would have written 'improve my mental health' on their list of top life goals. But in my recent survey, 71% list achieving good mental health as one of their top life priorities for this decade. But they're not there yet.

Only 12% of 20-somethings feel they have achieved good mental health, and 35% say their mental health is worse than expected. Women in their early 20s, and those identifying as gay, bisexual or other, are more likely to report poor mental health during this life stage.

It seems that today's 20-somethings, particularly those in their early 20s, really are suffering more than previous generations. A recent study by EY reported that the percentage of Gen Z respondents feeling moderately, very or extremely worried in general jumped from 30% in 2019 to 54% in 2023. The American Psychological Association reported that all other generational groups enjoy better mental health than Gen Z-ers, with Boomers reporting the very highest levels of mental health.

Anxiety appears to be a particular problem for today's 20-somethings. In my study, 'anxious' is the word most commonly chosen to describe how respondents feel about the future. And what's more, according to the National Center for Health Statistics and the U.S. Census Bureau, 59% of Gen Z show symptoms of an anxiety disorder. Dipping into what my survey respondents had to say, it's clear that the struggles of this decade feel all too real – and the looming '30 deadline' only serves to compound their fears:

"The best way to describe my life over the past few years is a battle to be happy with being alive. I've regretted what I have done, and what I haven't done. I'm apprehensive about getting older, fearing these thoughts will get worse, and I am depressed about how long it has taken me to be a functional human being. My mental health has been all over the place and I am not seeing many positives to turning 30"
(USA, 29rs)

"The closer I get to 30, the more anxiety it gives me. I am trying, but it makes me sad when I don't see any change in myself and the way I feel"
(USA, 27yrs)

Anxious At 30: Am I Normal?

If you're feeling anxious in the run-up to 30, it might help to know you are not alone.

The Myth: CAREFREE AT 30. Our 20s are the best years of our lives – a decade in which we are at our most beautiful, happy and carefree. This is the decade of living in the moment, going on endless adventures, and having limitless fun

The Reality: ANXIOUS AT 30. Our 20s are amongst the most stressful and challenging years of our lives, in which the uncertainties of the future make it almost impossible to enjoy living in the moment. In fact, many young adults are living in the future, with 40% of 20-29

year olds feeling anxious about what's to come. A further 20% feel 'apprehensive;' 14% feel 'afraid' and 13% feel 'panicked.' 20-22 year olds, single women and those identifying as gay, bisexual or other are more likely to report negative future-focused emotions.

Quarter-Life Anxiety: It's NOT You

1. The Situationship

2. The Happiness Gap

3. Generation Social

4. Frenemies

5. Acceptance

The Situationship

In her 2023 book 'The Twentysomething Treatment, Clinical Psychologist and 20-Something Guru Dr Meg Jay emphasises the important distinction between brain-based, enduring mental illnesses, and temporary, situation-based episodes of poor mental health. Based on years of clinical work with Quarter-Lifers, she observes that many of the negative feelings they experience are attributable to temporary situational factors such as unemployment, relationship breakdown, or relocation – and not to chemical imbalances in the brain. Sometimes her work has involved 'un-doing' a self-diagnosis that her clients have presented with.

In reality, our 20s are a 'situationship' in which, almost every trigger for poor mental health, is in abundance: uncertainty, unemployment, geographic mobility, the removal of support networks, unstable relationships, unhealthy lifestyles... need I go on? This DM, typical of the kind of messages I receive, perfectly captures the conflicting pressures and priorities that make 20-something life feel so chaotic and stressful:

"I'm not 30 yet but I've been feeling overwhelmed, chasing time and feeling lost. It all hits you in one go – where is time going, have I lived my 20s to the fullest, why am I feeling stagnant, I lost my job. I feel like I've wasted time, and I worry about the unknown, and I'm always comparing where I am to other people. There are a lot of things on my mind..."
(Roxy, 28, Instagram DM)

In her viral video, Founder of Truly Twenties Elle Wilmot described this decade as 'The Panic Years,' a turbulent time of life characterised by both huge uncertainty, and massive pressure to get it all figured out fast. And the real kicker is that young people often have fewer resources with which to make the best life choices – with limited life experience, underdeveloped skills, still growing brains and limited financial means.

"In your 20s you're expected to choose a career, choose a life partner, and make all these big life decisions in just a couple of years, without really being connected to yourself yet, it's not hard to see why it feels so hard"
(Maren Ashford, Co-Founder, Tapestry)

My data adds support for this - suggesting that the more 'unsettled' a Quarter-Lifers' situation appears to be, the more negative feelings they experience, and the more fear they have for the future. Being unpartnered, on a low income and not owning a home are all correlated with more negative emotions including anxiety.

The good news is that the data indicates that most 20-somethings recognise their current negative sentiment as a 'right now' problem more than an ongoing issue. For 88%, declining mental health is not a top concern when it comes to getting older – meaning, they see it as a present problem more than a future fear. Encouragingly, 51% believe that their 30s will be better than their 20s, especially women already in their late 20s. Perhaps the best evidence for the 'situational' theory of poor mental health though, is that most people are able to pinpoint a specific uncertainty that is causing them to feel anxious at the moment. For example:

"I don't have a job or any income, so my mental health is bad. I had

hoped to have had a job years before turning 30, but haven't achieved that, so the prospect of turning 30 and still having no job is making me stressed, depressed and panicked"
(UK, 28yrs)

"I'm anxious because I feel like I'm losing time to have children and buy a house of my own"
(UK, 26yrs)

"I wanted to have children younger but it didn't work that way, so I'm worried about hitting 30 and still not having a baby"
(UK, 27yrs)

"I'm scared of ageing because I'm single and I'm worried I'll be alone forever"
(UK, 28yrs)

"I'm afraid the future won't ever be what I wished to achieve. I'm not financially where I need to be, I haven't found my purpose, and I'm afraid my situation won't get any better"
(USA, 26yrs)

In the midst of confusing and tumultuous times, it can be easy to confuse temporary situation-based feelings of anxiety with genuine anxiety disorders.

"Anxiety typically comes from worrying about the future – it's no surprise that worrying about your future and the pressure to have certain things in place would happen around milestones (like turning 30). Generalised anxiety, on the other hand, is worrying about multiple areas of your life, most of the time, for an extended period of time, and not just constrained to milestones"
(Tonya Kelly, MSW, RSW and Dr. Erica Martin, Ph.D. C. Psych.)

The important takeaways for me are;

a) poor and inconsistent mental health in our 20s is absolutely normal, and understandable

b) these feelings are most likely temporary.

Dr Jay says she often advises her anxious young patients that "you'll feel more settled when life gets more settled." And having lived through my turbulent 20s and come out the other side feeling decidedly more stable, I'm inclined to agree.

The Happiness Gap

One thing that's always baffled me is how readily older generations deny the experiences of younger ones, especially when they've already lived these years for themselves. 20-somethings appear to be a particular target. When opening up with their very real emotional struggles, they're often dismissed with cliches such as 'you've got nothing to worry about,' 'just don't sweat it,' 'youth is wasted on the young,' or the grand old chestnut, 'these should be the best days of your life!'

For Quarter-Lifers in crisis, this dismissive attitude is decidedly unhelpful. Not least because it sends the message that if we're not, in fact, having the time of our life (while locking in the perfect partner, property and pension of course), then we're doing it all wrong. It serves to widen the gap between the level of happiness we expect to feel in our 20s, and our lived reality.

"People are quick to forget just how challenging your early 20s can be. The struggle to financially stand on your own two feet, to find a job you like, to meet new people, to 'find yourself.' It doesn't always last long, but this period of time can be so testing. Never underestimate what a 20-something is going through"
(Gaby Mendes, Founder TalkTwenties and TwentiesFest)

Most importantly, both anecdote and scientific data categorically disprove the 'best days' argument. My experience, and the experience of almost every woman I know is that life, in fact, feels better with age – so the idea that we reach 'peak happiness' in our 20s is actually a myth. There's even a name for it. 'The Happiness Curve.' In his 2018 book of the same name, Jonathan Rauch used well-being data to show that happiness starts to decline in our 20s, and only starts to rise again as we move towards mid-life. Rather than despairing about the present, I find it reassuring to think that my best days are most likely yet to come.

I asked a variety of experts and wise women why they think we tend to get happier with age, and their explanations were largely consistent – happiness is found when we disconnect from external influences and expectations and connect more strongly with ourselves. Greater self-connection gives us a greater sense of control, or agency, over our own lives and guides us towards more aligned and authentic life choices. In essence, the more we know ourselves, the more we can be ourselves, and the happier we become:

"In my 20s, I was being pushed through life by societal expectations and my inner critic. That only changed when I learned about self-clarity, meaning knowing who I am, knowing what my values are, and knowing what my life purpose is. But getting to that takes a lot of time and practice"
  (Maren Ashford, Co-Founder, Tapestry)

"I believe that life is one journey around the clock face. In the first half of your clock, which lasts into the 20s or even the 30s, you're not in control, you're learning, you're making mistakes, you're working out what you like, you're being pushed and pulled by friends, partners, neighbours and teachers. In the second half, that is when you realise that every step you take is within your control. You suddenly realise it's down to me now. That's when the anxiety disappears, because you can't be anxious about something you know, that you're in control of"
  (Sally Bee, Broadcaster, Author & Coach)

In explaining the 20-something Happiness Gap, Psychologists Tonya and Erica reference 'The Paradox of Choice,' a renowned book by American Psychologist Barry Schwartz. In it, Schwartz argues that whilst most human beings desire choice, too much choice can actually make us incredibly unhappy, unsettled, and anxious. And modern life, with its myriad options and endless streams of small choices to be made, can get incredibly stressful:

"The endless options that exist in every facet of life - what milk to buy, brand of jeans, mortgage vs rent, can be very overwhelming, and inaccurate information can lead to confusion, and chasing happiness. The constant search for "happier" leaves us not feeling happy and grate-

ful for what we already have, and can lead to anxiety and depression when the next thing doesn't in fact make us happier"
   (Tonya Kelly, MSW, RSW and Dr. Erica Martin, Ph.D. C. Psych.)

On top of the small everyday choices we all have to make, it strikes me that our 20s are the decade of indecision – when our entire futures are still unwritten, our lives could still go in any direction and our identities still feel fluid. Exciting, sure. Stressful? You betcha! For the human brain, constantly making choices saps energy and creates stress.

This is exactly why tech billionaires like Steve Jobs and Mark Zuckerburg famously saved energy for the big stuff by eliminating everyday choices such as what to wear. I live with one of these people. Peek inside the closet of my Entrepreneur husband and you'll still see row upon row of identical white t-shirts and black shorts. He doesn't believe in wasting valuable brain power on his wardrobe. You probably know someone like this too. She's the girl who spends Sunday afternoons meal prepping and planning outfits for the week to save time and stress in the week ahead.

Generation Social

On Sunday nights my husband and I always sit down to watch a film. We take great care to choose something of mutual interest, which is easier said than done when my preferred genre is slashers and his is historical biopics. Nonetheless we always settle on something we both really want to watch. But ten minutes in, my hand inevitably starts to twitch. My eyes flick down to the left. And when something flashes out of the corner of my eye I give into temptation and pick up my iPhone. I click onto WhatsApp, I furtively scroll Instagram... until I catch my beloved glaring at me and hastily put down my device, feeling ashamed.

> *My name is Kate, and I'm a smartphone addict. I am not alone. According to data the average person checks their phone every twelve minutes, and I'm betting that's an under-statement for many Quarter-Lifers. So, let's try an experiment. Just keep doing what you're doing right now – reading this book, walking, working out, cooking,*

whatever... and see how long it takes before you're tempted to reach for your phone. Scary, isn't it?

Jonathan Haidt certainly thinks so. In his ground-breaking 2023 book, 'The Anxious Generation' Haidt explains in terrifying detail how exposure to social media during childhood and early adulthood correlates with a sharp decline in young adult mental health. Those in their early 20s right now, he argues, are a generation of guinea pigs. The first to grow up immersed in an online world which we now know to be incredibly damaging, particularly for still-developing brains. He talks about how the switch from a 'play-based childhood' to a 'phone-based childhood' essentially re-wired the brains of an entire generation (Gen Z), triggering a global surge in anxiety, depression and body image issues.

A growing body of research is linking heavy social media use (which has been defined as 3 hours or more a day) with poorer mental health outcomes, particularly amongst young women. In my survey 91% of 20-29s say they use social media daily, and I'd bet that many of them are heavy users. As a content creator, I would certainly fall into that category myself. Studies into the impacts of social media on young minds make for grim reading – with regular use linked to sleep disruption, decreased real-life interactions, increased loneliness and decreased resilience. Not to mention the normalisation of dangerous behaviours like starvation, self-harm and substance abuse, plus increased exposure to cyberbullies and sexual predators.

The pervasive impact of social media came up often in my expert interviews. Several warned that technology encourages unhealthy external validation, and unrealistic social comparison:

"Social media has been used by many to project something that is false. Teenagers and young adults are bombarded with images of others that they believe to be true, and they're making comparisons. Just at the time when they are trying to figure out who they are, they have no access to true role models, authentic people and real life. That is very confusing"
   (Vassia Sarantopoulou, Psychologist)

"Social media provides a platform to continuously compare yourself

to others, who in fact, are only showing the world the best parts of their life. This leads to inaccurate comparisons, decreased confidence, and added pressure to measure up to unrealistic standards"
(Tonya Kelly, MSW, RSW and Dr. Erica Martin, Ph.D. C. Psych.)

One thing that social media has been praised for in recent years, is the way in which it has opened up the conversation about mental health, and made young people who are suffering, feel less alone.

And believe me when I say, I am here for all of this.

However, it would be amiss of me not to point out the slightly less functional flip side as well. Recent years have seen stacks of amateur content popping up on TikTok and Instagram in which creators both 'diagnose' and 'un-diagnose' serious mental health conditions. While this may have increased awareness and understanding in some cases, experts have warned against misinformation and over-simplification of complex health conditions. And consuming information from unreliable sources can lead to self-diagnosis, over-diagnosis, misdiagnosis and over-identification with mental illnesses. All of which can make it more difficult for health professionals to get young people the help they need. It can lead to wrongful or over-use of powerful prescription medications. And importantly, it can foster feelings of permanence or helpless thinking that removes the possibility that things will either get better on their own, or that we can take action to make things better for ourselves. Psychologists Erica and Tonya are mindful of the risks of self-diagnosis:

"Young people do seem to be suffering more than previous generations. And some of that is because of increased awareness (which is positive). Dr. Google helps with self-diagnosis, but we must remember that diagnosis is an art, not a science, so you cannot rely on tick boxes alone. The risk is that otherwise normal human experiences can become pathologised, or put into the diagnosis box, when not all of life's hardships warrant a diagnosis"
(Tonya Kelly, MSW, RSW and Dr. Erica Martin, Ph.D. C. Psych.)

Clearly more nuance is required when it comes to understanding our mental health – and if in doubt, we should consult a mental health professional and not our favourite TikTocker. Encouragingly though, when it comes to the confusing, or negative influence of social media, there is light at the end of the tunnel. Studies show that the negative mental health effects of social media are reversible. Taking a significant break from social media has been shown to improve feelings of happiness and life satisfaction in a relatively short space of time. Time for a social media break!

Frenemies

If you've ever watched any of the 'Real Housewives' franchise, you'd be forgiven for assuming that female friendship is mostly about getting glammed up for raucous dinner parties in which you quaff champagne and viciously tear down your closest friends over the canapes. A former die-hard fan myself, I've recently quit my RHOBH (if you know you know) habit owing to its depiction of friendship - which is untrue and overblown at best, and downright toxic at worst. Either way, those ladies that lunch should know better.

Thankfully, aside from enjoying the odd glass of fizz, my girlfriends are nothing like the Real Housewives. But what are yours like? Take a minute to consider your five closest friends. What are they like? What do they do for a living? What are they into? How do they talk about themselves? How do they talk about, and to, other people? How do they make you feel about yourself?

I'm asking these questions for good reason. Motivational speaker Jim Rohm famously stated that we are the average of the five people we spend the most time with. So, if in answer to my questions you were envisioning your close-knit group of positive, supportive, open-minded and healthy-living girlfriends, the chances are, you're ticking most of those boxes too. But, what if the first qualities that came to mind were negativity, criticism, gossiping, bitching, conflict or complaining? If that sounds closer to the truth, it could be that your inner circle, your supposed support system, is actually bringing you down rather than lifting you up.

Serial Founder Lindsey Kane told me about the impact of toxic friendships on her younger self:

"I didn't realise until recently the impact of the people around you and the impact that negativity has, it's like a cancer. Who is in your circle is so important for how you feel and the wrong people will really hold you back. I think about being in a bucket of crabs, and you're trying to escape and trying to get out, but all of these crabs are just pulling you back down into the bucket because they don't want you to leave. They don't want you to try and aspire to do anything better. I've gone on a massive journey with this, and I've kind of audited my friend group"
(Lindsey Kane, Founder of Jolt)

Lindsey is not alone in her experiences. In a study by the UK Mental Health Foundation, 68% of people admitted that a toxic friendship had negatively impacted their mental health.

And lest we forget that we ourselves can be our own worst frenemy. Perhaps the only thing more damaging than criticism from other people, is the criticism we constantly level at ourselves. The monkey brain, gremlin, inner saboteur, inner judge, limiting beliefs, negative self-talk, critical parent, Sheila... however you refer to your own inner critic, I'm guessing that you know exactly who I'm talking about. The tricky part is that, unlike a neggy next-door neighbour, we live with ourselves 24/7, making negative self-talk a heck of a lot harder to hide from.

Psychologists have found strong and undeniable links between self-criticism and a range of nasty mental health outcomes, including depression, eating disorders and anxiety. This is why mental health experts advise that understanding, and interrupting, our inner critic is THE key to improving our mental health:

"Research shows that our relationships are the single most important predictor of our happiness. And what relationship is more important than the one you have with yourself? I am yet to meet a person who thinks that life is a breeze. Studies overwhelmingly show the many benefits self-compassion has for all areas of life"
(Dr Maike Neuhaus, Positive Psychologist)

"Our inner Saboteur is our survival mind. It's designed to keep us safe, but it also keeps us small, and tuning into it makes us very unhappy. Mental health, or mental fitness, is about learning how to inter-

cept your inner saboteur and learning how to connect to what we call your Sage, which is the regions of your mind that house your positive thoughts, your positive emotions and your greatest powers like creativity, curiosity, calm and decisive action"
(Maren Ashford, Co-Founder, Tapestry)

Science has proven, unequivocally, that while self-criticism can trigger mental health challenges, self-reassurance protects against it. And this is especially important for young adults. One study found that reduced self-criticism between the ages of 23 and 29 significantly improved mental resilience and psychological health at age 35. Proof positive that getting a handle on your self-talk now, will set you up for success in the future.

"I think about mental fitness in the same way as physical fitness. When you put a 'mental mountain' in front of someone who is not mentally fit, they're going to feel overwhelmed. But the great news is that just like physical fitness, we can develop the muscles of our mental fitness, through training and positive mind habits"
(Maren Ashford, Co-Founder, Tapestry)

Quarter-Life Anxiety? Get Unstuck In 4-Steps

By now we have established that 20-something life, with all of its ups, downs and uncertainties can give us major anxiety. We also know that feeling anxious in turbulent times is absolutely normal, and hopefully temporary. Most importantly, we have learned that suffering in silence is not the solution. Fortunately, there are plenty of things we can do to improve our mental fitness and feel better fast. Expert tips incoming.

How To STOP Looking Out

- **Stop Consuming Junk**

"Stop and think about what you're consuming, what you are filling your time and your mind with. If you're spending 5 hours on social media every day and you're consuming negative messages or looking

at stuff that's making you feel bad about yourself, that is feeding into your mindset. Look to consume more positive, realistic and fulfilling messages"
(Lindsey Kane, Founder of Jolt)

- **Audit Your Network**

"Do an audit of your inner circle. Think about how your friends make you feel, and the value they bring to your life. Do they support you and encourage you to be a better person, or do they try to discourage you and hold you back? Do they make you laugh, or do they make you cry? Do you feel better or worse about yourself after you see them? It sounds ruthless, but if they bring negative energy, or make you feel shit, it could be time to cut ties"
(Lindsey Kane, Founder of Jolt)

- **Combat Saboteur With Sage**

"You can't control what other people think, say or do, and some people are always going to bring Saboteur Energy, which is contagious. If someone is judging you or giving opinions about your life choices, it's going to naturally trigger your inner saboteurs. If that happens, know that the person is speaking from their saboteur. Have compassion and recognise that they're not actually speaking from their true self. Feel sorry for them because they are stuck in their negative mind chatter, and they're not able to escape from it. You can. Always come back to yourself – and when they go saboteur, you go sage"
(Maren Ashford, Co-Founder, Tapestry)

- **Communicate Your Limits**

"I have health problems, and I get very tired. So I've learned to be very clear about my boundaries. I'll go into a party for example, walk straight up to the host and say thanks for inviting me, I'm going to stay as long as I can. But once I need to go, I need to go. So, I'm saying right now 'hello' and 'goodbye', thanks for having me and I'm having a great time'. I'll tell them that I'm just going to do the French exit and when the time comes, I'll simply quickly disappear without saying anything. And I have never had anybody hate me for it"
(Sally Bee, Broadcaster, Author & Coach)

- **Take A Mental Health Day**

"If you're really struggling, give yourself a break. You wouldn't feel guilty about letting people down if you broke your leg and had to take a day off work, so treat a mental health emergency in the same way. Take time to feel better and don't beat yourself up over it"
   (Sally Bee, Broadcaster, Author & Coach)

How To START Looking In

- **Validate Your Own Feelings**

"Instead of thinking that you shouldn't feel this way, try to acknowledge that you ARE feeling this way and probably for a good reason. Offer yourself a listening ear, check in with your feelings and needs"
   (Dr Maike Neuhaus, Positive Psychologist)

- **Know Your Inner Critic**

"Do the Positive Intelligence Saboteur Assessment (www.positiveintelligence.com/saboteurs). It's a five-minute online quiz that can be truly game-changing. Once you understand your inner saboteur or inner critic, you are in a better position to defeat it"
   (Maren Ashford & Rosanna Ruff, Co-Founders, Tapestry)

- **Trust Yourself**

"Trust that however you feel right now, you will get yourself in the right position. Trust that everything will be alright, that everything will happen at the right time for you, if you follow your natural path. Don't try to force things and don't rush. Rushing doesn't solve the problem. And neither does worrying. If worrying made a problem go away, I'd say worry like crazy, but it doesn't"
   (Sally Bee, Broadcaster, Author & Coach)

- **Consume Consciously**

"Are you reading, listening to and looking at content that will empower, motivate or inspire you in some way? Are you spending time with

people who encourage you to look at different perspectives? When you consume positive things and surround yourself with people who lift you up, you'll feel happier"
(Lindsay Kane, Founder of Jolt)

- **Be Mindful For 10 Seconds**

"Mindfulness is the gateway to your calm centre. And all it takes is 10 seconds. Bring mindfulness into your daily routine. When you brush your teeth or have a shower, notice the sensations in your mouth, or on your body, the tastes, the textures, the changing pressure or temperature... really get present for a few moments. The more you do this, the more you build the muscle that takes you out of that negative mind chatter and centre yourself again"
(Maren Ashford & Rosanna Ruff, Co-Founders, Tapestry)

- **Create The Conditions For Happiness**

"You can't just be happy; you have to create the conditions for happiness. To be well, you need four things to be working – your physical health, your mental health, your emotional health and your spiritual health. Think about what you are doing to nurture each of these spheres, and look at which areas may need a little more attention"
(Michelle Hawkins-Collins, Founder, The Wisdom Space)

- **Practice Pausing**

"If something happens that frustrates you, upsets you or makes you feel anxious, take a moment to breathe before you react. Let your emotions come down. When emotions are heightened, we can get into very black and white thinking, and it becomes harder to regulate our emotions"
(Michelle Hawkins-Collins, Founder, The Wisdom Space)

How To REFRAME Your Goals

- **Know It's Temporary**

"Understand that much of the way you're feeling right now is down

to uncertainty and many of your problems are temporary. You most likely won't be broke, single, lonely or living with your parents forever. Remind yourself that these things are now problems, not forever problems"
(Kate Berski, Author)

- **Don't Self-Diagnose**

"Periods of mental poor health do not make you mentally ill. Try not to self-diagnose or label yourself for life. Leave diagnoses to medical professionals, and bring your current circumstances into the conversation to rule out situational factors that could be improved"
(Kate Berski, Author)

- **Separate Fears From Facts**

"Watch the stories you tell yourself – are you making assumptions, being overly negative, engaging in self-blame, jumping to conclusions, or catastrophising... if you're feeling anxious, ask yourself is this based on fear or fact?"
(Tonya Kelly, MSW, RSW and Dr. Erica Martin, Ph.D. C. Psych.)

- **Get Support**

"Don't feel you have to go through the overwhelm alone, and don't feel embarrassed to seek help – even therapists need therapists! It's easier to navigate transitional times with the right support, whether that's a therapist, a coach, a trusted friend or an astrologer... find what works for you"
(Caitlan Siegenthaler, IFS Therapist & Podcaster)

- **Choose Your Words**

"If you're worrying about the 'what ifs...' of the future, change the words "what if..." to "even if..." Instead of "What if I don't get married/get the job/have a baby?" it becomes "Even if that doesn't happen..." It helps you see that there are other paths, alternative opportunities. Trust that if one thing doesn't come to you straight away, the doors will open for something else"
(Sally Bee, Broadcaster, Author & Coach)

- **Play The Worst-Case Scenario**

"Ask yourself, what's the worst that could happen? Often the consequences of not doing something are not as catastrophic as you think. Talk yourself into seeing a different perspective"
　(Sally Bee, Broadcaster, Author & Coach)

- **Don't Forget The Basics**

"Good mental health starts with simple self-care – make sure you have good sleep hygiene, eat well and exercise. Put your phone away and invest in real-time connections instead. We need authentic connections to be healthy"
　(Tonya Kelly, MSW, RSW and Dr. Erica Martin, Ph.D. C. Psych.)

- **Re-Wire Your Thinking**

"Neurons that fire together, wire together – meaning, our ways of thinking and talking to ourselves become 'automatic' over time. If you start telling yourself more compassionate and helpful statements, you will create new neural pathways that will help you feel better and lead a more productive life. Stick positive mantras on your mirror, create screensavers for your device or send yourself reminders through your day. For example, "I don't need to worry – I trust that my future self will figure it out; I am enough just as I am; I can learn from past mistakes; I am worthy"
　(Tonya Kelly, MSW, RSW and Dr. Erica Martin, Ph.D. C. Psych.)

How To Celebrate The Small Wins

- **Embrace Self-Praise**

"Instead of criticising yourself for the things you haven't achieved yet, practice praising yourself for the things you have already achieved"
　(Dr Maike Neuhaus, Positive Psychologist)

- **Practice Gratitude**

"Start every day by saying out loud or writing down three things that

you're grateful for. Doing that at the beginning of your day is really powerful, because you go into that day with a much more positive mindset"
(Maren Ashford & Rosanna Ruff, Co-Founders, Tapestry)

- **Be Happy Now**

"Stop yourself from saying or thinking 'I'll be happy when...' Instead focus on the glimmers, the things that make you happy now, in this moment"
(Gaby Mendes, Founder TalkTwenties)

MINDHACKER QUESTIONS

- Can I explain WHY I feel anxious or sad right now? What situational factors could be playing a part? Are these things likely to change in the future?

- How do the accounts I follow on social media make me feel about my own life and my progress? Is it time to hit 'unfollow' on anyone?

TURNING 30 GOALS - REGROUP

Take a look back at your original list of Turning 30 Goals – did you write a mental health goal on there? How high up your list is it sitting? What words did you use to express it?

Now you've learned more about the external influences that might have shaped your expectations about what your 20s should be like, or your experience of what living this decade actually is like, does that make you feel any differently about your current situation?

Now let's think about some 'BABY GOALS.' What daily habits or small actions could you commit to doing every day to help improve your mental well-being over time? Remember – keep these small, and achievable and if you're struggling right now, recognise that the way you're feeling is not wrong. It is normal for mental health to go up and down. Your feelings are unlikely to last forever.

So You Don't Have A Dream Job

"I don't have a dream job because I don't dream of labour."
(Anon)

Career Anxiety Is Real

If the disparaging headlines about Gen Z are to be believed, this confession should come with a trigger warning. But here goes. I love to work. In my twenty-ish-year career as a Marketer, Entrepreneur and Writer, I've been fortunate to work for, and with, many brilliant and beautiful people. I've travelled the world, immersed myself in different cultures, enjoyed a lot of laughs and had conversations that have changed the way I look at the world. I've built competence, confidence and self-esteem through the opportunities, challenges, achievements and rewards that my career has brought my way.

I've also experienced toxic corporate cultures, soul-crushing bullying, 'character building' rejections, multiple burnouts (see Chapter 9), moments of complete disillusionment and recurring existential crises. Not to mention periods of extreme emotional, practical and financial insecurity that have triggered my anxiety, my insomnia, and my eczema.

And I know I'm not the only one.

Wherever you are in your career, working life can be fraught with uncertainties. But this is especially true in our 20s – the decade in which society expects us to figure out 'what we are doing with our lives' at the exact same time as locking down a place, a plus one, and a pension plan. 30 appears to be the socially accepted deadline for finding your path, and your purpose in the world. Failure to do so can result in feelings of anxiety, pressure and even panic as the milestone birthday looms closer. This is probably why career anxiety emerged as one of the most common themes in the comments sections of my survey:

"I feel like I sat in a dead-end job too long, and I wasted all that time I could have put towards building a meaningful career"
(USA, 26yrs)

"I'm trying to find a new career. It feels like starting over again, whilst my peers appear to be at much higher levels of seniority in their role. I made a choice to travel, hence using up my savings. So again, I am starting over in a financial sense"
(UK, 27yrs)

"When you turn 30, society expects you to have a career, which, at the moment, I don't have. I am getting close to 30 and I worry that I won't have my career sorted when I turn 30"
(USA, 28yrs)

"I'm unemployed, and the prospect of turning 30 and still having no job is making me stressed, depressed and panicked"
(UK 28yrs)

"I had planned to have a well-paid job and buy a house by the time I turned 30, but at 28 I have neither!"
(UK, 28yrs)

Unfortunately for those of us who are not Trust Fund Babies, paid work isn't optional. Moreover, despite accusations to the contrary, it seems that most 20-somethings are working. In my survey, 75% of all 20-somethings are working or studying full-time at the moment, rising to 83% at age 29.

I've never really bought into the 'work to live' argument either. Since the average person will spend 90,000 hours, that's a full third of their life at work, it seems to me that finding an occupation that doesn't make you want to scratch your eyes out on a daily basis might spill over into a happier life overall. We've all had 'living for the weekend' eras and we all know how miserable that can be. The endless cycle of wishing away the weekdays to live it large, or wilfully hibernate, for

24 hours, only to feel the Sunday Scaries creeping in... and repeat.

The problem is, not all jobs are born equal. Whilst it's relatively easy to get a job, it's far trickier to find *the job*. It's all very well being advised to 'follow our dreams,' but what if we don't dream of working in the first place? And is there really such a thing as a dream job anyway, or is everyone 'living the dream' on Instagram telling big fat porkies?

Career Anxiety At 30: Am I Normal?

If you're feeling anxious about your current career status, you are most certainly not alone, and here's the proof.

The Myth: Everyone else knows exactly where they're going in life and is doing what they love. I'm the only one who feels confused, stuck, or anxious about the future of my career.

The Reality: The average career satisfaction for 20-somethings is 5/10, and only 8% describe themselves as 'very satisfied' in their current job. While 92% stated a career-orientated goal, 36% fear they will never find a job they love and 48% worry they won't find a job that pays them enough to live on.

Career Anxiety: It's NOT You

In the past year, I've spoken to 20-somethings who are employed, unemployed, under-employed and everything in between. And I've noted that career anxiety afflicts people at all levels of employment. Whatever their individual situation, many young adults describe a general sense of anxiety that they're not where they should be by this point in life, or they don't feel how they're supposed to feel about their job. Basically, their working reality has fallen far short of their careering expectations.

In my experience, behind every Quarter-Life career crisis is one of these three unmet expectations. Can you relate?

Disorientation: *'I expected to know what I wanted to do by now, but*

I don't'

Dreaming: *'I know where I want to go, but I don't know how to get there'*

Disillusionment: *'I expected to be happy when I achieved my goal, but I'm not'*

Yes! The Expectation Gap is back, and it's the reason you feel disappointed with your career trajectory. But hold on for a second. Where do these expectations actually come from? Why do we feel under so much pressure to pinpoint our dream job? And who decided 30 was the deadline to figure it all out anyway?!

I am about to break it all down, and in the process expose multiple 'Milestone Myths' that are making us feel like we're failing or falling behind in our careers when we are absolutely not.

On your behalf, I will be going to town on the many outdated, irrelevant and unhelpful socially constructed 'truths' that make us feel bad about our work life and hold us back from having the career we want. I hope that by busting some of the craziest career myths, I can make you feel better about where you are now, and help you unlock a future that fits. Let the myth-busting bonanza commence!

1. The Love Myth

2. The What Myth

3. The Security Myth

4. The Arrival Myth

5. The Purpose Myth

6. The Headhunter Myth

7. The 30 Myth

The Love Myth

I blame Mark Twain (or Confucius, depending on who you're asking) for a good slug of the career disillusionment experienced by Quarter-Lifers. "Find a job you love, and you'll never work a day in your life."

It's absolute nonsense.

If there is a person in this world who relishes every God-given second of their current employment, I for one am yet to meet them. Because, just to shatter your illusions from the outset, there really is no such thing as a dream job.

And yet, it's a message 20-somethings have already taken to heart. In my survey, 53% chose finding a job they love as a top turning 30 goal, rising to 70% amongst 21-22-year-olds. 40% feel they're falling behind on this goal too.

I'm living proof of that there's no such thing as a perfect job. Having gone around the Ferris wheel of various employment, self-employment and pseudo-employment options in the past few decades, I've been lucky enough to be living my lifelong dream of being a writer. Crafting words, creating content I believe in, connecting with like-minded women, and doing this from wherever in the world I choose. It really doesn't get better than this. And yet... there are mornings when I wake up at 4.30am after a broken night with a sick child and I think, I'd really rather go to brunch.

While I love coming up with content ideas, I have little energy for editing or hacking the social media algorithms that could surely bring abundant new followers in my direction. While writing is my passion, the operational side of the book business is less inspiring. I'd much rather while away an afternoon watching The Kardashians than absorbing YouTube tutorials on setting up an Amazon marketplace. You get the picture.

The truth is, even in the best-case scenario, there are always going to be parts of your job, and whole days, weeks or even months at work when you absolutely do not feel like you're living the dream. But it doesn't necessarily mean that it's not the best job for you right now. The problem with the 'Dream Job' narrative is that it sets the expectation that we should be loving our work life at all times.

So, when we inevitably find that we're not, we conclude that;

a) there's something wrong with our job,

b) there's something wrong with us. Cue dissatisfaction, disillusionment, inner turmoil, identity crises, wild escapist fantasies and frantic CV titillation, on loop, until we make the leap to our next role, when the whole cycle starts again.

Podcast Host and Founder of Talk Twenties Gaby Mendes (another woman who's created her Dream Job, but not without a lot of hard work and heartache) tells me that many of her 20-something listeners suffer from career anxiety too. She questions the expectation that work should be consistently enjoyable, when other aspects of life are absolutely not. She counsels young women to ride out the inevitable ups and downs of working life, before jumping to radical career decisions that may not leave them any happier:

"There's a whole narrative saying you should love what you do. Society tells us we should feel fulfilled all the time. So, people think to themselves, everyone else is loving their job, why don't I love mine? I DO love my job overall. But I also don't believe that there is this magic job where you'll love every single second of the day. There are always going to be downsides, and tasks you don't enjoy, there are negatives in every fairy tale. I mean, do you wake up every day and love your wardrobe? Do you love your partner the same every single day? The way you feel about work naturally ebbs and flows, like everything else..."

(Gaby Mendes, Podcast Host & Founder of Talk Twenties)

The What Myth

This enduring work myth was actually busted back in the 1930s by jazz musician Ella Fitzgerald in the song "It Ain't What You Do (It's the Way That You Do It) sing it with me now 'that's what gets results.'

This tune has been my earworm since I started considering career anxiety. And that's because when it comes to jobs, we tend to get incredibly fixated on what it is we are doing. The job title, the job description, the tasks in hand. And those things are important for sure. But they're only part of the picture.

When it comes to work, most of us under-estimate how much influence 'the way that we do it' has on our resulting happiness levels. We fixate on the what, and forget about the where, the when, the who, the how and the why.

Looking back, some of the unhappiest moments of my own working life have had to do with these lesser discussed 'Ws'. The wheres (an airless, windowless sweatshop in rainy Acton), the whens (evenings, weekends and holidays...), the whys (because a lazy team member f*cked something up) and so on and so on.

A growing body of psychological research suggests that living and working in adverse conditions radically impacts our mental wellness and can even change the structure and function of our brain. A huge number of factors impact the way we feel at work - from light levels, temperature and clutter to corporate communication styles, culture and conflict. And none of these factors could ever be appreciated from the job description.

I've learned this from bitter experience. You might recall my 'job from hell' from Chapter 9. Well, even before the horrible bosses, came the horrible office - an early red flag which I overlooked to my detriment. My first interview was at a bar in central London. And since it went well, I was invited back to the office a few days later. I remember stepping into that trendy Soho studio and feeling immediately oppressed. Distracted by my nerves and eager to impress, I pushed aside the sinking feeling that something didn't feel right. Shuffling awkwardly past rows of tightly packed desks towards the meeting room, I should have taken note of the cramped conditions. The floor to ceiling black paint punctuated by feeble mood-lighting added to the sense that the walls were closing in on me – but I convinced myself I just wasn't used to the hipster dive bar vibe. I took the job anyway. And while things went south for myriad reasons, I can see that the working environment had messed with my mood from the outset. Since then, I've insisted on working only in offices flooded with natural light, and have a SAD lamp permanently stationed on my desk, for emergencies.

To be doubly sure that I'll never be left in the dark again, I'm currently in the process of moving someplace sunny – having come to the realisation that living in the 'grizzly' (my word for 'grey' and 'drizzly') British climate was impacting my energy levels, and my productivity. Fortunately for me, work is now, wherever I can carry my laptop. And whilst I've changed nothing else about what I'm doing, simply changing where I'm working has made a world of positive difference.

I realise that not everyone is quite so flexible. But being able to pinpoint exactly what's making you feel 'meh' about your job can be the first step in creating positive change. It's exactly what I used to do for my clients as a Brand Consultant. The first stage of almost every project involved digging into 'The 5 W's' (Who/Why/Why Not/ When/ Where) to understand where exactly a brand was going wrong or leaving money on the table. Maybe it was a who problem –targeting the wrong consumers; a why problem – not giving people a good reason to buy; a where problem – not being in the right places... I won't bore you with brand geekery, but you get it right?

You can use the same tool for yourself to find out exactly why your current work situation is not working for you. It could be that you identify an easy fix (changing teams to escape a toxic boss, or working with your line manager on prioritisation, or delegation). And if not, you'll be armed with a better brief for landing your next role. When you know what you're looking for (and what you're definitely not looking for), you'll be better placed to apply for better-fitting jobs, ask better questions at interviews and ultimately land a better job for you.

The Security Myth

When I quit my lucrative agency job to go freelance at the age of 32, my mum thought I was mad. I had a non-compete clause in my contract which meant I couldn't work with any of my existing clients, and didn't have a single scrap of work lined up. I'd just got married and was co-founder of a pre-revenue beauty start-up. I had no 'slow month' savings, and no contingency plan. It felt like a huge risk.

But a few months in, it struck me that the risks of self-employment were actually a lot lower than I'd imagined. Instead of putting all my eggs in one basket – tying myself to a single employer who could blindside me with redundancy at any moment – I'd actually spread my bets. Now I had a healthy roster of clients across several countries. If budgets got tight for one, I'd pick up work with another. If the UK economy turned sketchy, American jobs swooped in to fill the gap. That's when I knew that job security is a cosy corporate myth, and not necessarily a reality.

As many employees discovered during the Covid pandemic. Career Coach Berta explains:

"But when COVID hit, people realised that everything can disappear in a blink of an eye. They were holding on to their jobs because they valued that feeling of security, but it made them realise that there is no such thing as security, not even a corporate job, because you can lose these overnight. And it's not only the poor performers that lose their jobs, you can be really good at what you do and still get made redundant. So, you cannot even rely on your talent to secure your income. Keeping all your eggs in one basket can no longer support a mortgage, a family and a life. Many people don't go for their dream job to keep the security of the job they already have, but these world events remind us that this is a false feeling of security"
(Berta Maso, Career Coach)

I wanted to give an honourable mention here to the 'job for life' myth. The tired old social construct that still pressures us to pick a path at 29 and stay in our lane for the rest of eternity. It simply isn't realistic, or even true.

The average American will have 12 jobs in their lifetime, and job hop 8 times between the ages of 18 and 34. Employees are not sticking to one track either. According to a recent poll by The Fast Company, 52% of Americans are considering a major career change this year. Perhaps more encouragingly, the average age for a career pivot is age 39. So, if you're still in your 20s and contemplating starting over, you're actually ahead of the game!

You'd also be in great company.

I've been fortunate enough to interview over 40 objectively successful women in the writing of this book. And what struck me is that all of them found success, and true job satisfaction, after 30, often by switching lanes entirely. I met a teacher turned content creator, a marketer turned motherhood mentor, an event planner turned media mogul. As an entrepreneur turned writer myself, making my major career pivot at age 39, I'm bang on schedule. The good news is most career 'pivoters' never look back. Almost everyone reaches career crisis point at one time or another:

"In my group of friends, I was the first one to have the career crisis. I was around 25, and I really felt like everyone else had got it together, everyone else was settled in their careers and their jobs were going so well. I felt like I was the only one. At 25 I decided to tear it all up and start again – I left my job, my relationship and my flat. Later on, almost all of my friends hit the same point. I'm so grateful I did it now, I'm so much happier and more fulfilled"
(Ellie Austin-Williams, Financial Educator)

Job security, it seems, is not only a myth, but it can also be a millstone around workers necks. Career Coach Berta believes the days of the traditional 9 to 5 office job are numbered – with Millennials and Gen Z blazing the trail for better days:

"9 to 5 traditional employment was associated with the Baby Boomers. But the next generation are challenging everything. They're not putting all their eggs in one basket; they're coming up with all sorts of new ways to generate an income and diversify their income stream. They're going to be telling their children that back in the day people used to go to the office every single day to sit at a desk from nine to five, and the kids are not going to believe them"
(Berta Maso, Career Coach)

The Arrival Myth

What does 'success' mean to you? Take a second, if you will, to think about your working definition of success. How will you know that you've really 'made it'? Maybe write it down if you're feeling especially energetic.

Usually, when I ask people to define success, they'll write down a specific job title, a salary band, a number they hope to read on their bonus cheque, a social media follower count... They'll also capture concrete goals like publishing a book, filming a movie, or winning an industry award.

These are all very worthy and admirable ambitions. They also have one thing in common - they're outcomes. Big Wins. End-Goals. And it's no surprise to me that we define success in these terms.

After all, we have been conditioned to see success as an outcome.

Now don't get me wrong, goals can be great things, and I'm not anti-ambition by any means. I am, however, concerned that adopting a future-orientated 'milestone mentality' can make people incredibly unhappy in the present. It gives rise to the 'I'll be happy when...' type thinking. It puts us 'in the waiting room' of our own lives. When we should be centre stage.

Psychologists have a phrase for this: *The Arrival Fallacy* – referring to the deep-held human belief that if we can only reach our goal, we will be happy forever.

If this assumption were true, then every single Gold Medal Athlete, Lottery Winner and Love Island victor would be living in eternal bliss. And they're not.

The unpopular truth is that happiness, like all emotions, is temporary. And while achieving our goals might create a short-term uplift in our mood, that high won't last forever. And real people remind me of this every day. My inbox is bulging with DMs from disillusioned high achievers who have finally reached their lifelong career goal, only to find that it's not all it's cracked up to be. This is exactly the experience of corporate success story turned Wellness Entrepreneur Maren Ashford:

"In my 20s I had no idea who I was. I had no idea what my purpose was in life. And I was just achieving. Achieving what society, my school, or my workplace defined as success. And I ticked lots of boxes. At school, I was told that achievement was being a straight-A student.

So, I became a straight-A student. Then I was told achievement was getting into Oxbridge. So, I got into Oxbridge and got a fancy degree. And then I went and got a series of impressive-sounding jobs. And I worked hard and was successful. I was also deeply unhappy. Because I had no self-clarity, I didn't know my values, I didn't know my purpose"
(Maren Ashford, Co-Founder, Tapestry)

Career Coach Berta also sees career disillusionment as a product of blindly accepting societal definitions of, and pathways to, success:

"Society tells you what success is and how to get there. So, you chase this idea of success, and you follow the expected path without ever questioning it. But why do you have to study at university? Why after the degree comes a masters? Why after the masters do you apply for the internship in the big corporation? Then get the fancy corporate job. It's because we don't question these things, or stop to think about our own definition of success, that so many of us get 20 years into our careers and wonder why we don't feel happy, or even successful"
(Berta Maso, Career Coach)

For today's 20-somethings, social media has brought a cacophony of noise that makes it almost impossible to tune out unhelpful external definitions of success. From amping up traditional success symbols (flash cars, bling watches, ravishing real estate...) to offering new, yet equally unachievable alternatives (travelling the world indefinitely on an apparently unlimited budget). Whichever end of the spectrum, these visions of success can make mere mortals grinding away 9-5 in a grey cubicle, feel like abject failures. Or at the very least, incredibly confused about the kind of life they should be building for themselves.

"20-somethings are tasked with finding a career. But this generation has gone through a long period of over-stimulation. They have been bombarded by society's expectations and other people's standards. They find it impossible to figure out who they really are or how to create more meaning and purpose in their own lives. They've never had the space and silence to connect with themselves. Instead, they are constantly looking for something, chasing something, pursuing something until they reach the point of existential crisis... Who am I? Why have I chosen this career? Is it actually my decision? Is it because I

saw it on Instagram? Is it because my parents pushed me towards it?"
(Vassia Sarantopoulou, Psychologist)

So, we've established that societal standards and milestone-thinking is making us miserable. But what then, is the secret to long-term career contentment? According to Daniel Pink, author of Drive, it's actually quite the opposite. Pink argues that most workers are more motivated by internal, meaningful, process-led goals than by traditional external rewards. Seeking autonomy, mastery, and purpose at work is more likely to lead to job satisfaction than chasing a specific salary for example. Turns out, it's not achieving our goals that makes us whistle while we work, but rather the process of driving towards them. We really start to thrive in our careers when we start to enjoy the journey.

The Purpose Myth

I blame the Silicone Valley tech companies with their lofty visions of 'making the world a better place' for this most modern of myths. In recent times young adults have been subjected to a new societal pressure - purpose pressure. Now, not only are we expected to love what we do, we need to be doing something genuinely worthwhile. We don't need a career; we need a cause!

Nearly half of the women I surveyed, included 'finding a job with purpose' as one of their turning 30 goals – and 40% of them already feel like they're falling behind on achieving this goal. 36% went on to say they fear they will never find their calling in life.

Finding your purpose sounds wonderful in theory, and it's certainly a popular topic on the career corners of Instagram. Believe me, nobody was a bigger fan of Simon Sinek's seminal work, 'Start with Why' than this girl. Of course, he's right - we all derive more satisfaction from our work when we actually believe in what we are doing. My own work is infused with purpose – helping Quarter-Lifers overcome life goal anxiety and start building a life on their terms, brings me untold joy every day.

However, it's taken me almost forty years, multiple miss-steps and several career pivots to arrive at this purposeful place. And the same can be said for most individuals who feel they've finally found their purpose in life. It's not the principle that bothers me, it's the deadline. Expecting baby adults fresh out of uni to not only find a career path, get really good at it and make lots of money doing it but to also save the world at the same time, all before their 30th birthday, starts to feel a bit much, don't you think?

My personal problem with purpose goals is that they're often wildly unachievable, vague, or impersonal. Getting clear on your core values, so say my experts, is a much better way to find purpose in the work you do. Values are the personal beliefs that guide our lives. Your values might be loyalty, kindness, freedom, or generosity for example. When our values are aligned with the work we do, we feel good. But when our values are violated, we get the professional 'ick.' For example, if integrity was one of your core values, yet your company expected you to 'stretch the truth' when reporting data to consumers, or higher powers, that would be a source of significant stress. But how do we know if this is the source of dissatisfaction in our job?

"We often feel unhappy at work when we are neglecting our values, or when our values are being stepped on by other people or by circumstances, things just don't feel right inside. There's this sense of kind of dissonance, you feel out of tune. And the person next to you might be fine with it, we're all completely unique. You have to trust your gut, your intuition, if it doesn't feel right, if you feel uncomfortable, even if you can't quite put your finger on it. The reason you can't quite put your finger on it is because you haven't discovered your values yet. But just trust that feeling. If it doesn't feel right, then do something about it"
(Maren Ashford & Rosanna Ruff, Co-Founders of Tapestry Design Life)

Therapist Caitlan tells me that continuing to work in a career that's misaligned with our values doesn't just give us the heebie-jeebies, it's a one-way ticket to burnout, a mentally and emotionally depleted state more often associated with straightforward over-working:

"I think there's a bit of a misunderstanding about burnout being just working too hard, working too many hours. Actually, you can work

really, really hard but not be burnt out because your career is aligned with your values. You know when you're on the right path, because you feel at peace. But I see so much burnout in women who are sticking in that misaligned career"
(Caitlan Siegenthaler, IFS Therapist and Podcaster)

The Headhunter Myth

Have you ever sat with friends grumbling away about your job, bemoaning how under-paid and under-appreciated you are, secretly wishing some mysterious talent agent would swoop in to discover your untapped potential as a (model/actor/influencer/singer/ballerina/insert fantasy job here)? And how quickly have you taken positive action to rectify the above injustices inflicted upon you by going out and scoring a more suitable career? I will forgive you if you're looking sheepishly at your feet right now, because we have all been there.

In the past, I was certainly one for wishful thinking, lavish procrastinations and bouts of wine-fuelled entitlement. And I'm not alone. I come across so many adults, young and old, who are patiently waiting to be discovered. Hiding at home anticipating a knock at the door that will change their life. Not realising the truth of the enlightened. Change happens only when you change something.

It's not all our fault either – we've been brought up on TV talent shows in which bakery assistants, plucked from obscure Northern towns become global pop phenomena virtually overnight (shout out to the Harry Styles fans out there!) Moreover, we've bought into the Headhunter myth. Sure, there's a job of the same name, but we all know they're just recruiters in fancier suits. And I hate to burst any bubbles, but the job of a recruiter is to force-fit you into an employment gap that already exists, not to perfectly tailor a dream role around your exquisite delectations. And whatever they might tell you on that clandestine inbound call to your office, their client has probably not asked for you by name either. In other words, the best roles are rarely advertised, and many don't even exist – because they're created only when the right people come together:

"20-something me thought that I had to wait until a really good job

was posted, apply for that job and fit myself into it. Now what I understand is that there are better ways that do not include looking for an advertised job. Many of the best jobs don't even exist yet. Your dream role is more likely to come from a conversation you have that leads to something you never expected"
    (Berta Maso, Career Coach)

Like Berta, I may have been a passive optimist in my 20s, but my mindset flipped entirely in my 30s. Partly because I've changed. Mostly because the world has changed.

Naturally in the writing of this book, I read up on the competition. Over the past 18 months, I've consumed so many self-help books and motivational masterpieces that I'm now dreaming in positive affirmations.

One book that struck a particular chord was Ash Ambirge's 'Middle Finger Project'. Not just because there's an expletive in the sub-line, although that always helps, but because her career advice is so simple it actually hurts.

Ash argues that dutifully scrolling the LinkedIn listings and attempting to match your CV to the available positions is old-hat, and it won't land you the job of your dreams anyway. The way to get the job you really want, is to just do the job already! So simple. So brilliant. If you want to sing, she says, start singing. If you want to be a photographer, start taking photos. If you want to write, Just. Start. Writing. And thanks to the social media-crazed, platform-driven world we now live in, if you keep doing what you're doing, eventually somebody will notice, and your dreams of being discovered just might become a reality.

I unwittingly put the 'just do it' principle into practice when I started the 30-Phobia project. I had no background in publishing, zero industry contacts and a social media following of approximately nil. All I had going for me was a lifelong dream, a well-worn MacBook and an inescapable urge to put words on paper. But I didn't let a little thing like lack of experience get in my way. I soon discovered that pivoting careers in the social media age is as simple as updating your LinkedIn and tapping a few words on an Instagram bio. I was now a writer. Because I said so. And more importantly, because I did so. And I kept on doing so until my words, and my ideas, started to get noticed. The very fact you're reading this book right now means my trickery worked! I am an author because I made a book! And you can too. You just need to give lady luck a little helping hand.

The 30 Myth

I could write a whole book about this one – oh wait, I just did! As many of us have experienced, the pressure to decide 'what you want to be when you grow up' starts practically from birth. And for those planning to leave school at sixteen, or eighteen, I imagine that decision gets pretty real, pretty soon.

For me, career pressure hit a little later. Despite having aspirations to work in Advertising from the age of around 15, by 21 I hadn't exactly made any moves. A diligent student, and even more diligent drinker, I'd thrown myself whole-heartedly into life at Leeds University, only concerning myself with the most immediate of deadlines. I didn't worry about my future employment. I assumed, quite naively in retrospect, that I'd slide straight from the university steps into a cushy Ad Exec role in a London agency.

But little did I know, my peers hadn't taken quite such a laissez-faire approach to career planning. Suddenly in the final term, people started talking about the Grad Schemes they'd scored places on, and the cool-sounding Internships they'd surreptitiously been lining up while I was busy lining my stomach with doner kebabs. That was the first time I remember feeling I'd been left behind. I was 21. And the feeling only got worse when I returned to my family home to take up a temp job at a local hospital, where the closest thing I got to Advertising was pointing people in the direction of the toilets.

I'd thought then that everyone else was 'sorted' – that they'd figured out what they wanted to do with their life and all they had to do now was cruise on up the corporate ladder where piles of cash and infinite acclaim awaited them. I would have been firmly amongst the 70% of 21-year-olds who believe that 'other people find life easier than me.' A statistic which I love, especially coupled with the fact that only 4% of

21-year-olds believe that they find life easier than other people. This means that all of these sickening high achievers we read about in the 30 under 30 lists are most definitely the exception and not the rule.

But try telling this to 20-somethings.

According to my study, Milestone Anxiety peaks in the early 20s. Perceived pressure to achieve certain life goals by 30 is highest amongst 21-year-olds. The feeling of 'running out of time' and anxiety induced by '30 Under 30' lists also top out at 21. Young adults appear to have accepted 30 as the deadline of professional life, by which time they will either 'make it,' or peace-out into lifelong oblivion. Perhaps this false deadline harks back to traditional timelines that expected a woman to play at work only until she landed the real prize - a handsome husband, stylish home, and beautiful baby. In which case, she'd need to crack on and find a job before fertility pressure forced her to give it all up. I read a quote recently that said, 'tradition is just peer pressure from the past'. So, I suggest we leave it there.

Along with the turning 30 career deadline, real women continue to prove that there really are no deadlines on dreams (I've spoken to at least forty of them in the writing of this book). And if that's not enough, many of the world's most famously successful women found their feet well after 30. To name but a few:

- JK Rowling finally got the first Harry Potter book published at age 32

- Vera Wang launched her first fashion line at 40

- Actor Kathy Bates didn't land her break-out role until she was 43

- Olivia Coleman won her first Academy Award at 45

- Legendary TV Chef Julia Childs published her first cookbook at 49

- Dame Judi Dench didn't appear in an American movie until her 60s

- Arianna Huffington didn't start her media career until her 50s

- Astronaut Wally Funk completed her first space mission at 82
- Fashion Ikon Iris Apfel rose to fame at age 84

Success After 40

"My 20s and early 30s were a bit of a mess. I didn't really have any clear vision and I wasn't very focused, I was doing a bit of everything. But in my mid-30s it all changed. I started seeing people around me hitting milestones that I wasn't hitting - buying their own flats, getting married, and having promotions. I was watching peers in comedy go from strength to strength while I was treading water. I got to 35 and thought, this is nuts. I need to get a grip. That five-year countdown to 40 was a real kick up the bum for me. I don't know why I made 40 such a big deal. But for me, it was a milestone in terms of changing my attitude towards my career and really buckling down. It was the start of my trajectory as a successful stand-up comedian. I decided to just focus on stand-up and to get really good at that one thing. When I was younger, I had decided in my head that if it didn't happen in my 30s it was never going to happen. But that is not true. As my career has proven, everything really came together in my 40s, but all the groundwork was in my 20s and 30s"
(Jen Brister, Stand-Up Comedian)

Before we wrap, I must lodge my dislike of the phrase 'late bloomer.' As well as reinforcing the implicit deadline, it's also irrelevant in this context. Given our previous discussion on the death of jobs for life and the normalisation of career pivots, nowadays very few individuals are doing the same job the day they retire as their first ever day of work. So, what's the actual point of all the pressure to pick a horse by 30? Entrepreneur Lindsay Kane, who founded her supplements business in her late 30s believes society should give young people a break:

"People in their teens and 20s are made to feel like they should know what they want to do for the rest of their lives. I think we need to normalise it being okay not to know. The truth is, no one knows. Even as adults, no one really truly knows what they want to do until the day they die. Trying things, changing your mind and trying something

else is part of life, and life about is experiencing everything that you possibly can. We need to give ourselves a break"
(Lindsay Kane, Founder of Jolt)

Like Lindsay, I believe it's OK to be uncertain, it's advisable to try on a few roles before fully committing, and it's perfectly OK to change your mind many times along the way.

Moreover, it keeps things spicy. For the lucky ones, life is too long not to keep trying new things. The older I get, the less I care for deadlines, and the more I embrace experiences. I love the idea of lifelong learning and genuinely believe that it is never too late to pursue your passions. In my 20s, career uncertainty gave me anxiety, now it feels more like opportunity. And I for one, am excited for what's still to come.

Career Anxiety? Get Unstuck In 4-Steps

Friend, the incoming career advice is GOLD! My juicy expert tips are designed to help you overcome anxiety about not having your dream job right now and guide you to find a path that fits the future.

My incredible panel of coaches, mentors, psychologists and highly successful women had a LOT to say about how to get unstuck and unlock future career success. I'm genuinely pumped to be sharing their advice here. Oh, the sleepless nights and tears in the office toilets I could have avoided if only known all of this when I was in my 20s!

Of course, everyone is in a slightly different situation personally and professionally, and we all have different dreams in mind. So, feel free to take the tips that fit and skim past those that don't. This is your journey after all.

How To STOP Looking Out

- **Drop The Deadline**

"Deadlines create stress when it's not really there. They're constructs

of our mind that aren't real. If anything, they cripple people. People think they need to get there by 30 and if they don't, they give up. Don't fall into that trap! You can find success at any time, so take age out of the equation"
(Laurie Jennings, GM, Good Housekeeping Institute)

- **Forget 30 Under 30**

"Those 30 under 30 lists are not helpful. Our society is too obsessed with speed and fetishises young success. But 30 is only a third of our lives, assuming we'll all live to about 90, and for most of that time, we were children! So, at 30 we really haven't got a lot of adult experience. You can be a high-achieving person at any age, so take the pressure off"
   (Caitlan Siegenthaler, IFS Therapist & Podcast Host)

- **Stop Clock-Watching**

"My mum always said, there's no stopwatch, you're constantly working against a clock that only exists in your head. It's not real. You can get success too early, but you can never get it too late. So, if it comes to you in your 40s or if it comes to you in your 50s, like it did for me, that's no bad thing"
   (Jen Brister, Stand-up Comedian)

- **Challenge Societal Norms**

"If you chase what society deems to be a great life, you'll always feel like you're living life on someone else's terms. Sure - creating a multi-million-dollar business might look great on paper - but would you personally want the constant hustle, let alone the legal and administrative burden that comes with that? Instead, take your journal and write about what happiness and success look like to YOU"
   (Dr Maike Neuhaus, Positive Psychologist)

- **Stop Comparing**

"My career took off when I had complete tunnel vision, I stopped comparing myself to other people and stopped worrying about where other people's careers were going. Because it doesn't matter. You're

doing your own thing"
(Jen Brister, Stand-up Comedian)

- **Beware Of External Pressure**

"External conditioning and expectations could be pushing you to want to achieve certain goals or reinforcing certain patterns of behaviour. Try to listen to your gut instead, reconnect to yourself and your needs"
(Aleks Malkin, Health & Beauty Influencer)

- **Stop Fearing Failure**

"Wayne Gretzky, the famous Canadian hockey player always said, you miss 100% of the shots, you don't take, and you miss some of the shots that you do take, but at least you're taking them, and you also get some of the unexpected shots, and some of the unexpected shots actually go in. So shoot your shot. If you never try, you'll never know"
(Laurie Jennings, GM, Good Housekeeping Institute)

- **Let Go Of Limiting Beliefs**

"Identify the beliefs and negative self-talk that is holding you back from chasing your dream job. Ask yourself - what one limiting belief about myself or my capabilities can I let go of today?"
(Dr Maike Neuhaus, Positive Psychologist)

- **Don't Be A Tree**

*"There is so much bullshit around about the milestones we should be hitting at certain ages, and some weird belief that the older you get the more stuck you are in your decisions. It's b*llocks. You can change anytime you want to. If you don't like where you are at in life. Move. You are not a f*cking tree"*
(Jordan Stachini, Founder Co & Co)

- **Don't Obsess About The End Goal**

"You can't really control how successful you will be, but you can control what you put into it. So just pick one thing and try to get really good at it. My goal wasn't to get an agent, get on the telly and get two

million followers. My goal was to pick one thing and do it well. I just focused on getting good at stand-up comedy, and all the other things came from that"
(Jen Brister, Stand-up Comedian)

How To START Looking In

- **Know Your Priorities**

"If you can unpack and understand what your priorities are early on, then you've got a kind of North Star to keep coming back to when you face those crossroads. For example, know whether freedom is more important to you or financial security. Do you take the job, which is going to pay you 20 grand more, but requires you to work every other weekend? Or do you value your weekend enough to stay with a job that pays you less? If you haven't been through that process of figuring out what matters to you, then it's easy to just follow the money and ignore everything else"
(Ellie Austin-Williams, Financial Educator)

- **Do Your W's**

"Look beyond the job description. What the job entails can be less critical to your happiness and satisfaction than where you're based, when you're working, who you're working with and why your role exists. Dig into the things that have really made you happy or unhappy in previous jobs, and look for roles that offer a set-up in which you can thrive"
(Kate Berski, Author)

- **Clarify Your Values**

"A quick way to get a sense of what your values are is to visualise a peak moment in your life. It doesn't have to be work-related. Think about why that moment was important to you, where you were, what you were doing, and who else was there.... write it all down. Then unpick the themes that sit behind it, and work out what it says about the things that are important to you. My moment was hosting a charity event in a beautiful garden square in Notting Hill, and my family was

there. Suddenly, it was very clear that my values were beauty, integrity and compassion"
(Maren Ashford, Co-Founder of Tapestry)

- **Know Your Patterns**

"If you're unhappy or feeling stuck with your career, you have to start by looking within. Really understand the working patterns that keep creating your unhappiness, or that busyness or overwhelm. It doesn't matter how many times you change the working context, and it won't matter if you change the company. It doesn't even matter if you leave corporate to start a business, you will create that situation wherever you go. Unless you break the patterns that create a situation in the first place, you're going to keep recreating that negative situation"
(Berta Maso, Career Coach)

- **Trust Ongoing Feelings**

"Career dissatisfaction is often temporary, or fixable, and your negative feelings might actually be about something outside of work. But if it's clear that everything else in your life is pretty good, and if work is consistently bringing you down, if that feeling is continuous, then it might be time to move on"
(Gaby Mendes, Founder Talk Twenties)

- **Beware Sunday Scaries**

"You will know when enough is enough when Sunday comes, and you feel your soul die. You know enough is enough when you're living for the weekends, or that next holiday. You know, enough is enough, when Monday is the worst day of the week, and Fridays are the best. You don't have to remain in a place you don't belong"
(Berta Maso, Career Coach)

- **Find Your Joy**

"If you're self-employed, a business owner, or aspiring to go in that direction, tap into what gives you joy and where you can really add value. Your time is finite, and you can't do everything. Identify the tasks that drain your time and energy and work out how to outsource

them"
(Berta Maso, Career Coach)

How To REFRAME Your Goals

- **Think Life First**

"Instead of fitting your life around your work, first define what is the life you want to live, and then fit your professional reality around it. Do you want to be flexible? What working days or hours do you realistically have available? How much time do you want to spend with your family? How much time do you need to dedicate to yourself? When and where do you work best? That's your brief – find a way to fit your work around this"
(Berta Maso, Career Coach)

- **Turn Envy Into Admiration**

"Who do you envy or compare yourself to? What happens if you reframe that feeling of envy as admiration? What is it about this person or their life that you admire? What does this reveal about your own goals, purpose or values? Does it show up something that's missing from your life? How can you incorporate more of this into your professional life?"
(Camille Cook, Host of Unfulfilled Podcast)

- **Play The Long Game**

"The rush to have it all figured out as fast as possible is something we created as a society, but it's more helpful to think about the whole lifespan of your career. We tend to focus on that first five to ten years, but we don't think about what's going to happen when we get there. You're probably going to be working into your 60s or 70s. So there isn't actually a rush. What's the point of rushing to the top in your 20s, and then just sitting still for 40 years? It's a journey, it's meant to be a process. My advice is to zoom out and look at the bigger picture"
(Ellie Austin-Williams, Author & Financial Educator)

- **Find A Path, Not A Destination**

"Don't let achievement anxiety get in your way. Stop thinking about the ultimate goal and instead try to find the right path. You'll know you're going in the right direction when it feels natural, you feel aligned, and useful, like you're making a meaningful contribution. Trust that if you follow this path, you'll get yourself in the right position to be successful on your terms"
(Lindsay Kane, Founder of Jolt)

- **Stop Job Hunting**

"All the best jobs are invisible and un-advertised, so don't wait for roles to come to you. Network before you need a new job, before you want something from someone, and before you become unsatisfied in your role. Put yourself centre stage and make connections – then the jobs will come to you"
(Berta Maso, Career Coach)

- **Just Do It**

"You don't need to wait for the perfect role to fall into your lap, now you can create it for yourself! Changing your job title is as simple as updating your LinkedIn, changing your job is as simple as getting started. So just start doing what you love, consistently, and telling everyone about it online and IRL. If you keep showing up, eventually you'll get traction. As soon as you have a platform, opportunities will come to you, and you can start getting paid for pursuing your passion"
(Kate Berski, Author)

- **Be Helpful**

"If you're looking to grow your network, instead of asking people to help you, ask how you can help them. If we all help each other, we all grow together"
(Lindsay Kane, Founder of Jolt)

- **Be Giving**

"Luck doesn't just happen to you, you create your own luck. Start by being a good person, be good to others, be generous with your time, generous with your praise and your partnership. It will come back to

you, maybe not by 30 but it will come... and then you'll be ready to go through the open door"
(Laurie Jennings, GM, Good Housekeeping Institute)

How To CELEBRATE The Small Wins

- **Love The Job You Have**

"It sounds counter-intuitive, but if you don't love your job, show it more love. Be more present, more curious, more positive, more open-minded, show up more, and talk to more people. You may well find yourself enjoying work more, and more opportunities are coming to you"
(Kate Berski, Author)

- **Find Your Purpose**

"Don't put pressure on yourself to change the world in a big way. Do look for purpose in your current job. However small, however local, you are making an impact, you are making your corner of the world a little brighter, making someone's day a little better. You'll get more out of work when you understand why you're doing it"
(Kate Berski, Author)

- **Utilise Social Media**

"Social media platforms have made everybody accessible, and this creates huge opportunities. You could send a message to anyone in the world right now and they just might read it, they just might reply. You can join a Facebook group and get instantly connected to people who are already doing what you want to do. You can start a TikTok or Instagram page, host a podcast, or write a LinkedIn newsletter right now. People get discovered on these platforms every day, so use them to your advantage"
(Berta Maso, Career Coach)

- **Celebrate Progress**

"Write down the steps you have already taken towards achieving your goal, however small they may seem. For example, have you created an

Instagram profile, started a blog or a journal connected to your chosen career? Have you connected with someone who's already doing that job? Give yourself credit for the steps you have already taken in the right direction"
(Kate Berski, Author)

MINDHACKER QUESTIONS

- Which one activity makes me forget to eat, drink or scroll? How can I do more of this? (Don't worry about getting paid for it yet!)

- What is the one thing I've always wanted to try but haven't because of fear of judgement?

- How can I redefine success in a way that feels authentic to me?

TURNING 30 GOALS - REGROUP

Take a look back at your original list of Turning 30 Goals – did you write a career goal on there? How high up your list is it sitting? Which words did you use to express it?

Now you've learned more about the external influences that might have shaped your expectations around career, would you re-prioritise or re-define your goals in any way?

Before moving on, take a minute to re-draft your career goals on the 'NEW GOALS' list at the back of this book, or wherever you're taking your notes. Don't forget to add to your 'BABY GOALS' Column. What small steps could you start taking that could inch you closer to your dream job? Remember – there are no deadlines on dreams, and there is no stopwatch for success. Keep moving along that path at your own pace, and you will get there when the time is right.

Life Starts At 30

The Truth About 20-Somethings

In many ways, 30-Phobia is nothing new. 20-somethings have always felt under pressure to 'get it all figured out by thirty.' However, I believe the struggle is more real for the current generation for one key reason. The negative influence of social media during their formative years.

Social media appears to have super-sized the age-old struggles of finding a place, a partner and a passion in life. It's exposed baby adults to more extreme visions of success, more unachievable beauty standards, more people with which to compare their lives and more options for how to live than ever before. Higher standards have elevated expectations and reduced life satisfaction in the process. And greater perceived choice has amped up anxiety levels (just think about how easy it is to order off a set menu compared to scanning through hundreds of food options).

It feels like social media, and the rise of self-help culture to an extent (controversial to say in a self-help book I know!) has added more conditions to traditional life goals too.

It's no longer enough to get a job that pays the rent, now we have to love what we do and change the world while we're doing it. Now we're not just looking for a passable life partner, we must find a best friend, passionate lover, business partner, co-parent, therapist and life coach all in one. Mothers are no longer charged with simply keeping their kids alive, they are housekeepers, teachers, mentors, therapists, nutritionists and psychologists – and that's not including their paid job. Yes, the Expectation Gap is widening in all areas – and young people are becoming less happy as a result. I think we can all agree by now that our 20s are not in fact 'the best days of our lives.' For many of us,

'Shit Show' comes closer to the mark.

In this book, I've made it my mission to tell the truth about 20-somethings, and here are some of the biggest truths I've learned along the way:

12 Truths About Your 20s

1. Your 20s are not the best days of your life

2. Literally, nobody has it all figured out by 30

3. Wherever you're at, you are normal, and you're not alone

4. There's no such thing as ahead or behind, because we are all on our own path

5. You'll find your way faster by looking IN, instead of OUT

6. Everything is temporary, especially feelings

7. Trying to short-cut the sh*t bits won't help you in the long run

8. Uncertainty can be great, because it signals opportunity

9. 30 is not the deadline, it's the start line

10. Your best days are still ahead of you

11. You have time to get your act together – one small step at a time

12. Life won't turn out how you expected, but it might be better

The Happy Ending

Despite my best efforts, I've always been a glass-half-empty gal, and I admit that large sections of this book may be validating, but not uplifting. At one point my Editor instructed me to pepper in a few more 'mini orgasms' and stop making my readers wait for the Happy Ending.

Maybe I did go a bit hard on the 'why your 20s suck' side of things... And if that's the case, dear reader, this IS the happy ending you have been waiting for.

When I asked young women how they feel about turning 30, second only to 'anxious,' they selected 'hopeful.' And the majority believe that their 30s will be better than their 20s. This is one of the things I love about this decade. Yes, everything is up in the air. Yes, everything is confusing as hell. But also, there's everything to play for. Your 20s are the decade of opportunity.

Sure, you're making a lot of mistakes, which is a necessary part of the process, but you still have plenty of time to course correct. If you're feeling all at sea right now, it's totally normal, you won't feel this way forever. A decade will make all the difference.

Having studied Psychology, I gained a newfound respect for the word 'hope.' Because it doesn't mean what you think it does. 'Hope in a jar' 'Hope for the best' 'Hoping to win the lottery,' we often use it in a relatively passive sense to express a desirable, yet unlikely future outcome. But according to Psychologists, 'hope,' unlike 'wishing,' means more than aspiring to something, it means taking positive action towards it.

They've even discovered that 'hope-based' therapy can significantly improve symptoms of depression. It turns out, it's not the hope that kills you, it's the very thing that's keeping you alive. So, this is your signal to stay hopeful, even when you're knee-deep in the sh*t show that is Quarter-Life.

I personally find the most hope in the squiggly success stories of other women. This is why I felt so inspired when Jordan's story slid into my LinkedIn DMs. Her incredible journey teaches valuable life lessons about letting go of external definitions of success and situations that no longer serve you, and pursuing your most authentic path, one small step at a time.

Jordan's Story

"At 30 I had the 'perfect life'. I was flying high in my career. I lived in a beautiful house. I was in a long-term relationship with a great guy. We had a little dog. Luxurious holidays. High disposable income... and I was so fucking unhappy.

The 'perfect life' that the world had always told me to strive for was unfulfilling, and empty, and left me with an overwhelming feeling of 'Is this really it?'.

The reality was, I was in a job which made me miserable. I was five stone overweight. And I was no longer in love with my partner.

I decided to change one thing. Starting with my job. I handed in my notice and started my own business. Then I got a PT and committed to training twice a week. This is where it all changed for me.

I went into PT sessions with a desire to look different – but I underestimated the impact exercise and nutrition would have on my mental state. Suddenly I was able to see a way out of that overwhelming feeling of unhappiness.

So, at 32, when my peers were getting married, having kids, or worrying about 'the clock ticking', I decided to start again. I ended my relationship of 7 years, sold the house and bought one of my own. I focused on my business and being healthy.

That was two years ago. There have been ups and downs, and moments of 'what the fuck have I done?' But never moments of regret. Throughout the dismantling of my 'perfect life', I stayed true to one belief, that you are only ever answerable to your future self.

You must live every single day of your life with yourself. So, you need to make sure that in 1, 5, 10 years' time, you can sit down with yourself, look yourself in the eye, and say 'It might not have been easy, but I made the right choices'.

Now I am 34. Single. Unmarried. Childless. Living alone with my dog. Running a business.

And I have never felt more strongly that I am right where I need to be"
(Jordan Stachini, founder of Co & Co)

Surviving Quarter-Life

No post ever (not even my cat memes) got the 'grammers going more than this one question: What advice would you give your 20-year-old self? Cue hundreds of jewels of hard-won wisdom from the over 30s. Not to mention a bang-up list of recommendations should I ever be in the market for Psychic Moon Readings or Coaching on becoming a Crypto Millionaire in ten days.

What struck me most though was that amongst the hundreds of comments, everyone appeared to be saying the same thing. And when five hundred smart women are saying something, it's probably worth printing it in a book!

Survival Tips from the Over 30s

#1 Trust Yourself

It's natural to second-guess yourself in turbulent times but hang on in there. However out of control you might feel, you have actually got this!

"Have blind faith in yourself girl!"
@theflourishingdoc

"Trust yourself more than anything"
@theheadspacelab

"Embrace your inner strength"
@theallyrose

"Believe in yourself"
@studio.pink.lens

#2 Trust The Process

You might feel like a hot mess at the moment, but know that disappointments, setbacks and missteps are a normal, and necessary, part of the journey. Have faith that even if you're not living the dream right now, you will reach your goals when the time is right.

"Be patient, it will all work out"
    @time4changesorg

"Wait, you're in for a treat"
    @thealphabrain.co

"One thing at a time"
    @_ely.03

"You can make mistakes and still be happy"
    @sneakylittlebrownnoser

"Nothing lasts forever, good or bad"
    @helvii

#3 Be Brave

Don't let fear stop you from building your best life. Be brave, be open-minded, worry less, say yes and go with the flow. You'll be amazed where this mindset will take you.

"Leave your comfort zone and travel"
    @syed_nauman

"Take more risks"
    @pzetti

"Take that chance, see what happens"
    @thebrittlebrownie

"Go through the open door"
    @lauriejenningsnyc

"Always shoot your shot"
@laura_ann_moore

#4 Love Yourself

Don't waste any more energy on self-criticism. Practice self-compassion, self-acceptance and self-care instead. Over time, you'll feel more and more confident in yourself.

"Be kinder to yourself"
@hegogym

"You are enough"
@eddieeyebrows

"Be happy without being perfect"
@lead_succeed_with_iman

"Love yourself before anyone else"
@newlifeparadigm

"Enjoy your own company"
@dr_sidrah

#5 Live For YOU

Comparison is the thief of joy and ultimately you are answerable only to yourself. So stop trying to live up to other people's expectations. Live life on your own terms.

"It's OK if everybody doesn't like you"
@aka_zuda

"Live the life you want, not what others want"
@tarekwahdann

"Don't worry what others think"
@just_peachy0227

"Be your priority. You don't have to please others"
@marucarillo84

"Live. Your. Damn. Life"
@Jud_prve

Alternative Milestones

Much of the Milestone Anxiety experienced by Quarter-Lifers relates to not having reached traditional life goals – like not being married, owning property or having children by 30.

Society conditions us to believe that achieving all of these goals is an essential part of living a successful and happy life. But what message is this sending to those who have yet to reach these socially approved goalposts? Or those who find themselves wondering if they even want these things anyway? In the absence of valid alternatives, outliers are often made to feel abnormal, less than, failures. The way we are taught to pity and placate unmarried, childless women for example,

"Oh you poor thing, you'll find someone soon..."

The thing is, real people are proving a lot of our social conditioning wrong. Not only are there more single women than ever before, meaning that being single makes you normal, and not a weirdo. But it seems that being single makes you happier too.

Data shows that single childless women are significantly happier than married mothers.

And having spoken to a close friend who is a divorce lawyer, I can understand why. For women, getting married and having children often means taking on greater responsibilities and working more unpaid hours – which can lead to conflict, resentment and disengagement. While for men, taking a wife still seems to go hand in hand with a lightening of the domestic load. Which explains why married men are just as happy as single women.

I'll spare you further feminist rantings, because my real point is this.

We see ourselves as an inclusive society, but by perpetuating traditional milestones, we are excluding vast chunks of the population from our celebrations. And I, for one, feel that there's a lot more worth celebrating. Here are a few suggestions for alternative milestones to shout about. I cordially invite you to add your own!

- Getting over a breakup
- Ending a toxic relationship or friendship
- Friendship anniversaries
- Becoming a pet parent
- Starting therapy
- Moving abroad
- Starting a new hobby
- First solo trip
- Sober-versaries
- Finishing medical treatment
- Paying off a loan
- Becoming debt-free
- Going back to school
- Getting your VISA
- Starting a new side hustle
- Taking a 'single moon'
- Starting a new career

- Getting your first pay cheque
- Moving out of the family home
- Leaving a toxic job
- Recovering from a mental health crisis
- Getting a full night's sleep

Emergency Affirmations

Positive thinking can take us a long way. But there are always going to be wobbly moments when it really feels like life isn't going to plan. So, I wanted to leave you with some Emergency Affirmations. Simply break glass in case of emergency and find a mantra that makes you feel better:

- This is temporary
- I embrace the process
- I have time, and I'm doing fine
- I'm enjoying the journey
- Life is too long not to enjoy myself
- I am collecting experiences, not achievements
- I'm excited for what's to come
- I'm not anxious, I'm excited
- I'm just doing me
- The older I get, the better my life becomes
- Uncertainty means opportunity

- I am right where I need to be
- I can't be behind, because I'm on my own path
- Look how far I've come!
- I'm not anxious, I'm excited
- Good things are coming for me
- My best days are yet to come
- It's not a no, it's a not now
- Life starts at 30
- 30 is not the deadline, it's the start line

The Truth About Turning 30

I spent the week before my 30th birthday in a mild state of panic. My expectations of life at 30 were in wild contrast to my lived reality. I was turning 30 and my ring finger was still empty. I was still in my overdraft. And my flat still smelled of damp. Added to this were fears that nobody would turn up to my birthday brunch and I'd have to go bottomless all on my own. But my fears turned out to be unfounded. All the people that mattered showed up, the waiters were incredibly free-flowing with their top-ups and I soon forgot about my turning 30 fears.

The morning after, aside from a raging fizz-over, I had no regrets. It struck me that my pre-30 panic had been pointless.

I couldn't stop the clock.

I'd turned 30 anyway.

And no bombs went off.

No mad Aunties came out of the woodwork to scold me for missing the marriage deadline.

I realised that I had a fresh new decade to play with, which was bursting with opportunities. My 'scary age' suddenly felt like the first page of a beautiful new Moleskine notebook. And as my story unfolded, I learned that 30 wasn't the deadline after all. It was only the start line.

Epilogue: Behind The Book

When I got pregnant, aged 35, I didn't tell anyone aside from my partner for four months. Maybe it was superstition, waiting for the all-clear at the twelve-week scan, especially since society was telling me my 'Geriatric pregnancy' would be fraught with risks. Maybe it was slight embarrassment too.

I'd been vocally 'childfree' up until that point, then changed my mind at the eleventh hour (PSA: it's OK to change your mind!). This was such a pivot from my previous stance that when I finally WhatsApp'd my baby scan to my besties, they thought it was an April fool!

Keeping things to myself didn't come naturally at all. I'm an awful liar, mostly because my memory is rubbish, but also because my poker face is naff, and I have been blessed with an over-active conscience.

My biggest test came when I took a hiking trip to Chamonix, Switzerland with my dad. He knew something was up when I refused a lovely bottle of red on night one, not to mention when I started scarfing down raclette at an alarming rate in the middle of the afternoon. But even though I knew he knew, 'Mum' was still the word, so to speak. Looking back, I realise that for me, the decision not to share was stupid. Because in all honesty if something had gone wrong down the line, I'm certain I would have told my parents, and my closest friends, anyway, because surviving tough times requires support. Getting through those early days of pregnancy deserves celebrating. And the experience of having an alien body growing inside your body is weird and confusing, to say the least. So, I definitely could have benefitted from the collected wisdom of the women who had gone through this before. I missed out on all of that by abiding by the traditional rule.

I wasn't about to make the same mistake twice. So, when I started growing this 'book baby' I took the exact opposite approach. I told everyone who would listen I was writing a book. I bored people silly with my bookish questions and growing body of data. I made it official by opening a shiny new Instagram account. I decided to write 30-Phobia in real time, documenting the highs and lows, the little wins and the epic fails. I knew that this time, I needed the village. I also wanted the book to be great. And I've learned from business that most ideas get better when you share them with the right people. I decided early on that if it all went sideways, I'd divulge that too. It's often said that a problem shared is a problem halved. And now thanks to the power of social media, a problem shared is a problem normalised. By telling the hard truths, we make others feel less alone.

The journey to publishing this book has been squiggly, to say the least. It's taken me at least twelve months longer than originally planned to squeeze this little baby out.

I've enjoyed countless rejections and much ghosting from publishing professionals, and I've made the acquaintance of some especially salty internet trolls. But I'm still glad I did it my way. It made sense for me to break the rules of book publishing by 'writing in public,' because very little else about my life journey so far has been expected, so why stop here.

The best part about putting myself out there has been the connections I've made along the way. This project has opened the door to thousands of like-minded, wickedly relatable women and inspiring experts from across the globe. The words in this book have been shaped by every interview, comment, critique and email. It truly feels like a community effort.

At this point, I feel like I've been through a year of free therapy. What started out as a scientific study of turning thirty has evolved into a more personal transformation. I've noticed my own mindset shifting with every expert I've interviewed and every chapter that's unfolded. I note that I'm no longer seeking external validation – I've written this book to my own satisfaction, and if anyone else likes it, that'll be a lovely bonus.

I've started looking IN to really understand the core values that drive me (like empathy, community, integrity and helpfulness). I've reframed the way I see success – I no longer obsess about the end goals; I acknowledge that life is the process of pursuing our dreams.

True success is a feeling, not a list of accolades to reel off at dinner parties.

I think more about how my life feels, and less about how it looks from the outside.

And I've made a point of enjoying the journey this time, by celebrating every small win and 'inch stone' along the way.

I've awarded myself a virtual high-five, and popped a wee bottle of fizz, for every single chapter I've filed. And I'm about to crack open a whole bottle to celebrate this grande finale.

All of this means that even if I never sell a single book, secure another speaking engagement, or read one single positive review, it really doesn't matter, because I've already won.

Notes

My Turning 30 Goals

By the time I turn 30, I will...

1. _____

_____

_____

2. _____

_____

_____

3. _____

_____

_____

4. _____

_____

_____

5. _____

_____

_____

What emotions come up for you?

How achievable do they feel?

How will you feel if you don't achieve them by 30? Or ever?

New Goals

Baby Goals

Your Notes

Notes

Notes

30-Phobia

Notes

Acknowledgements

This book has truly been a community effort, and I'm so grateful to everyone who helped make the 30-Phobia project a reality.

Particular thanks to all of the experts who agreed to share their experiences and wisdom in these pages. Jen Brister, Vassia Sarantopoulou, Ellie Austin-Williams, Laura Ann Moore, Tonya Kelly, Erica Martin, Maren Ashford, Rosanna Ruff, Georgie Davies, Laura Guckian, Tricia Rosas, Lindsey Kane, Maike Neuhaus, Gaby Mendes, Sally Bee, Berta Maso, Caroline Tolman, Barbara Escolme, Mindi Palm, Jay Richards, Carrie Eaton, Dani Weiss, Alyssa Montagna, Angharad Rudkin, Bethan Rose Jenkins, Caitlan Siegenthaler, Bindi Gauntlett, Laurie Jennings, Michelle Hawkins-Collins, Federica Amati, Mary Hutchings, Michelle Mikulsky, Jordan Stachini.

Thank you to my Publisher, Editor and Mentor Sally Bee, for empowering me to publish this book my way. Thanks for breathing life into the project when it needed it most, for pushing me to share more of myself, and for painstakingly editing every inch of the text. Not to mention being the 'voice of the experts' in the audio book. This book would not be here without you.

Thanks to Kat Erbesova for all of the amazing content you've created, for keeping my Instagram running like clockwork and for helping me spread the word to 20-somethings everywhere that it's OK not to have it all figured out by 30, or ever.

Thank you to John Alexander for crunching all the numbers and answering all my silly questions. To Stephen Power for starting the conversation that shaped the direction of the book. And to Hannah Power (no relation) for encouraging me to share my own turning 30 story.

Thanks to author Neil Strauss, who encouraged me to write the story that only I could write, and who showed me that writing can happen anywhere, in whatever time you have. And thank you to Liz, for the last minute, late night, proof reading.

Thank you Bex for being the first person to tell me I needed to write a self-help book!

Thank you to my friends and family, who have supported my writing ambitions from the off, and who trusted me to tell their stories in these pages. Special thanks to my husband Michal, who has always been my number one fan. You're very brave to let me publish this without reading it first!

Finally, I would like to acknowledge the incredible online community that has grown up around me over the past 18 months. Every conversation, email, WhatsApp message, DM and comment has shaped the content of this book. Each follow, like and share has spurred me on. 30-Phobia is more than a book, it's part of an ongoing live conversation. And you can join in now on Instagram @kate.berski or tiktok @30_phobia.

References

- Turning 30 study by Kate Berski & John Alexander, August 2023 (2,500 women aged 20-29, UK & USA)
- 2014 Alter and Hershfield
- https://www.oceanfinance.co.uk/blog/cost-of-being-single/
- https://onepoll.com/blog/2019/07/25/cost-of-dating/
- https://inews.co.uk/inews-lifestyle/money/singles-tax-alone-serious-hit-finances-255749
- https://www.bbc.com/future/article/20210408-the-sexist-words-that-are-harmful-to-women
- https://theconversation.com/spinster-old-maid-or-self-partnered-why-words-for-single-women-have-changed-through-time-126716
- https://localhistories.org/life-in-the-17th-century/
- https://www.ons.gov.uk/peoplepopulationandcommunity/birthsdeathsandmarriages/lifeexpectancies/bulletins/nationallifetablesunitedkingdom/2015to2017
- https://www.babbel.com/en/magazine/language-of-being-single
- https://www.nbcnews.com/better/lifestyle/emma-watson-says-she-s-self-partnered-here-s-what-ncna1078871
- https://www.researchgate.net/publication/234767557_Imagining_Romance_Young_People's_Cultural_Models_of_Romance_and_Love
- https://www.researchgate.net/publication/263521659_From_Love_at_First_Sight_to_Soul_Mate_The_Influence_of_Romantic_Ideals_in_Popular_Films_on_Young_People's_Beliefs_about_Relationships
- https://medium.com/hello-love/study-predicts-45-of-women-will-be-single-by-2030-1fbc99bad6a8
- https://www.entitymag.com/millennials-pressured-to-get-married/
- https://match.mediaroom.com/2017-02-06-Singles-in-America-Match-Releases-Largest-Study-on-U-S-Single-Population
- https://www.echineselearning.com/blog/feeling-pressure-to-get-married-youre-not-the-onlyone#:~:text=The%20feeling%20of%20being%20urged%20to%20get%20married,get%20married%20around%202030%20years%20old%20or%20earlier.

References

- https://www.immediate.co.uk/hitcheds-annual-national-wedding-survey-reveals-latest-trends-and-truth-about-cost-of-getting-married-in-britain/
- https://www.hitched.co.uk/wedding-planning/organising-and-planning/average-uk-wedding/
- https://www.huffingtonpost.co.uk/2016/02/12/viral-proposal-videos-impact-on-relationship_n_9158550.html
- https://www.ons.gov.uk/peoplepopulationandcommunity/birthsdeathsandmarriages/marriagecohabitationandcivilpartnerships/bulletins/marriagesinenglandandwalesprovisional/2019#age-at-marriage
- https://www.statista.com/statistics/371933/median-age-of-us-americans-at-their-first-wedding/#:~:text=In%202021%2C%20the%20median%20age,men%20and%20women%20since%201998.
- https://www.ons.gov.uk/peoplepopulationandcommunity/birthsdeathsandmarriages/marriagecohabitationandcivilpartnerships/bulletins/marriagesinenglandandwalesprovisional/2019
- https://www.prnewswire.com/news-releases/national-survey-finds-most-engaged-couples-are-interested-in-eloping-this-year-301583425.html
- https://www.apa.org/monitor/2023/06/cover-story-science-friendship
- https://www.euronews.com/health/2023/02/15/fewer-friends-less-time-to-hang-out-what-data-says-of-our-friendships-post-pandemic-world#:~:text=Similarly%2C%20the%20number%20of%20respondents,cent%20to%2048%20per%20cent.
- https://yougov.co.uk/society/articles/38493-yougov-friendship-study-part-1-close-friends-and-b?redirect_from=%2Ftopics%2Fsociety%2Farticles-reports%2F2021%2F12%2F16%2Fyougov-friendship-study-part-1-close-friends-and-b
- Evans & Alexander 2022, Turning 30 Study
- https://medium.com/heart-affairs/according-to-a-recent-survey-this-is-the-age-when-youll-meet-the-one-2b496337183#:~:text=People%20Often%20Meet%20'The%20One,to%20be%20closer%20to%2028.
- https://opportunityinsights.org/national_trends/
- https://www.theguardian.com/world/2016/mar/07/revealed-30-year-economic-betrayal-dragging-down-generation-y-income
- https://assets.ey.com/content/dam/ey-sites/ey-com/en_us/topics/consulting/ey-2307-4309403-genz-segmentation-report-us-score-no-20902-231us-2-vf4.pdf
- https://www.tsb.co.uk/news-releases/young-people-most-reliant-on-debt-as-cost-of-living.html#:~:text=TSB%27s%20own%20data%20shows%20that,going%20overdrawn%20is%2010%25%20higher.
- https://commonslibrary.parliament.uk/research-briefings/sn01079/

- https://wordsrated.com/student-loan-debt-in-the-united-kingdom/
- https://www.bloomberg.com/graphics/2023-06-reed-jobs-report-graduates-face-worst-market-in-five-years/?embedded-checkout=true
- https://royalsocietypublishing.org/doi/10.1098/rsos.160097
- https://www.amigoloans.co.uk/press-releases/article/what-is-the-true-cost-of-friendship
- https://www.squaremeal.co.uk/wedding-venues/wedding-news/average-cost-wedding-guest-set-to-increase-2023_10470
- https://wwd.com/business-news/business-features/gen-z-millennials-losing-friends-spending-habits-1235723309/
- https://explodingtopics.com/blog/bnpl-stats
- https://www.theguardian.com/commentisfree/2023/mar/16/tiktoks-shoppertainment-model-gen-z-debt
- https://assets.ey.com/content/dam/ey-sites/ey-com/en_us/topics/consulting/ey-2307-4309403-genz-segmentation-report-us-score-no-20902-231us-2-vf4.pdf
- https://moneytalkwitht.com/blog/gen-z-financial-literacy/
- https://www.oecd-ilibrary.org/sites/a9f80ab9-en/index.html?itemId=/content/component/a9f80ab9-en#:~:text=On%20average%2C%20men%20score%20higher,10%20points%20(Figure%2012.1).
- https://www.personneltoday.com/hr/graduate-jobs-market-2023/
- https://propertyindustryeye.com/rental-affordability-at-its-worst-for-a-decade-as-rents-continue-to-rise/
- https://www.pewresearch.org/short-reads/2007/01/23/gen-nexters-say-getting-rich-is-their-generations-top-goal/
- https://www.lendingtree.com/credit-cards/study/emotional-spending/#:~:text=Almost%2070%25%20of%20Americans%20admit,that%20fuel%20the%20shopping%20sprees.
- https://www.regenesys.net/reginsights/the-power-of-dopamine-understanding-its-influence-on-spending-behaviour#:~:text=The%20excitement%20of%20browsing%2C%20creating,of%20dopamine%20in%20the%20brain.
- https://www.amazon.com/Algebra-Wealth-Formula-Financial-Security/dp/0593714024
- https://www.hommati.com/blog/how-generation-z-will-change-the-housing-market-forever#:~:text=Gen%20Z%20believes%20in%20the,have%20already%20purchased%20a%20home.
- https://www.sciencedaily.com/releases/2016/03/160329101037.htm
- https://www.uswitch.com/mortgages/first-time-buyer-statistics/
- https://thenibbler.com.au/article/two-thirds-of-millennials-and-gen-z-rath-

References

- er-travel-than-buy-a-home-in-coming-year
- www.axios.com
- https://www.ncbi.nlm.nih.gov/pmc/articles/PMC7537569/
- https://www.census.gov/library/stories/2023/06/more-than-a-quarter-all-households-have-one-person.html
- ons.gov.uk
- jchs.harvard.edu
- https://www.lhsdoi.com/20712/showcase/searching-how-psychology-explains-our-need-for-community/
- https://www.linkedin.com/pulse/lifegoals-social-construct-stick-your-own-agenda-when-buyers-agent/
- https://ourworldindata.org/life-expectancy#:~:text=Across%20the%20world%2C%20people%20are,has%20this%20dramatic%20change%20occurred%3F
- https://www.pewresearch.org/social-trends/2024/01/25/financial-help-and-independence-in-young-adulthood/
- https://www.pewresearch.org/short-reads/2023/05/23/young-adults-in-the-u-s-are-reaching-key-life-milestones-later-than-in-the-past/
- https://www.census.gov/content/dam/Census/library/publications/2017/demo/p20-579.pdf
- https://medium.com/@heysuryansh/exploring-instagrams-algorithmic-bias-towards-attractive-women-and-its-impact-on-users-case-79a4c7e6583f
- https://www.cbsnews.com/miami/news/20-somethings-are-paying-up-for-cosmetic-procedures-to-prevent-aging/
- https://www.independent.ie/news/men-and-women-happiest-with-their-bodies-at-age-60-study-finds/40716831.html
- https://www.independent.co.uk/life-style/30th-birthday-anxiety-b2356628.html
- https://downloads.ctfassets.net/inb32lme5009/7BkRT92AEhVU51EIzXXUHB/37749c3cf976dd10524021b8592636d4/The_Friendship_Report.pdf
- https://www.cbsnews.com/news/value-of-intergenerational-friendships/
- https://www.sportpsychologytoday.com/sports-psychology-articles/outcome-goals-vs-process-goals/
- https://www.ons.gov.uk/peoplepopulationandcommunity/birthsdeathsandmarriages/conceptionandfertilityrates/bulletins/childbearingforwomenbornindifferentyearsenglandandwales/2020
- https://www.statista.com/statistics/241535/percentage-of-childless-women-in-the-us-by-age/
- https://www.uclahealth.org/news/understanding-pregnancys-biological-clock

- https://www.morganstanley.com/ideas/womens-impact-on-the-economy#:~:text=Based%20on%20Census%20Bureau%20historical,up%20from%2041%25%20in%202018.&text=What's%20driving%20this%20trend%3F,in%20their%2050s%20and%2060s
- https://www.nhs.uk/conditions/artificial-insemination/
- ONS in https://getpenfold.com/news/childcare-cost
- https://www.ons.gov.uk/peoplepopulationandcommunity/birthsdeathsandmarriages/livebirths/bulletins/birthcharacteristicsinenglandandwales/2021#:~:text=In%202021%2C%20the%20standardised%20mean,being%20delayed%20until%20older%20ages.
- https://www.nbcnews.com/news/motherhood-deferred-us-median-age-giving-birth-hits-30-rcna27827
- https://www.gov.uk/government/news/looking-after-the-grandchildren-make-sure-it-counts-towards-your-state-pension#:~:text=Grandparents%20who%20provide%20childcare%20for,%C2%A37.3%20billion%20a%20year
- https://assets.ey.com/content/dam/ey-sites/ey-com/en_us/topics/consulting/ey-2307-4309403-genz-segmentation-report-us-score-no-20902-231us-2-vf4.pdf
- https://www.apa.org/monitor/2019/01/gen-z
- https://www.freshbooks.com/hub/productivity/how-many-hours-does-the-average-person-work#:~:text=Don't%20worry%2C%20you',at%20work%20over%20your%20lifetime.
- https://www.verywellmind.com/how-your-environment-affects-your-mental-health-5093687
- https://www.apollotechnical.com/career-change-statistics/
- https://www.amazon.com/Drive-Surprising-Truth-About-Motivates/dp/1594484805/ref=as_li_ss_tl?ie=UTF8&qid=1469394402&sr=8-1&keywords=daniel+pink&linkCode=sl1&tag=mewilm-20&linkId=8ec7db32048e14a2a89e55d5a4e8d9eb
- The Middle Finger Project, Ash Ambirge
- https://www.apa.org/monitor/2024/01/trends-hope-greater-meaning-life
- https://www.psychologytoday.com/gb/blog/why-bad-looks-good/202102/why-so-many-single-women-without-children-are-happy

Let's Chat

This isn't just a book, it's a small part of an ongoing live conversation. As I put pen to paper, I also put myself out there, sharing my writing journey, emerging insights, mindset hacks and relatable memes with a growing community of 20-somethings on Instagram @kate.berski and TikTok @30_phobia. So, join me, say Hi and feel free to ask me any questions.

Website: www.kateberski.com